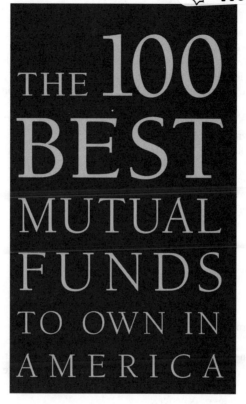

THE 100 BEST MUTUAL FUNDS TO OWN IN AMERICA

THIRD EDITION

Gene Walden

Dearborn
Financial Publishing, Inc.®

This publication is designed to provide accurate and authoritative information in regard to the subject matter covered. It is sold with the understanding that the publisher is not engaged in rendering legal, accounting or other professional service. If legal advice or other expert assistance is required, the services of a competent professional person should be sought.

Editorial Director: Cynthia Zigmund
Managing Editor: Jack Kiburz
Project Editor: Trey Thoelcke
Interior Design: Elizandro Carrington
Cover Design: S. Laird Jenkins Corp.
Typesetting: Elizabeth Pitts

Library of Congress Cataloging-in-Publication Data

Walden, Gene.
    The 100 best mutual funds to own in America / Gene Walden—3rd ed.
        p.   cm.
    Includes index.
    ISBN 0-7931-2859-5 (pbk.)
    1. Mutual funds—United States—Directories.   I. Title.
HG4930.W35   1998
332.63′27—dc21   98-12372
                                                                          CIP

Dearborn books are available at special quantity discounts to use as premiums and sales promotions, or for use in corporate training programs. For more information, please call the Special Sales Manager at 800-621-9621, ext. 4514, or write to Dearborn Financial Publishing, Inc., 155 N. Wacker Drive, Chicago, IL 60606-1719.

Dedication

To Brenna, Phoebe, Patrick, and Corinne

Contents

100 Best Funds Listed Alphabetically

100 Best Funds by Investment Objective

Aggressive Growth Funds	Ranking
AIM Constellation Fund	99
Alger Spectra Fund	2
Alliance Quasar Fund	75
American Century Income and Growth Fund	51
American Century–Twentieth Century Giftrust	98
American Century–Twentieth Century Ultra Fund	58
Baron Asset Fund	4
—Fidelity Emerging Growth Fund	(100)
Invesco Dynamics Fund	43
Kaufmann Fund	42
Managers Special Equity Fund	63
MFS Capital Opportunities Fund	50
PBHG Growth Fund	41
Putnam Voyager Fund	90
Stein Roe Capital Opportunities Fund	55
T. Rowe Price Small Cap Stock Fund	59
Van Campen American Capital Emerging Growth Fund	87
Warburg Pincus Emerging Growth Fund	61

Growth and Income Funds	Ranking
Dreyfus Disciplined Stock Fund	40
Enterprise Growth and Income Portfolio	54
Kemper-Dreman High Return Equity Fund	74
MFS Massachusetts Investors Trust	77
Nationwide Fund	52
SAFECO Equity Fund	32
Selected American Shares	38
— Vanguard Growth and Income Portfolio	(35)
Victory Diversified Stock Fund	76

Long-Term Growth Funds	Ranking
AIM Value Fund	80
Alger Growth Portfolio	89
Alliance Growth Fund	86

Sector Funds

Small-Cap Stock Funds

Preface

The decade of the 1990s has been one of the best ever for stock market investors. Many of the stock funds from the last edition of *The 100 Best Mutual Funds to Own in America* have climbed 50 to 100 percent since the book was published. And their popularity continues to grow. There are now more than 8,000 different mutual funds, with well over $4 trillion in total mutual fund investments.

Americans continue to be drawn to mutual funds for several very good reasons. Mutual funds are professionally managed by experienced investment managers, they provide instant diversification by investing in a broad range of stocks or bonds, and they provide solid performance, particularly in a good market.

The purpose of this book is to help direct you to the funds that have done the best over the past few years. With more than 8,000 funds to choose from, narrowing the field to the top performing funds is no easy task. The 100 funds in this book all have several characteristics in common: they ranked among the top 5 percent of all funds in terms of total return over the past five years, they are all managed by experienced fund managers, and they are all geared to smaller individual investors.

Many of the funds from the second edition of this book have made a return visit to this third edition, although we've also included a number of exciting new funds that have enjoyed exceptional performance in recent years.

If you want to select from the cream of the crop, you've come to the right source. Choose carefully, diversify by including several different types of funds in your portfolio, and be patient. Ultimately, you should be able to enjoy the same type of investment returns that have made mutual funds the most popular form of investment ever invented. May all your picks go north!

—Gene Walden

Acknowledgements

As he has with many of my other books, Larry Nelson played a crucial role in helping put this book together. He helped wade through volumes of research material, crunched numbers, ferreted out vital fund information, and helped put together the many tables and graphs.

Thanks also to my editors at Dearborn Financial Publishing who helped shape the book, including editorial director Cynthia Zigmund, managing editor Jack Kiburz, and project editor Trey Thoelcke.

Introduction

For hurried Americans of the 1990s, mutual funds have become the fast food of investing.

Quick, convenient, and diversified, mutual funds give investors a chunk of the stock and bond markets without the hassle. No poring over stock tables, no thumbing through annual reports and corporate balance sheets, no restless nights fretting over the daily ups and downs of the markets. What could be simpler?

Well, maybe it's not quite as easy as it sounds. The selection process can be staggering. You must choose from more than 8,000 mutual funds—nearly four times the number of stocks on the New York Stock Exchange.

Despite their professional management, their diversification, and their finely honed trading strategies, however, not all funds are created equal. In fact, the vast majority of mutual funds have trailed the overall stock market over the past ten years. There are, however, exceptions that rise above the crowd.

The 100 Best Mutual Funds to Own in America is designed to ease your selection process by narrowing the field of choices to 100 truly exceptional funds. Each of the 100 best funds ranks in the top 2 percent of all mutual funds in terms of total return over the past five years.

In paging through this book, you'll find a detailed and individual overview of all the funds, with helpful insights on their investment objectives and strategies, their top ten holdings, sales charges and annual fees, fund manager's experience, special shareholder services, minimum investment requirements, performance records, asset mix, toll-free number, fax line, and a wealth of other vital information.

You'll also get a chance to tap the minds of America's top investment managers and learn their secrets on what to buy, when to buy, and when to sell.

A special honorable mention section of about 100 other outstanding stock and bond funds is also included. The honorable mention roster is divided into several sections, including growth funds, growth and income funds, bond funds, high-yield bond funds, tax-exempt bond funds, sector funds, international funds, and aggressive growth funds—all ranked based on five-year performance records.

WHY MUTUAL FUNDS?

What is a mutual fund? Technically, a mutual fund is a "company" that pools investment contributions from shareholders to buy stocks, bonds, or other investments. When you invest in a mutual fund, you are buying shares of the mutual fund "company," and you share in the success of that company.

But for all practical purposes, you can think of a mutual fund simply as a portfolio of investments such as stocks and bonds. You become a part owner of that portfolio when you buy shares in the fund. With a single investment, you suddenly hold a diversified portfolio of dozens of investments. Most funds have 25 to 300 stock or bond holdings. When you own shares in a fund, your share price directly reflects the net asset value of the stocks in the fund, and the investment value of your shares fluctuates as the fortune of the fund's holdings fluctuate.

In addition to diversification, convenience, and professional management, mutual funds offer several other benefits:

- *Liquidity.* With most funds, you can pull your money out simply by calling the company and telling them to sell your shares.
- *Low investment requirements.* It usually doesn't take a lot of money to invest in a mutual fund. Initial minimum investment requirements vary from about $250 to $2,500, although a few funds require as much as $100,000 to $500,000. Once you're a shareholder, most funds allow you to contribute even smaller subsequent amounts— usually from $50 to $250—so it becomes very easy even for small investors to build a position in a fund.
- *Direct purchases.* Although brokers are often helpful in recommending good mutual funds to their clients, you don't have to use a broker to buy shares in a mutual fund. You can buy shares directly from the company simply by calling the company's toll-free sales line.
- *Low (or no) sales fees.* Many companies allow you to purchase fund shares with no sales fee. These are called *no-load funds* or just *no-loads* (which mean they have no sales "load" or fee). Load funds vary in the fees they charge investors. Some *low-load* funds charge about 3 percent, although most load funds charge from 4.5 to 8 percent. Some funds charge what is known as a *back-end load,* which is a sales charge you pay when you sell your shares in the fund. Typically, back-end load funds charge 5 percent if you sell the first year, 4 percent the second year, and so on with the fee diminishing to zero after the fifth year. Funds also charge annual expense fees that usually vary from about 1 percent to 3 percent, depending on the fund.

- *Checking deduction plans.* With most funds, you can have money automatically withdrawn from your checking account and invested in the fund each month or each quarter.
- *Automatic withdrawal.* Retired investors sometimes opt for withdrawal plans which authorize the fund to pay out a set amount to the investor from his or her fund account each month or each quarter.
- *Retirement account access.* Most companies allow investors to use their funds in IRAs, SEPs, and other retirement accounts.
- *Telephone exchange.* Investors who wish to switch from one fund to another within the same family of funds are usually allowed to make that switch commission-free simply by calling the company and ordering the change.
- *Automatic reinvestment.* With most mutual funds, investors can have their dividends and capital gains distributions automatically reinvested in additional shares of the fund with no additional sales fee.

FUNDS FOR EVERY TASTE

A wide variety of mutual funds meets the tastes and risk thresholds of nearly everyone who invests. The original mutual funds were designed to produce a combination of growth and income by investing in a diversified portfolio of dividend-paying blue chip stocks. Many types of funds are offered today, including:

- *Growth and income funds.* These funds are appropriate for investors who want a steady stream of income along with some appreciation. They are not appropriate for high-income investors who want to minimize their taxes, because the additional income adds to the investor's tax burden. And because they invest in more well-established companies, growth and income funds are among the least risky types of mutual funds.
- *Growth funds.* These funds invest primarily in stocks of fast-growing companies in order to provide long-term appreciation (with minimal current income) for shareholders. While growth funds tend to be more volatile in the short term than income-oriented funds, they tend to provide better long-term returns. Because of their diversification, growth funds, too, are among the least risky types of funds.
- *Aggressive growth funds.* These stock funds normally come in many forms. Some invest in depressed stocks that have turnaround potential. Others look for trendy stocks. Most of the top aggressive

growth funds in recent years have had large positions in high-tech stocks. Other funds look for good start-up companies that could blossom into major corporations. And still others invest in potential takeover stocks that could experience a sharp run-up in prices. With aggressive funds, the portfolio managers play a numbers game. Some of their picks pan out; others fall flat. Their hope is to make enough money on the winners to more than compensate for the losers. In truth, the label "aggressive growth" applies more to the types of stocks that these funds invest in than to their overall performance. Although a large share of the top-ranked funds in this book are aggressive growth funds, many aggressive growth funds have proven to be no more profitable than other stock funds—just more volatile. These funds tend to be riskier than growth funds and particularly over the short term.

- *International and global funds.* These funds give investors a stake in the international market. *Global funds* are funds that invest in both U.S. and foreign stocks, whereas *international funds* invest strictly in foreign stocks. Because they invest in foreign stocks, international funds can be somewhat riskier than U.S. growth stock funds. However, by investing in an international fund as part of a diversified portfolio, you add foreign diversification, which actually reduces the overall risk of your portfolio.

- *Sector funds.* These specialty funds invest strictly in stocks of one specific sector. There are funds for almost any market sector you could name—precious metals, utilities, high technology, medical technology, and financial services, among others. If you think gas and oil stocks are ready to take off, you might invest in an energy fund. If you want a hedge against inflation, you might invest in a gold fund that buys the stocks of gold mining companies. Although specialty funds have broad stock holdings within a specific sector, they lack the diversity and safety of traditional stock funds. If the sector is faring poorly, so will the fund. For instance, medical funds experienced phenomenal growth in 1991 when the medical sector was hot, but when medical stocks cooled off amid political discussions of medical cost containment, health care sector funds became the worst-performing funds of 1992. Sector funds are the riskiest of all funds.

- *Index funds.* These are funds designed to mirror the overall market. By buying an index fund, you can expect to achieve a return similar to the growth of the overall market. That may not seem particularly adventuresome, but index funds do tend to outperform about 80 percent of all mutual funds simply because index funds are 100 percent invested in stocks at all times. Some index funds are tied to the Dow Jones Industrials Average while others are designed to reflect the Standard & Poor's 500-stock index.

- *Money market funds.* Although money market funds are a form of mutual fund, they are considered a separate class. Brokerage firms use money market fund accounts for clients who want to continue drawing interest on the money in their account when it is not invested in securities or other investments. Banks also offer money market accounts for clients who want to get a slightly higher return than they would get through a standard savings account. These are the safest of all funds but generally provide the lowest long-term return.

- *Bond funds.* Bond funds first became popular in the 1970s, when investors began opting for managed portfolios of corporate bonds rather than individual bonds. An offshoot of the traditional bond fund is the *high-yield bond fund*—a portfolio of low-rated *junk bonds* that pays an interest rate three or four points higher than that paid by many of the AAA-rated bonds. With individual junk bonds, safety is a major concern because of the risk of default, although the diversification of a portfolio of bonds reduces the risk substantially. In reality, all bond funds—even government bond funds—carry a great deal more risk than most investors expect. Bond values rise and fall as interest rates fluctuate. When interest rates rise, bond values drop. A 2 percent rise in market interest rates can push the value of a bond fund down by 10 percent or more. In 1994, when interest rates were dropping steadily, bond funds declined in value—many dropped as much as 5 to 10 percent. Conversely, when market rates are falling, bond funds enjoy excellent appreciation, although the best bond funds generally fall far short of the best stock funds over the long term. This book covers bond funds—both high-quality and high-yield funds—in the honorable mention section.

- *Tax-exempt bond funds.* These funds invest in municipal bonds, which provide a tax break for investors. The dividends they pay are exempt from federal taxes, and in the case of funds that are comprised of tax-exempt bonds from the investor's state, they are also exempt from state taxes. The problem, however, is that the returns these funds provide are among the lowest in the industry—even after taking the tax break into account. Municipal bonds also carry a degree of risk. It is possible for bond issuers to default, creating major losses for bondholders, as was the case in Orange County, California, in 1994.

- *Closed-end funds.* A closed-end fund is a professionally managed diversified portfolio that is closed to new investors. As with stock offerings, investment companies underwrite such funds to raise a limited amount of money. Once the cutoff point has been reached, no new investments are accepted, and the fund begins trading on the open market like a stock. Some of the best-known closed-end funds include the Mexico Fund, the Korea Fund, the Brazil Fund, and the Taiwan Fund, all of which trade on the New York Stock Exchange. By contrast, open-end funds can continue to issue new shares as shareholders contribute new investment dollars. Investors buy shares directly from the mutual fund company rather than through a stock exchange. (Closed-end funds are not covered in this book; only the traditional open-end funds are featured.)

RATING THE TOP 100 FUNDS

From 8,000 funds, my objective was to sift out the 100 best. I began by focusing on the top 2 percent of all funds based on total return over the past five years. Of those top-ranking funds, I eliminated from consideration all funds that were closed to new shareholders, all funds with excessive minimum investment requirements (anything over $25,000), and funds with new fund managers. (I made an exception for some Fidelity funds because the company has a policy of shifting fund managers from fund to fund every few years. It is a policy that has worked well for Fidelity because the funds are all managed more or less on a team basis anyway.) Then I looked at the track histories of the funds and eliminated funds that had been particularly volatile over the past few years.

I also eliminated two well-performing funds because of poor service. Even after requesting each fund's annual report and prospectus on three separate occasions, the fund companies never bothered to send that material. That's not just bad service—it's bad marketing. So both funds, the Lord Abbott Developing Growth Fund and the OakMark Value Fund, were scratched from the list.

Once I had assembled the list of 100, the next step was to rank the funds from 1 to 100. The ranking system revolved around the following three categories, each worth a maximum of 5 points (for a maximum total of 15 points):

- *Performance.* Each fund was graded based on its five-year total return record (through mid-1998). The system ranks the funds relative to other funds from the top 100—not relative to all mutual funds. If I had graded them relative to all funds, then all 100 of the funds in my list would have scored a perfect 5 because they all rank in the top 2 percent of all mutual funds over the five-year period. Instead, I graded on a curve, with roughly the top 25 funds receiving a perfect 5, the next 25 receiving a 4, and so on down to 2 points.

- *Consistency.* Rather than looking at day-to-day volatility, I graded each fund's consistency on a year-to-year basis. I compared the performance of each fund to the Dow Jones Industrial Average each year over a six-year period from 1993 through 1997 (and part of 1998). A fund would score a perfect 5 if it outperformed the Dow (or ended the year virtually even with the Dow) each of the six years. Generally, if it trailed the Dow in one of the six years, the fund would score a 4; if it trailed the Dow in two of the six years, it would score 3 points; if it trailed the Dow in three of the six years, it would score a 2 for the category; and if it trailed in four of the six years, it would score a 1 (although if it were that volatile, I would have dropped it from the list—no fund scored less than a 2 in consistency). There were a few exceptions. For instance, in some cases when a fund trailed the Dow for three years, but only by one or two percentage points each time, I deducted 2 points instead of 3.

- *Fees/Services/Management.* This is the most subjective of the three categories with certain guidelines. With this category, it was more a matter of deducting points than awarding them. To receive a perfect 5, a fund would need to (1) be a true no-load fund (with no sales fee to buy or sell); (2) have a fund manager who had been with the fund at least four years; (3) offer the full range of standard services that most funds offer (checking account deduction, automatic withdrawal, retirement account availability, instant telephone redemption, and free switching between funds within the family by telephone); and (4) have reasonable minimum investment requirements (no more than a $5,000 initial investment minimum and $500 subsequent investment minimum).

A normal load fund—with a front-end or back-end sales fee of 4 percent or above—would automatically lose 2 points in this category, whereas a low-load fund (with a sales fee of 3 percent or less) would have just 1 point deducted. If the fund manager had been with the fund less than four years, another point would normally be deducted. (The only exceptions would be for a veteran fund manager who had been with the fund for a minimum of three years after establishing an impressive track record with another fund.) If a fund didn't offer most of the standard mutual fund services mentioned above, another point was deducted. If its minimum investment requirement is excessive (for instance, one fund in the book requires a $25,000 minimum investment), yet another point would be subtracted.

BREAKING TIES

With 100 funds graded on a 15-point rating system, many funds scored the same. How did I break the ties? I looked at several factors:

- *Diversification.* A fund that is well diversified across industry lines ranked above sector funds, which invest exclusively in a specific industry. The reason: the risk factor is much higher with sector funds. Although they may have done well over the most recent five-year period, they would stand to fall much faster than the broadly diversified funds if their sector should suddenly fall out of favor.
- *Five-year total return.* If all other factors were about equal, I rated funds with the best five-year performance records ahead of those with lesser records.
- *Management.* For funds with identical five-year returns, I looked at the fund manager. A fund with a manager who had been with the fund five to ten years would be rated above a fund with a relatively new manager.

AND THE WINNERS ARE . . .

If mutual funds are the fast food of investing, then Fidelity must be the McDonald's. The Boston-based investment giant offers more than 200 different funds. Seventeen of the top 100 funds were Fidelity funds.

As in past editions of this book, the hottest area was the high-tech sector funds, which accounted for about a dozen of the top 100 funds. In fact, many of the other high-ranking diversified funds were also loaded with technology stocks. Otherwise, the list was dominated by small company funds, aggressive growth funds, growth funds, and a few growth and income funds.

All of the funds in this book have doubled or tripled in value over the past five years. Keep in mind, however, that strong past performance does not guarantee similar future performance. It makes sense to invest in funds with solid, consistent track records and experienced management, but even the best funds have some down years. That is why investors should consider buying shares in more than one fund.

Patience is also important. Nothing goes straight up, but over time the best funds with the best managers tend to reward their patient shareholders with superior long-term returns.

MUTUAL FUNDS AND TAXES

There's no question that mutual funds are an investment conceived in convenience—you get diversity, professional management, and a host of special services, all for a simple investment. But the convenience ends when the taxes begin. Unless you invest strictly in tax-exempt municipal bond funds, or tuck your mutual funds safely away in a tax-sheltered retirement plan, you're likely to encounter some confusing twists when calculating your taxes.

Each year most stock and bond funds pay interest and dividends and make capital gains distributions (from profits made on trades within the fund). As a shareholder, you are liable for taxes on those gains even if you had those distributions automatically reinvested in additional shares. Your fund will send you a Form 1099-DIV (or similar form) annually that details your taxable gains for the year.

You are also liable for taxes on the appreciation of your fund shares when you sell your holdings. But take special care in calculating your gains, particularly if you have your fund distributions automatically reinvested. The tendency among investors is to overpay because they forget they've already paid taxes on the reinvested share of their holdings.

For instance, if your total holdings went from $1,000, when you bought the fund, to $2,000, when you sold, that doesn't mean you owe taxes on the full $1,000 gain. Part of that gain came from reinvested dividends and capital gains for which you would already have paid taxes.

To determine your true taxable total:

1. Add up all the dividends and distributions from the fund that you have had reinvested in additional shares.
2. Subtract the total value of your holdings when you bought the shares from the total value when you sold the shares to determine your total gain.

3. Subtract #1 (your reinvested distributions) from #2 (your total gain). That is your taxable income.

Example: You paid $1,000; you reinvested $100; you sold at $2,000.

Value at sale	$2,000
Initial investment	– $1,000
Reinvested distribution	– $ 100
Taxable income	$ 900

For investors who have accumulated shares over time, the IRS offers the following options for calculating taxable gains on the sale of a portion of those shares.

- *First in, first out (FIFO)*. You sell the first fund shares you purchased and pay taxes on the gains. The best situation for using FIFO is when your fund shares have recently declined. That means you may have paid the most for your earliest shares, which therefore would represent the smallest taxable gain.
- *Average cost*. Your taxes under this option are based on the average price you paid for shares you accumulated over time. To calculate the average, divide your total investment in the fund (including reinvested gains) by the number of shares you own. That works best when share prices have surged over time because you probably paid the least for your earliest shares—and would show the biggest gain for those shares if you used FIFO. But by using cost averaging, you can push up the average purchase and cut down the total taxable gain.
- *Specific identification*. This option allows you to identify the specific shares you are selling, which enables you to select the shares that will give you the smallest taxable gain.

Tax-averse investors may prefer municipal bond funds. The dividends they pay are exempt from federal taxes, and in the case of funds that are comprised of tax-exempt bonds from your state, they may also be exempt from state taxes. But you are still subject to taxes on any capital gains you earn on those funds by selling bonds at a profit.

Despite the tax breaks, however, it would probably be a mistake to put too much of your money in municipal bond funds. They tend to be among the worst-performing funds on the market over the long term. Even with the tax savings, their total after-tax return is likely to trail that of most taxable stock and bond funds over the long term.

TAKING ACTION

The 100 Best Mutual Funds to Own in America helps reduce your universe of choices from the roughly 8,000 funds currently on the market to the much more manageable level of 100 (plus the honorable mention funds). But, ultimately, it is you who must take action if you are to profit from the information in this book.

How should you select the fund or funds that are right for you? Here is a simple action plan:

1. Skim through the book to find a few funds that look promising to you.
2. Once you've selected a handful of good funds, call each fund's toll-free number (or send a fax) and request the fund's most recent annual or semiannual report and prospectus. The phone numbers you need are listed along with the profiles of each fund.
3. Read through the fund information. Many funds will also send some helpful marketing brochures that allow you a better glimpse of their company and the fund for which you've requested information.
4. Weigh all the factors that are important to you—total five-year performance, sales loads, annual fees, minimum investment requirements, services, type of fund, and any other factors you consider important.
5. Decide which fund (or funds) you want to buy.
6. Call the fund's toll-free number and place your order.
7. To go one step further, you can track the progress of your fund each day in the mutual fund section of *The Wall Street Journal, Investor's Business Daily, USA Today,* and many major metropolitan daily newspapers. A newsletter you can subscribe to that specifically covers the 100 mutual funds in this book is *The Best 100 Update,* which comes out twice a year and costs $12.95. (It also tracks the stocks in my other book, *The 100 Best Stocks to Own in America.)* You can order by calling 800-736-2970 or by writing P.O. Box 390373, Minneapolis, MN 55439.

THE COMPLETE PORTFOLIO

For a diversified approach, you will probably want to invest in several different funds, depending on your investment objectives. For instance, you should consider buying a broadly diversified stock growth fund, an aggressive growth fund, an international stock fund, perhaps an income fund such as a bond fund or high-yield bond fund, and a sector fund such as a high-tech fund. This book helps you choose from the best of each category.

Here are several factors to consider in making your selection—and several ways this book can help you assess those factors:

- *Investment objectives.* Do you want income, capital appreciation, safety, or aggressive growth? While the top 100 funds are nearly all geared to total capital appreciation, the honorable mention section covers several dozen income funds.
- *Performance.* You want a fund that has provided superior long-term performance because good performance in a single year means very little. Very often, the best-performing funds one year become the worst-performing funds the next. This book takes a long-term perspective, featuring funds based on superior five-year performance records.
- *Consistency.* Are you willing to put up with some volatility in hopes of getting better long-term returns? Or would you rather have a fund that tends to match the market year in and year out but may not offer quite the long-term potential of more volatile funds? This book rates funds on their year-to-year consistency.
- *Fees.* If you plan to hold a fund for years to come, the initial sales load won't make a lot of difference. But if you expect to move in and out of various funds from year to year, then the 4 to 8 percent fee that most load funds charge would make a significant difference in your total return. Investors who do a lot of buying and selling of mutual funds should seriously consider using only no-load or low-load funds. Also take a look at the fund's annual expense ratio. Those fees can vary from as little as .70 percent to as high as 3 percent, which can make a big difference over time. This book details all the fees associated with each of the featured funds—both the top 100 and the honorable mention picks.
- *Management.* A fund is truly a reflection of its manager. A fund with a great track record may not be such a great fund if the manager leaves. If you are selecting a fund based on its past performance, make sure the manager responsible for that performance is still running the fund.
- *Services.* As mentioned earlier, mutual funds offer a variety of services, such as automatic checking account deduction, periodic fund withdrawal plans, and IRA accounts. Make sure the fund you are interested in offers the services you need.

LONG TERM

Excelsior Value and Restructuring Fund

Excelsior Funds
73 Tremont Street
Boston, MA 02108-3913

Fund manager: David J. Williams
Fund objective: Long-term growth

Toll-free: 800-446-1012
In-state: 617-456-9394
Fax: 617-557-8610

Performance	★ ★ ★ ★ ★
Consistency	★ ★ ★ ★
Fees/Services	★ ★ ★ ★ ★
UMBIX	**14 Points**

The Excelsior Value and Restructuring Fund focuses on stocks of companies in transition. Its portfolio is stocked with candidates for restructuring, mergers, consolidations, liquidations, spin-offs, and reorganizations. A few solid blue chips are also in the portfolio, such as Philip Morris, IBM, and Bristol-Myers, but most of its holdings are lesser-known small and midsize companies.

The fund has enjoyed outstanding performance since its inception in 1992. Over the past five years, it has posted an average annual return of about 28 percent. Fund manager David Williams takes a fairly conservative trading approach; the annual portfolio turnover ratio is 62 percent.

The fund's leading industrial sectors include technology, 20 percent of assets; consumer staples, 18 percent; financial companies, 15 percent; consumer cyclicals, 13 percent; and banking-related companies, 11 percent.

PERFORMANCE

The fund has enjoyed exceptional growth over the last five years. Including dividends and capital gains distributions, the Excelsior Value and Restructuring Fund has provided a total return for the last five years (through mid-1998) of 245 percent. A $10,000 investment in 1993 would have grown to about $35,000 five years later. Average annual return: 28.1 percent.

CONSISTENCY

The fund has been very consistent recently, outperforming the Dow Jones Industrial Average in four of the last five years through 1997 (and again through the first few months of 1998). Its biggest gain came in 1995, when it jumped 38.8 percent (compared with a 33.5 percent rise in the Dow).

FEES/SERVICES/MANAGEMENT

Like all Excelsior funds, the Value and Restructuring Fund is a true no-load fund—no fee to buy, no fee to sell. The fund's total annual expense ratio of .91 percent (with no 12b-1 fee) compares very favorably with other funds.

The fund offers all the standard services, such as retirement account availability, automatic withdrawal, and automatic checking account deduction. Its minimum initial investment of $500 and minimum subsequent investment of $50 compare favorably with other funds.

David Williams has managed the fund since 1992. The Excelsior family of funds includes 19 funds and allows shareholders to switch from fund to fund by telephone.

Top Ten Stock Holdings

1. Suiza Foods
2. IBM
3. Bristol-Myers Squibb
4. Fannie Mae
5. Nabors Industries
6. Philip Morris
7. Texas Instruments
8. Avon Products
9. PNC Bank
10. Mellon Bank

Asset mix: common stocks—98%; cash/equivalents—2%
Total net assets: $230 million
Dividend yield: 0.39%

Fees

Front-end load	*None*
Redemption fee	*None*
12b-1 fee	*None*
Management fee	0.56%
Other expenses	0.35
Total annual expense	0.91%
Minimum initial investment	$500
Minimum subsequent investment	$50

Services

Telephone exchanges	*Yes*
Automatic withdrawal	*Yes*
Automatic checking deduction	*Yes*
Retirement plan/IRA	*Yes*
Instant redemption	*Yes*
Financial statements	*Semiannual*
Income distributions	*Quarterly*
Capital gains distributions	*Annual*
Portfolio manager: years	6
Number of funds in family	19

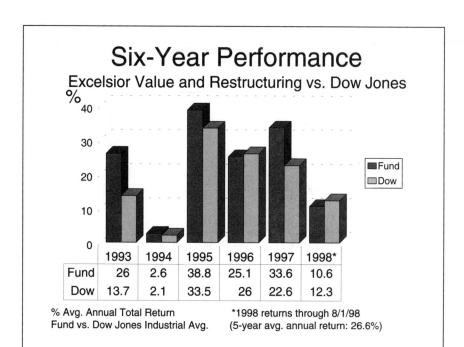

Six-Year Performance
Excelsior Value and Restructuring vs. Dow Jones

	1993	1994	1995	1996	1997	1998*
Fund	26	2.6	38.8	25.1	33.6	10.6
Dow	13.7	2.1	33.5	26	22.6	12.3

% Avg. Annual Total Return
Fund vs. Dow Jones Industrial Avg.

*1998 returns through 8/1/98
(5-year avg. annual return: 26.6%)

2

Alger Spectra Fund

AGGRESSIVE

Alger Funds
30 Montgomery Street
Jersey City, NJ 07302

Fund managers: David Alger,
   Seilai Khoo, and Ronald Tartaro
Fund objective: Aggressive growth

Toll-free: 800-992-3863
In-state: 201-547-3600
Fax: 201-434-1459

Performance	★ ★ ★ ★ ★
Consistency	★ ★ ★ ★
Fees/Services	★ ★ ★ ★ ★
SPECX	**14 Points**

The Alger Spectra Fund invests in a wide variety of stocks that are in a period of rapid growth. The fund managers look for two key profiles in selecting stocks for the portfolio. They want companies of any size that provide goods or services for a rapidly expanding marketplace. And they want companies that are going through changes that could make them more profitable, such as new management, new products or technologies, restructuring or reorganization, or mergers and acquisitions.

The fund, which was a closed-end fund until 1996, has enjoyed tremendous long-term growth. Over the past ten years, the fund has posted an average annual return of 23 percent. A $10,000 investment in the fund ten years ago would now be worth about $80,000.

The Spectra Fund has about 70 stock holdings in all. The leading sector is financial services stocks, which account for about 14 percent of total assets. Other leading sectors include retailing, 12 percent; pharmaceuticals, 11 percent; computer software, 8 percent; and communications, 7 percent.

The fund stays almost 100 percent invested in stocks most of the time. The fund managers maintain a fairly aggressive trading approach; the annual portfolio turnover ratio is 134 percent.

PERFORMANCE

The fund has enjoyed tremendous growth over the last five years. Including dividends and capital gains distributions, the Spectra Fund has provided a total return for the last five years (through mid-1998) of 253 percent. A $10,000 investment in 1993 would have grown to about $35,000 five years later. Average annual return: 27.9 percent.

CONSISTENCY

The fund has been very consistent recently, outperforming the Dow Jones Industrial Average in four of the last five years through 1997 (and again through the first few months of 1998). Its biggest gain came in 1995, when it jumped 47.7 percent (compared with a 33.5 percent rise in the Dow).

FEES/SERVICES/MANAGEMENT

The Spectra Fund is a true no-load—no fee to buy, no fee to sell. It does have a very high annual expense ratio of 2.12 percent.

The fund offers many of the standard services, such as retirement account availability, automatic withdrawal, and automatic checking account deduction. Its minimum initial investment of $1,000 and minimum subsequent investment of $100 compare favorably with other funds.

Lead fund manager David Alger has been with the fund for 24 years. The fund is also managed by Seilai Khoo and Ronald Tartaro. The Alger family of funds includes six funds, but investors may not switch from Spectra to other Alger funds without paying a sales load.

Top Ten Stock Holdings

1. Guidant
2. America Online
3. Home Depot
4. Schering-Plough
5. Tyco International
6. Warner-Lambert
7. Wal-Mart
8. Rite Aid
9. Eli Lilly
10. Bristol-Myers Squibb

Asset mix: common stocks—93%; cash/equivalents—7%
Total net assets: $97 million
Dividend yield: none

Fees

Front-end load	*None*
Redemption fee	*None*
12b-1 fee	*None*
Management fee	1.50%
Other expenses	0.62
Total annual expense	2.12%
Minimum initial investment	$1,000
Minimum subsequent investment	$100

Services

Telephone exchanges	*No*
Automatic withdrawal	*Yes*
Automatic checking deduction	*Yes*
Retirement plan/IRA	*Yes*
Instant redemption	*Yes*
Financial statements	*Semiannual*
Income distributions	*Annual*
Capital gains distributions	*Annual*
Portfolio manager: years	24
Number of funds in family	6

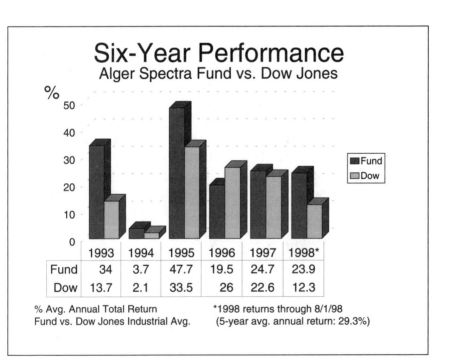

Six-Year Performance
Alger Spectra Fund vs. Dow Jones

	1993	1994	1995	1996	1997	1998*
Fund	34	3.7	47.7	19.5	24.7	23.9
Dow	13.7	2.1	33.5	26	22.6	12.3

% Avg. Annual Total Return
Fund vs. Dow Jones Industrial Avg.

*1998 returns through 8/1/98
(5-year avg. annual return: 29.3%)

LONG TERM

3
Mairs & Power
Growth Fund

Mairs & Power Funds
W-1420 First National Bank Building
332 Minnesota Street
St. Paul, MN 55101

Fund manager: George M. Mairs III
Fund objective: Long-term growth

Toll-free: 800-304-7404
In-state: 651-222-8478
Fax: 651-222-8470

Performance	★ ★ ★ ★ ★
Consistency	★ ★ ★ ★
Fees/Services	★ ★ ★ ★ ★
MPGFX	**14 Points**

Opened in 1958, the Mairs & Power Growth Fund has established itself as one of the most consistent long-term funds in America. After all these years, investors are finally discovering this diamond in the rough. Over the past two years, the fund's assets have grown nearly fivefold—from $87 million to over $400 million.

Over the past ten years, the fund has posted average annual returns of about 20 percent. A $10,000 investment in the fund ten years ago would now be worth about $60,000.

Fund manager George Mairs III invests primarily in large blue chip stocks, but he also includes some small and midsize companies in the portfolio. Mairs, who has managed the fund since 1980, looks for companies with reasonably predictable earnings, above average return on equity, market dominance, and financial strength. The fund has only about 35 stock holdings, more than half of which were plucked from its own backyard in Minnesota, such as Norwest, Dayton Hudson, General Mills, Medtronic, and 3M. The fund is big on large-cap blue chips, although it also owns some midsize stocks.

Mairs believes strongly in the buy-and-hold approach. His fund is the most conservatively traded fund in this book, with an annual portfolio turnover ratio of just 3 percent. He stays at least 90 percent invested in stocks almost all the time.

Although the fund has a solid stake in technology stocks, it is well diversified in other industries as well. The leading industrial sectors include consumer goods, 10 percent; financial services, 15 percent; technology, 17 percent; drugs and medical, 15 percent; retail, 5 percent; and chemicals, 5 percent.

PERFORMANCE

The fund has enjoyed tremendous growth over the last five years. Including dividends and capital gains distributions, the Mairs & Power Growth Fund has provided a total return for the last five years (through mid-1998) of 206 percent. A $10,000 investment in 1993 would have grown to about $31,000 five years later. Average annual return: 25.1 percent.

CONSISTENCY

The fund has been very consistent recently, outperforming the Dow Jones Industrial Average in four of the last five years through 1997 (but it trailed the Dow through the first few months of 1998). Its biggest gain came in 1995, when it moved up 49.3 percent (compared with a 33.5 percent rise in the Dow).

FEES/SERVICES/MANAGEMENT

The Mairs and Power Growth Fund is a true no-load fund—no fee to buy, no fee to sell. The fund's total annual expense ratio of just 0.89 percent (with no 12b-1 fee) compares very favorably with other funds.

The fund offers all the standard services, such as retirement account availability, automatic withdrawal, and automatic checking account deduction. Its minimum initial investment of $2,500 and minimum subsequent investment of $100 are a little high compared with other funds.

George A. Mairs III has managed the fund since 1980. The fund is the only one offered by Mairs & Power.

Top Ten Stock Holdings

1. Emerson Electric
2. Norwest
3. Medtronic
4. Pfizer
5. TCF Financial

6. Honeywell
7. U.S. Bancorp
8. Minnesota Mining & Manufacturing (3M)
9. Ecolab
10. Merrill Computer Systems

Asset mix: common stocks—95%; cash/equivalents—5%
Total net assets: $412.6 million
Dividend yield: 1.05%

Fees

Front-end load	*None*
Redemption fee	*None*
12b-1 fee	*None*
Management fee	0.60%
Other expenses	0.29
Total annual expense	0.89%
Minimum initial investment	$2,500
Minimum subsequent investment	$100

Services

Telephone exchanges	*Yes*
Automatic withdrawal	*Yes*
Automatic checking deduction	*Yes*
Retirement plan/IRA	*Yes*
Instant redemption	*Yes*
Financial statements	*Quarterly*
Income distributions	*Semiannual*
Capital gains distributions	*Annual*
Portfolio manager: years	18
Number of funds in family	1

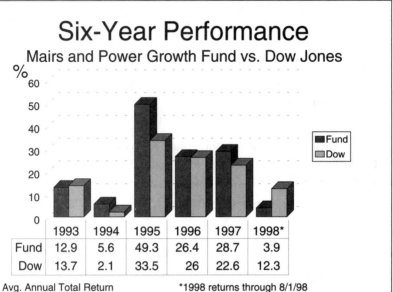

Six-Year Performance
Mairs and Power Growth Fund vs. Dow Jones

	1993	1994	1995	1996	1997	1998*
Fund	12.9	5.6	49.3	26.4	28.7	3.9
Dow	13.7	2.1	33.5	26	22.6	12.3

Avg. Annual Total Return
Fund vs. Dow Jones Industrial Avg.

*1998 returns through 8/1/98
(5-year avg. annual return: 23.9%)

AGGRESSIVE

Baron Asset Fund

Baron Funds
767 Fifth Avenue
New York, NY 10153

Fund manager: Ronald S. Baron
Fund objective: Aggressive growth

Toll-free: 800-992-2766
In-state: 212-759-7700
Fax: 212-583-2050

Performance	★ ★ ★ ★ ★
Consistency	★ ★ ★ ★
Fees/Services	★ ★ ★ ★ ★
BARAX	**14 Points**

Ronald Baron, the founder and portfolio manager of the Baron Asset Fund, has posted stellar returns since the fund was opened in 1987 by buying and holding stocks of fast-rising small and midsize growth companies. "We will not make an initial investment in a business unless we believe we can earn a return of at least 50 percent during the subsequent two years," explains Baron.

Baron is not quick to pull the plug on a stock even if its short-term prospects are less than stellar. "We will hold these investments if a business's prospects over the long term remain attractive." His long-term approach is reflected in the fund's extremely low annual portfolio turnover ratio of just 13 percent.

Over the past ten years, the fund has posted an average annual return of about 19.5 percent. A $10,000 investment in the Barron Asset Fund ten years ago would now be worth about $60,000.

The fund, which has about 80 stock holdings, is well diversified across industry groups. Its leading sectors include amusement and recreation services, 12 percent of assets; real estate–related businesses, 9 percent; media and entertainment, 12 percent; retail and restaurants, 8 percent; health services, 11 percent; hotels and lodging, 10 percent; and education, 6 percent.

The fund stays almost fully invested in the stock market most of the time.

PERFORMANCE

The fund has enjoyed exceptional growth over the last five years. Including dividends and capital gains distributions, the Baron Asset Fund has provided a total return for the last five years (through mid-1998) of 205 percent. A $10,000 investment in 1993 would have grown to about $30,000 five years later. Average annual return: 25 percent.

CONSISTENCY

The fund has been fairly consistent recently, outperforming the Dow Jones Industrial Average in four of the last five years through 1997 (but it trailed the Dow through the first six months of 1998). Its biggest gain came in 1995, when it jumped 35.3 percent (compared with a 33.5 percent rise in the Dow).

FEES/SERVICES/MANAGEMENT

Like all Baron funds, the Asset Fund is a true no-load fund—no fee to buy, no fee to sell. The fund's total annual expense ratio of 1.35 percent (including a 0.25 percent 12b-1 fee) is in line with other funds.

The fund offers all the standard services, such as retirement account availability, automatic withdrawal, and automatic checking account deduction. Its minimum initial investment of $2,000 and minimum subsequent investment of $1 compare favorably with other funds.

Ronald S. Baron has managed the fund since it opened in 1987. The Baron family of funds includes three funds and allows shareholders to switch from fund to fund by telephone.

Top Ten Stock Holdings

1. Manor Care	6. Polo Ralph Lauren
2. Choice Hotels International	7. AMF Bowling
3. Charles Schwab	8. Heftel Broadcasting
4. Sotheby's Holdings	9. Dollar Tree Stores
5. Vail Resorts	10. Bristol Hotel

Asset mix: common stocks—98%; convertible issues—1%; cash/equivalents—1%
Total net assets: $3.8 billion
Dividend yield: none

Fees

Front-end load	*None*
Redemption fee	*None*
12b-1 fee	0.25%
Management fee	1.00
Other expenses	0.10
Total annual expense	1.35%
Minimum initial investment	$2,000
Minimum subsequent investment	$1

Services

Telephone exchanges	*Yes*
Automatic withdrawal	*Yes*
Automatic checking deduction	*Yes*
Retirement plan/IRA	*Yes*
Instant redemption	*Yes*
Financial statements	*Quarterly*
Income distributions	*Annual*
Capital gains distributions	*Annual*
Portfolio manager: years	11
Number of funds in family	3

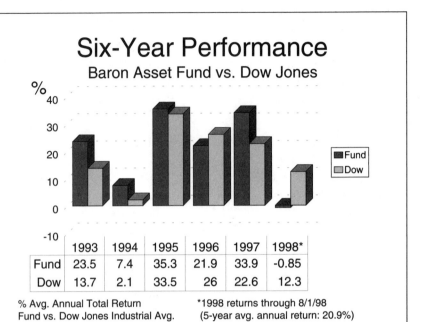

Six-Year Performance
Baron Asset Fund vs. Dow Jones

	1993	1994	1995	1996	1997	1998*
Fund	23.5	7.4	35.3	21.9	33.9	-0.85
Dow	13.7	2.1	33.5	26	22.6	12.3

% Avg. Annual Total Return   *1998 returns through 8/1/98
Fund vs. Dow Jones Industrial Avg.   (5-year avg. annual return: 20.9%)

LONG TERM

Gabelli Westwood Equity Fund

Gabelli-Westwood Funds
One Corporate Center
Rye, NY 10580-1434

Fund manager: Susan M. Byrne
Fund objective: Long-term growth
Web site: www.gabelli.com

Toll-free: 800-422-3554
In-state: 914-921-5100
Fax: 914-921-5118

Performance	★ ★ ★ ★
Consistency	★ ★ ★ ★ ★
Fees/Services	★ ★ ★ ★ ★
WESWX	**14 Points**

The Gabelli Westwood Equity Fund invests in a broad range of well-known companies, most of which pay dividends. The fund, which has been managed by Susan Byrne since 1987, is designed to provide both income and share price appreciation. Over the past ten years, the fund has posted an average annual return of about 17 percent. A $10,000 investment in the fund ten years ago would now be worth about $50,000.

In addition to blue chips such as IBM, Lockheed Martin, and GTE, the fund also invests in a few up-and-coming companies, such as Lucent Technologies, Sterling Commerce, and NextLevel Systems. The fund has about 50 stock holdings in all. Leading sectors include telecommunications, 12 percent of assets; real estate trusts, 9 percent; energy, 16 percent; health care, 7 percent; automotive, 5 percent; and insurance, 5 percent.

Byrne maintains a fairly conservative trading approach; the annual portfolio turnover ratio is 61 percent.

PERFORMANCE

The fund has enjoyed outstanding growth over the last five years. Including dividends and capital gains distributions, the Gabelli Westwood Equity Fund has provided a total return for the last five years (through mid-1998) of 186 percent. A $10,000 investment in 1993 would have grown to about $29,000 five years later. Average annual return: 23.4 percent.

CONSISTENCY

The fund has been extremely consistent recently, outperforming the Dow Jones Industrial Average for five consecutive years through 1997 (but it trailed the Dow through the first few months of 1998). Its biggest gain came in 1995, when it moved up 36.9 percent (compared with a 33.5 percent rise in the Dow).

FEES/SERVICES/MANAGEMENT

The fund is a true no-load—no fee to buy, no fee to sell. The fund's total annual expense ratio of 1.59 percent (including a 0.25 percent 12b-1 fee) is in line with other funds.

The fund offers all the standard services, such as retirement account availability, automatic withdrawal, and automatic checking account deduction. Its minimum initial investment of $1,000 and minimum subsequent investment of $50 compare favorably with other funds.

Susan Byrne has managed the fund since 1987. The Gabelli Westwood family of funds includes five funds and allows shareholders to switch from fund to fund by telephone.

Top Ten Stock Holdings

1. CVS	6. Eaton
2. IBM	7. ALCOA
3. Lucent Technologies	8. Campbell Soup
4. Bell Atlantic	9. SBC Communications
5. Conseco	10. Mobil

Asset mix: common stocks—93%; government securities—6%; corporate bonds—1%
Total net assets: $151 million
Dividend yield: 0.63%

Fees

Front-end load	*None*
Redemption fee	*None*
12b-1 fee	0.25%
Management fee	1.00
Other expenses	0.34
Total annual expense	1.59%
Minimum initial investment	$1,000
Minimum subsequent investment	$50

Services

Telephone exchanges	*Yes*
Automatic withdrawal	*Yes*
Automatic checking deduction	*Yes*
Retirement plan/IRA	*Yes*
Instant redemption	*Yes*
Financial statements	*Semiannual*
Income distributions	*Annual*
Capital gains distributions	*Annual*
Portfolio manager: years	11
Number of funds in family	5

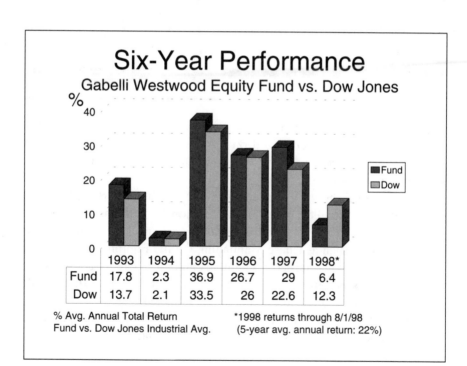

Six-Year Performance
Gabelli Westwood Equity Fund vs. Dow Jones

	1993	1994	1995	1996	1997	1998*
Fund	17.8	2.3	36.9	26.7	29	6.4
Dow	13.7	2.1	33.5	26	22.6	12.3

% Avg. Annual Total Return
Fund vs. Dow Jones Industrial Avg.

*1998 returns through 8/1/98
(5-year avg. annual return: 22%)

6

Legg Mason Value Trust

LONG TERM

Legg Mason Funds
100 Light Street, 29th Floor
Baltimore, MD 21202

Fund manager: William H. Miller III
Fund objective: Long-term growth
Web site: www.leggmason.com

Toll-free: 800-822-5544
In-state: 410-539-0000
Fax: 410-454-3445

Performance	★ ★ ★ ★ ★
Consistency	★ ★ ★
Fees/Services	★ ★ ★ ★ ★
LMVTX	**13 Points**

Legg Mason Value Trust manager William Miller III looks for stocks that appear to be undervalued based on the company's long-term earning power or asset value. That approach has helped propel the fund to outstanding growth over the past decade. The fund has posted an average annual return of about 19 percent over the past ten years. A $10,000 investment in the fund ten years ago would now be worth about $60,000.

Most of the fund's $3.7 billion in assets are invested in major blue chip companies, such as Chase Manhattan, Digital Equipment, IBM, and MCI. Its leading industrial sectors include computer systems and services, 20 percent of assets; financial services, 11 percent; banking, 16 percent; media, 6 percent; and telecommunications, 5 percent.

The fund manager takes a very conservative buy-and-hold approach. The annual portfolio turnover ratio is just 11 percent.

PERFORMANCE   ★ ★ ★ ★ ★

The fund has enjoyed exceptional growth over the last five years. Including dividends and capital gains distributions, the Legg Mason Value Trust has provided a total return for the last five years (through mid-1998) of 242 percent. A $10,000 investment in 1993 would have grown to about $34,000 five years later. Average annual return: 27.9 percent.

CONSISTENCY

The fund has been fairly consistent recently, outperforming the Dow Jones Industrial Average in three of the last five years through 1997 (and it led the Dow through the first few months of 1998). Its biggest gain came in 1995, when it moved up 40.8 percent (compared with a 33.5 percent rise in the Dow).

FEES/SERVICES/MANAGEMENT

Like all Legg Mason funds, the Value Trust is a true no-load fund—no fee to buy, no fee to sell. The fund's total annual expense ratio of 1.77 percent (including a 0.95 percent 12b-1 fee) is a little higher than most funds.

The fund offers all the standard services, such as retirement account availability, automatic withdrawal, and automatic checking account deduction. Its minimum initial investment of $1,000 and minimum subsequent investment of $100 are in line with other funds.

William H. Miller III has managed the fund since 1990. The Legg Mason fund family includes 14 funds and allows shareholders to switch from fund to fund by telephone.

Top Ten Stock Holdings

1. Dell Computer	6. Citicorp
2. America Online	7. MBNA
3. Fannie Mae	8. IBM
4. Chase Manhattan	9. Lloyds TSB Group
5. Storage Technology	10. Chrysler

Asset mix: common stocks—91%; government securities—1%; cash/equivalents—8%
Total net assets: $3.7 billion
Dividend yield: 0.07%

Fees

Front-end load	*None*
Redemption fee	*None*
12b-1 fee	0.95%
Management fee	0.72
Other expenses	0.10
Total annual expense	1.77%
Minimum initial investment	$1,000
Minimum subsequent investment	$100

Services

Telephone exchanges	*Yes*
Automatic withdrawal	*Yes*
Automatic checking deduction	*Yes*
Retirement plan/IRA	*Yes*
Instant redemption	*Yes*
Financial statements	*Semiannual*
Income distributions	*Annual*
Capital gains distributions	*Annual*
Portfolio manager: years	8
Number of funds in family	14

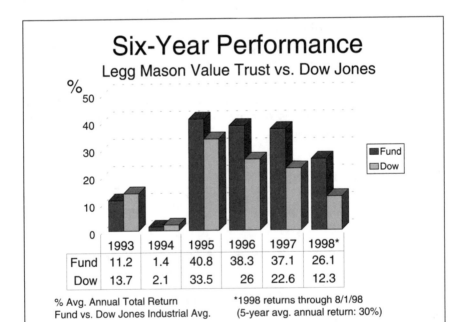

Six-Year Performance
Legg Mason Value Trust vs. Dow Jones

	1993	1994	1995	1996	1997	1998*
Fund	11.2	1.4	40.8	38.3	37.1	26.1
Dow	13.7	2.1	33.5	26	22.6	12.3

% Avg. Annual Total Return
Fund vs. Dow Jones Industrial Avg.

*1998 returns through 8/1/98
(5-year avg. annual return: 30%)

LONG TERM

7
White Oak Growth Stock Fund

Oak Associates Funds
P.O. Box 419441
Kansas City, MO 64141-6441

Fund manager: James D. Oelschlager
Fund objective: Long-term growth
Web site: www.oakassociates.com

Toll-free: 800-932-7781
In-state: 610-989-1000
Fax: 610-989-6088

Performance	★ ★ ★ ★ ★
Consistency	★ ★ ★
Fees/Services	★ ★ ★ ★ ★
WOGSX	**13 Points**

Solid as an oak, the White Oak Growth Stock Fund invests in fast-growing, but well-established, technology-related companies, such as Microsoft, Intel, Medtronic, and Cisco Systems. "We continue to believe that the health care, technology and financial services sectors offer the average investor the best opportunity for growth," says fund manager James Oelschlager.

Oelschlager's strategy is to buy the top blue chip stocks in the technology and financial sectors and hold for the long term. His annual portfolio turnover ratio is just 8 percent.

The fund has only about 25 stock holdings in all. Leading sectors include banks, 14 percent; computer communications, 12 percent; computer hardware, 12 percent; pharmaceuticals, 10 percent; semiconductor industry, 8 percent; and telecommunications equipment, 7 percent.

PERFORMANCE

The fund has enjoyed outstanding growth over the last five years. Including dividends and capital gains distributions, the White Oak Growth Fund has provided a total return for the last five years (through mid-1998) of 221 percent. A $10,000 investment in 1993 would have grown to about $32,000 five years later. Average annual return: 26.3 percent.

CONSISTENCY

The fund has been fairly consistent recently, outperforming the Dow Jones Industrial Average in three of the last five years through 1997 (and it led the Dow through the first few months of 1998). Its biggest gain came in 1995, when it jumped 52.7 percent (compared with a 33.5 percent rise in the Dow).

FEES/SERVICES/MANAGEMENT

The White Oak Growth Fund is a true no-load fund—no fee to buy, no fee to sell. The fund's total annual expense ratio of 0.98 percent (with no 12b-1 fee) compares very favorably with other funds.

The fund offers all the standard services, such as retirement account availability, automatic withdrawal, and automatic checking account deduction. Its minimum initial investment of $2,000 and minimum subsequent investment of $50 is in line with other funds.

James Oelschlager has managed the fund since 1992. The Oak Associates fund family has only two funds.

Top Ten Stock Holdings

1. Cisco Systems
2. Merck
3. Pfizer
4. Sun Microsystems
5. Linear Technology
6. Intel
7. Applied Materials
8. Medtronic
9. Ascend Communications
10. Tellabs

Asset mix: common stocks—95%; cash/equivalents—5%
Total net assets: $392 million
Dividend yield: 0.02%

Fees

Front-end load	*None*
Redemption fee	*None*
12b-1 fee	*None*
Management fee	0.59%
Other expenses	0.39
Total annual expense	0.98%
Minimum initial investment	$2,000
Minimum subsequent investment	$50

Services

Telephone exchanges	*Yes*
Automatic withdrawal	*Yes*
Automatic checking deduction	*Yes*
Retirement plan/IRA	*Yes*
Instant redemption	*Yes*
Financial statements	*Semiannual*
Income distributions	*Quarterly*
Capital gains distributions	*Annual*
Portfolio manager: years	6
Number of funds in family	2

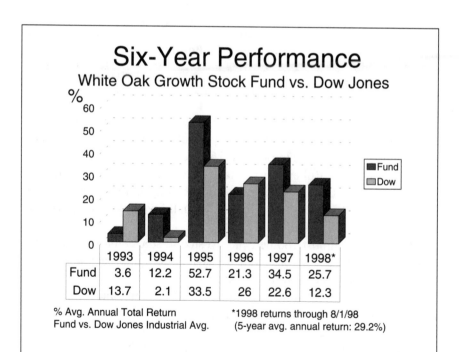

Six-Year Performance
White Oak Growth Stock Fund vs. Dow Jones

	1993	1994	1995	1996	1997	1998*
Fund	3.6	12.2	52.7	21.3	34.5	25.7
Dow	13.7	2.1	33.5	26	22.6	12.3

% Avg. Annual Total Return
Fund vs. Dow Jones Industrial Avg.

*1998 returns through 8/1/98
(5-year avg. annual return: 29.2%)

8
Torray Fund

LONG TERM

Torray Funds
6610 Rockledge Drive
Suite 450
Bethesda, MD 20817

Fund manager: Robert E. Torray
Fund objective: Long-term growth

Toll-free: 800-443-3036
In-state: 301-493-4600
Fax: 301-530-0642

Performance	★ ★ ★ ★ ★
Consistency	★ ★ ★ ★
Fees/Services	★ ★ ★ ★
TORYX	**13 Points**

The Torray Fund invests in solid, blue chip companies in fast-growing industries. The fund has enjoyed exceptional returns the past five years with an average annual gain of about 26 percent.

Fund manager Robert Torray takes a value approach in selecting stocks for the portfolio. "We are investing in long-term business values, not chasing stock prices," says Torray. "Usually we buy when prices are falling."

Torray stays almost 100 percent invested in stocks under normal circumstances. He takes a conservative buy-and-hold approach and has an annual portfolio turnover ratio of just 21 percent.

The fund has about 40 stock holdings in all. Leading industrial sectors include financial services, 13 percent of assets; media and entertainment, 10 percent; health care, 9 percent; aerospace, defense, and electronics, 9 percent; communications equipment, 9 percent; banking, 9 percent; computer systems, 9 percent; and telecommunications, 8 percent.

PERFORMANCE

The fund has enjoyed exceptional growth over the last five years. Including dividends and capital gains distributions, the Torray Fund has provided a total return for the last five years (through mid-1998) of 218 percent. A $10,000 investment in 1993 would have grown to about $32,000 five years later. Average annual return: 26 percent.

CONSISTENCY

The fund has been very consistent recently, outperforming the Dow Jones Industrial Average in four of the last five years through 1997 (and it led the Dow through the first few months of 1998). Its biggest gain came in 1995, when it moved up 50.4 percent (compared with a 33.5 percent rise in the Dow).

FEES/SERVICES/MANAGEMENT

The Torray Fund is a true no-load—no fee to buy, no fee to sell. Its total annual expense ratio of 1.09 percent (with no 12b-1 fee) compares favorably with other funds.

The fund offers some of the standard services, such as retirement account availability and instant redemption, but does not offer many of the other standard mutual fund services. Its minimum initial investment of $10,000 and minimum subsequent investment of $2,000 are much higher than most funds.

Robert Torray has managed the fund since 1990. The Torray Fund is the only fund offered by Torray Funds.

Top Ten Stock Holdings

1. AT&T
2. Travelers Group
3. Electronic Data Systems
4. SLM Holding
5. Loral Space & Communications
6. duPont (EI) de Nemours
7. Archer-Daniels-Midland
8. U.S. West Group
9. Northrop Grumman
10. Hughes Electronics

Asset mix: common stocks—98%; cash/equivalents—2%
Total net assets: $604 million
Dividend yield: 0.35%

Fees

Front-end load	*None*
Redemption fee	*None*
12b-1 fee	*None*
Management fee	1.00%
Other expenses	0.09
Total annual expense	1.09%
Minimum initial investment	$10,000
Minimum subsequent investment	$2,000

Services

Telephone exchanges	*No*
Automatic withdrawal	*No*
Automatic checking deduction	*No*
Retirement plan/IRA	*Yes*
Instant redemption	*Yes*
Financial statements	*Semiannual*
Income distributions	*Quarterly*
Capital gains distributions	*Annual*
Portfolio manager: years	8
Number of funds in family	1

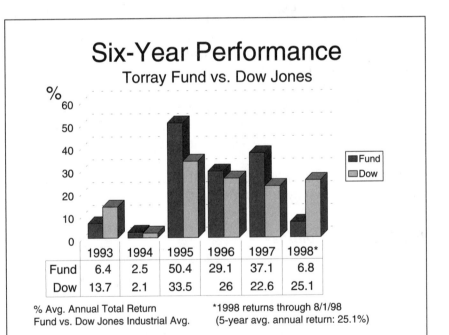

Six-Year Performance
Torray Fund vs. Dow Jones

	1993	1994	1995	1996	1997	1998*
Fund	6.4	2.5	50.4	29.1	37.1	6.8
Dow	13.7	2.1	33.5	26	22.6	25.1

% Avg. Annual Total Return
Fund vs. Dow Jones Industrial Avg.

*1998 returns through 8/1/98
(5-year avg. annual return: 25.1%)

SECTOR

9

Fidelity Select Home Finance Portfolio

Fidelity Investments
82 Devonshire Street
Boston, MA 02109

Fund manager: William Rubin
Fund objective: Sector fund
Web site: www.fidelity.com

Toll-free: 800-544-8888
In-state: 801-534-1910
Fax: 617-476-9753

Performance	★ ★ ★ ★ ★
Consistency	★ ★ ★ ★ ★
Fees/Services	★ ★ ★
FSVLX	**13 Points**

The new-home market continues to thrive along with the economy and so have the financial companies behind the home-building boom. For most of the past decade, mortgage lenders have enjoyed growing demand for their lending services—a trend that has helped make the Fidelity Select Home Finance Portfolio one of the nation's top-performing mutual funds. It has outperformed the Dow Jones Industrial Average in for seven consecutive years and has posted a 28 percent average annual return over the past ten years. A $10,000 investment in the fund ten years ago would now be worth nearly $120,000.

The home mortgage sector tends to do best when interest rates are low or falling and worst when they begin to edge back up. Volatility is something fund manager William Rubin has to live with. "The positive, near-term growth outlook for thrifts and banks should remain in place if companies continue their proactive management," says Rubin. "In addition, continued acquisitions will keep the industry consolidation trend intact and should support the high valuations we've seen."

The fund has about 140 stock holdings. Its leading segments include banks, 23 percent of assets; credit and other financial services, 16 percent; and savings and loans, 43 percent.

Rubin maintains a fairly modest trading policy. The annual average portfolio turnover ratio is 78 percent.

PERFORMANCE

The fund has enjoyed tremendous growth over the past five years. Including dividends and capital gains distributions, the Fidelity Select Home Finance Portfolio has provided a total return for the past five years (through early 1998) of 287 percent. A $10,000 investment in 1993 would have grown to about $39,000 five years later. Average annual return: 31.1 percent.

CONSISTENCY

The fund has been very consistent, outpacing the Dow Jones Industrial Average for the past five consecutive years (but it trailed the Dow through the first few months of 1998). Its biggest gains came in 1993 and 1995, when it moved up 27.3 and 53.5 percent, respectively (compared with a 13.7 and 33.5 percent gain for the Dow).

FEES/SERVICES/MANAGEMENT

The fund has a low front-end load of 3 percent and a maximum redemption fee of .75 percent if it's sold out within 29 days. Its annual expense ratio of 1.52 percent (with no 12b-1 fee) compares favorably with other funds.

The fund offers many of the standard services, such as retirement account availability and automatic checking account deduction. Its minimum initial investment of $2,500 and minimum subsequent investment of $250 are a little high compared with other funds.

William Rubin, who has been with Fidelity since 1994, has managed the fund since 1996. The Fidelity fund family includes more than 230 funds.

Top Ten Stock Holdings

1. Washington Mutual
2. Ahmanson
3. Dime Bancorp
4. Charger One Financial
5. Greenpoint Financial
6. TCF Financial
7. Astoria Financial
8. Peoples Heritage Financial Group
9. FIRSTPLUS Financial Group
10. Commercial Federal

Asset mix: common stocks— 95%; cash/equivalents—5%
Total net assets: $1.67 billion
Dividend yield: 0.45%

Fees

Front-end load	3.00%
Redemption fee	0.75
12b-1 fee	*None*
Management fee	0.61
Other expenses	0.91
Total annual expense	1.52%
Minimum initial investment	$2,500
Minimum subsequent investment	$250

Services

Telephone exchanges	*Yes*
Automatic withdrawal	*Yes*
Automatic checking deduction	*Yes*
Retirement plan/IRA	*Yes*
Instant redemption	*Yes*
Financial statements	*Semiannual*
Income distributions	*Semiannual*
Capital gains distributions	*Semiannual*
Portfolio manager: years	2
Number of funds in family	235

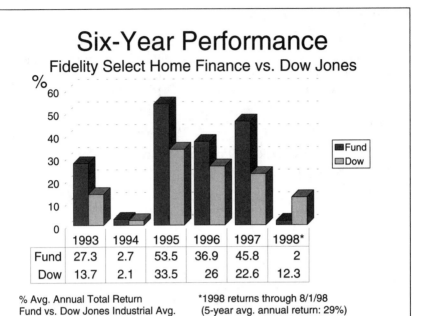

Six-Year Performance
Fidelity Select Home Finance vs. Dow Jones

	1993	1994	1995	1996	1997	1998*
Fund	27.3	2.7	53.5	36.9	45.8	2
Dow	13.7	2.1	33.5	26	22.6	12.3

% Avg. Annual Total Return   *1998 returns through 8/1/98
Fund vs. Dow Jones Industrial Avg.   (5-year avg. annual return: 29%)

SECTOR

10
Vanguard Specialized Portfolio: Health Care

Vanguard Group
P.O. Box 2600
Valley Forge, PA 19482

Fund manager: Edward P. Owens
Fund objective: Sector
Web site: www.vanguard.com

Toll-free: 800-635-1511
In-state: 610-669-1000
Fax: 610-640-1371

Performance	★ ★ ★ ★ ★
Consistency	★ ★ ★
Fees/Services	★ ★ ★ ★ ★
VGHCX	**13 Points**

The aging of America's baby boom generation is already starting to have an impact on the bottom line of the health care industry—an effect that should become even more profound in the years to come. The Vanguard Health Care Portfolio is positioned to take advantage of that growth. Over the past ten years, the fund has posted an average annual return of about 23 percent. A $10,000 investment in the fund ten years ago would now be worth nearly $80,000.

The fund invests in both large and emerging health-related companies, such as Abbott Labs, Bristol-Myers, Merck, Eli Lilly, and St. Jude Medical. The fund is worldwide in scope, and about 20 percent of its assets are invested in foreign health care stocks.

The fund has about 100 stock holdings in all. Leading sectors include drugs and pharmaceuticals, 46 percent; medical and dental instruments and supplies, 8 percent; health care management services, 5 percent; and health care facilities, 4 percent.

Fund manager Edward Owens takes a very conservative buy-and-hold approach. The annual portfolio turnover ratio is 7 percent.

PERFORMANCE

The fund has enjoyed tremendous growth over the last five years. Including dividends and capital gains distributions, the Vanguard Health Care Portfolio has provided a total return for the last five years (through mid-1998) of 246 percent. A $10,000 investment in 1993 would have grown to about $35,000 five years later. Average annual return: 28.2 percent.

CONSISTENCY

The fund has been fairly consistent recently, outperforming the Dow Jones Industrial Average in three of the last five years through 1997 (and it led the Dow through the first few months of 1998). Its biggest gain came in 1995, when it moved up 45.2 percent (compared with a 33.5 percent rise in the Dow).

FEES/SERVICES/MANAGEMENT

Like all Vanguard funds, the Health Care Portfolio is a true no-load fund—no fee to buy, no fee to sell. Its total annual expense ratio of just 0.38 percent (with no 12b-1 fee) compares very favorably with other funds.

The fund offers all the standard services, such as retirement account availability, automatic withdrawal, and automatic checking account deduction. Its minimum initial investment of $3,000 and minimum subsequent investment of $100 are a little higher than most funds.

Edward Owens has managed the fund since 1984. The Vanguard Group includes 95 funds and allows shareholders to switch from fund to fund by telephone.

Top Ten Stock Holdings

1. Pharmacia & Upjohn
2. Warner-Lambert
3. Pfizer
4. Bristol-Myers Squibb
5. Abbott Laboratories
6. McKesson
7. Merck
8. Zeneca Group
9. Johnson & Johnson
10. Allergan

Asset mix: common stocks—91%; cash/equivalents—9%
Total net assets: $4.5 billion
Dividend yield: 0.96%

Fees

Front-end load	*None*
Redemption fee	*None*
12b-1 fee	*None*
Management fee	0.24%
Other expenses	0.14
Total annual expense	0.38%
Minimum initial investment	$3,000
Minimum subsequent investment	$100

Services

Telephone exchanges	*Yes*
Automatic withdrawal	*Yes*
Automatic checking deduction	*Yes*
Retirement plan/IRA	*Yes*
Instant redemption	*Yes*
Financial statements	*Semiannual*
Income distributions	*Semiannual*
Capital gains distributions	*Annual*
Portfolio manager: years	14
Number of funds in family	95

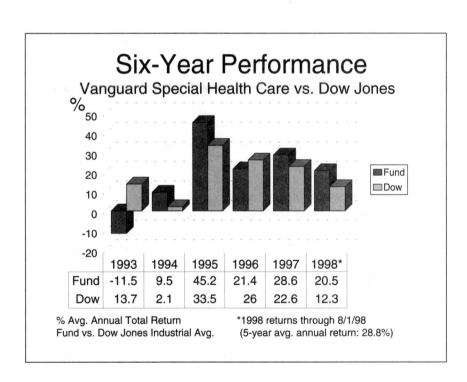

Six-Year Performance
Vanguard Special Health Care vs. Dow Jones

	1993	1994	1995	1996	1997	1998*
Fund	-11.5	9.5	45.2	21.4	28.6	20.5
Dow	13.7	2.1	33.5	26	22.6	12.3

% Avg. Annual Total Return
Fund vs. Dow Jones Industrial Avg.

*1998 returns through 8/1/98
(5-year avg. annual return: 28.8%)

11

T. Rowe Price Science and Technology Fund

SECTOR

T. Rowe Price Funds
100 East Pratt Street
Baltimore, MD 21202

Fund manager: Charles Morris
Fund objective: Sector
Web site: www.troweprice.com

Toll-free: 800-225-5132
In-state: 410-547-2000
Fax: 410-347-1572

Performance	★ ★ ★ ★ ★
Consistency	★ ★ ★
Fees/Services	★ ★ ★ ★ ★
PRSCX	**13 Points**

For several years, the T. Rowe Price Science and Technology Fund was one of the top-performing funds in America. All three of its key areas of concentration—computers, health care, and communications—were flying high through the high-tech boom of the 1990s. But all good things must come to an end. When the high-tech sector fell flat in 1996 and 1997, this high-flying fund fell with it. It was up just 14 percent in 1996 and a meager 1.7 percent in 1997. But for investors interested in participating in what is likely to be the fastest growth sector of the future, the Science and Technology Fund still holds great promise.

Over the past ten years, the fund has posted an average annual return of about 24 percent. A $10,000 investment in the fund ten years ago would now be worth about $83,000.

According to the fund's charter, the fund is limited to a maximum 25 percent threshold for any one sector. Whereas some technology funds specialize in computer stocks, others in health care, and still others in electronics or telecommunications, the Science and Technology Fund spreads its assets throughout a broad spectrum of technology issues. "With our diversification, we're not going to hit many home runs," says fund manager Charles Morris, "but we've caught a good portion of all the key waves."

Generally speaking, the fund may have the lion's share of its assets spread through six or seven different technology sectors, such as health care, wireless communications, computer software, semiconductors, and data services, with roughly 15 percent of its assets in each of the key categories. "That means we probably won't be among the top ten funds in any one quarter or even in any one year because we are too diversified," says Morris. "But we're able to ease the volatility a little by spreading our bets. I think consistency will be an enduring quality of this fund."

Morris tries to keep at least 85 percent of the fund's assets invested in stocks at all times, but he changes the mix continually. He loads up on stocks of the smaller, emerging companies when they seem undervalued and poised for a rebound. When their valuations get a little too high, he moves some of the assets into the more stable names and raises cash modestly. But under normal circumstances, smaller companies will dominate the fund. "We've tried to stay invested in the most dynamic small-cap and midcap stocks."

Morris is never shy about buying and selling stocks to stay on top of the trends. The fund has a fairly aggressive annual portfolio turnover ratio of 126 percent. "We understand that it's very important to keep moving. We try to stay on the leading edge of technology. It's easy to invest in the bigger technology companies like IBM or Hewlett-Packard, but we would rather invest in the one-product wonders like Cisco Systems—if we do our homework and make sure that their one product really is hot."

Although the fund's assets now exceed $3.5 billion, Morris still prefers to keep the portfolio at a manageable level of about 50 stocks.

PERFORMANCE

The fund has enjoyed excellent growth over the last five years. Including dividends and capital gains distributions, the T. Rowe Price Science and Technology Fund has provided a total return for the last five years (through mid-1998) of 203 percent. A $10,000 investment in 1993 would have grown to about $30,000 five years later. Average annual return: 24.9 percent.

CONSISTENCY

The fund has been fairly consistent recently, outperforming the Dow Jones Industrial Average in three of the last five years through 1997 (and it led the Dow through the first few months of 1998). Its biggest gain came in 1995, when it leaped 55.5 percent (compared with a 33.5 percent rise in the Dow).

FEES/SERVICES/MANAGEMENT

Like all T. Rowe Price funds, the Science and Technology Fund is a true no-load fund—no fee to buy, no fee to sell. Its total annual expense ratio of 0.97 percent (with no 12b-1 fee) compares very favorably with other funds.

The fund offers all the standard services, such as retirement account availability, automatic withdrawal, and automatic checking account deduction. Its minimum initial investment of $2,500 and minimum subsequent investment of $100 are a little on the high side compared with other funds.

Charles Morris has managed the fund since 1991. The T. Rowe Price family of funds includes 70 funds and allows shareholders to switch from fund to fund by telephone.

Top Ten Stock Holdings

1. Parametric Technology	6. Xilinx
2. Analog Devices	7. Cendant
3. Network Associates	8. ASM Lithography Holdings
4. First Data	9. Synopsys
5. Maxim Integrated Products	10. Microsoft

Asset mix: common stocks—93%; cash/equivalents—7%
Total net assets: $ 3.5 billion
Dividend yield: none

Fees

Front-end load	*None*
Redemption fee	*None*
12b-1 fee	*None*
Management fee	0.68%
Other expenses	0.29
Total annual expense	0.97%
Minimum initial	
investment	$2,500
Minimum subsequent	
investment	$100

Services

Telephone exchanges	*Yes*
Automatic withdrawal	*Yes*
Automatic checking	
deduction	*Yes*
Retirement plan/IRA	*Yes*
Instant redemption	*Yes*
Financial statements	*Semiannual*
Income distributions	*Annual*
Capital gains	
distributions	*Annual*
Portfolio manager: years	7
Number of funds in family	70

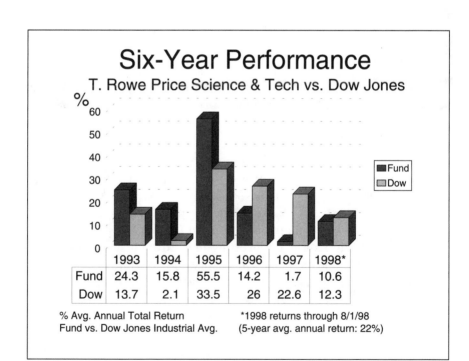

Six-Year Performance
T. Rowe Price Science & Tech vs. Dow Jones

	1993	1994	1995	1996	1997	1998*
Fund	24.3	15.8	55.5	14.2	1.7	10.6
Dow	13.7	2.1	33.5	26	22.6	12.3

% Avg. Annual Total Return   *1998 returns through 8/1/98
Fund vs. Dow Jones Industrial Avg.   (5-year avg. annual return: 22%)

12

Franklin California Growth Fund

LONG TERM

Franklin Strategic Funds
777 Mariners Island Boulevard
San Mateo, CA 94404

Fund managers: Conrad B. Herrmann, Nicholas Moore, and Kei Yamamoto
Fund objective: Long-term growth
Web site: www.franklin-templeton.com

Toll-free: 800-342-5236
In-state: 415-312-2000
Fax: 415-312-3642

Performance	★ ★ ★ ★ ★
Consistency	★ ★ ★ ★
Fees/Services	★ ★ ★
FKCGX	**12 Points**

There's no place on earth that's a more fertile incubator of hot young growth stocks than California. Silicon Valley is the true epicenter of the computer revolution. The Franklin California Growth Fund keeps at least 65 percent of its assets in California-based companies or companies conducting the majority of their operations in California. The fund has enjoyed outstanding returns by investing in California stocks. Over the past five years, the fund has posted an average annual return of 27 percent.

"As we continue to scan the investment horizon for opportunities, we find no shortage of potential investments for the Franklin California Growth Fund," says fund manager Conrad Herrmann. "California is fertile soil indeed for investment opportunity, and we shall continue to utilize the many resources at our command as we seek to take advantage of this fact."

The fund has about 90 stock holdings in all. Not surprisingly, the portfolio is heavily weighted in technology stocks. Leading sectors include electronic technology, 10 percent of assets; technology services, 20 percent; semiconductors, 4 percent; health-related companies, 6 percent; retail, 7 percent; financial services, 7 percent; and energy, 6 percent.

The fund managers maintain a fairly modest trading approach; the annual portfolio turnover ratio is 45 percent.

PERFORMANCE

The fund has enjoyed exceptional growth over the last five years. Including dividends and capital gains distributions, the California Growth Fund has provided a total return for the last five years (through mid-1998) of 231 percent. A $10,000 investment in 1993 would have grown to about $33,000 five years later. Average annual return: 27.1 percent.

CONSISTENCY

The fund has been very consistent recently, outperforming the Dow Jones Industrial Average in four of the last five years through 1997 (but it trailed the Dow through the first few months of 1998). Its biggest gain came in 1995, when it moved up 47.6 percent (compared with a 33.5 percent rise in the Dow).

FEES/SERVICES/MANAGEMENT

The California Growth Fund has a front-end load of 4.5 percent. The fund's total annual expense ratio of 1.08 percent (including a 0.22 percent 12b-1 fee) compares favorably with other funds.

The fund offers all the standard services, such as retirement account availability, automatic withdrawal, and automatic checking account deduction. Its minimum initial investment of $100 and minimum subsequent investment of $25 compare very favorably with other funds.

The management team of Conrad B. Herrmann, Nicholas Moore, and Kei Yamamoto has managed the fund since 1993. The Franklin family of funds includes 122 funds and allows shareholders to switch from fund to fund by telephone.

Top Ten Stock Holdings

1. Cisco Systems
2. Electronic Arts
3. Mattel
4. Hilton Hotels
5. Oracle

6. BankAmerica
7. Atlantic Richfield
8. Synopsys
9. Autodesk
10. Remedy

Asset mix: common stocks—91%; cash/equivalents—9%
Total net assets: $573 million
Dividend yield: 0.53%

Fees

Front-end load	4.50%
Redemption fee	*None*
12b-1 fee	0.22
Management fee	0.56
Other expenses	0.30
Total annual expense	1.08%
Minimum initial investment	$100
Minimum subsequent investment	$25

Services

Telephone exchanges	*Yes*
Automatic withdrawal	*Yes*
Automatic checking deduction	*Yes*
Retirement plan/IRA	*Yes*
Instant redemption	*Yes*
Financial statements	*Semiannual*
Income distributions	*Semiannual*
Capital gains distributions	*Semiannual*
Portfolio manager: years	5
Number of funds in family	122

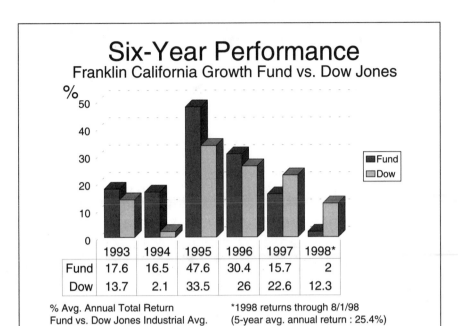

Six-Year Performance
Franklin California Growth Fund vs. Dow Jones

	1993	1994	1995	1996	1997	1998*
Fund	17.6	16.5	47.6	30.4	15.7	2
Dow	13.7	2.1	33.5	26	22.6	12.3

% Avg. Annual Total Return
Fund vs. Dow Jones Industrial Avg.

*1998 returns through 8/1/98
(5-year avg. annual return : 25.4%)

13

SAFECO Growth Fund

SAFECO Funds
P.O. Box 34890
Seattle, WA 98124-1890

SMALL CAP

Fund manager: Thomas M. Maguire
Fund objective: Small-cap stocks
Web site: www.safecofunds.com

Toll-free: 800-624-5711
In-state: 206-545-7319
Fax: 206-548-7150

Performance	★ ★ ★ ★ ★
Consistency	★ ★
Fees/Services	★ ★ ★ ★ ★
SAFGX	**12 Points**

The SAFECO Growth Fund invests primarily in little-known, small, emerging growth companies with big potential, such as Spartech, Dynamex, and Ultrak. About 70 percent of the fund's assets are in companies with less than $1 billion in total assets, while 10 percent are in mid-cap stocks, and 15 percent in large-cap stocks of over $4 billion, such as Philip Morris and Boston Scientific.

Over the past ten years, the fund has posted an average annual return of about 19 percent. A $10,000 investment in the fund ten years ago would now be worth about $60,000. "My favorite stocks continue to be those that haven't been discovered," says fund manager Thomas M. Maguire. "I hope to uncover and take opportunities that others fail to see."

Maguire takes a fairly active trading approach; the annual portfolio turnover ratio is 83 percent. The fund stays almost 100 percent invested in stocks under normal circumstances.

The fund has nearly 100 stock holdings in all. Its leading industrial sectors include health care, 13 percent of assets; broadcasting, 10 percent; computers, 7 percent; retail, 11 percent; office equipment and supplies, 7 percent; leisure, 7 percent; and financial services, 6 percent.

PERFORMANCE

The fund has enjoyed exceptional growth over the last five years. Including dividends and capital gains distributions, the SAFECO Growth Fund has provided a total return for the last five years (through mid-1998) of 227 percent. A $10,000 investment in 1993 would have grown to about $33,000 five years later. Average annual return: 26.7 percent.

CONSISTENCY ★ ★

The fund has been somewhat inconsistent recently, outperforming the Dow Jones Industrial Average in only two of the last five years through 1997 (but it led the Dow through the first few months of 1998). Its biggest gain came in 1997, when it jumped 50 percent (compared with a 22.6 percent rise in the Dow).

FEES/SERVICES/MANAGEMENT

Like all SAFECO funds, the SAFECO Growth Fund is a true no-load fund—no fee to buy, no fee to sell. The fund's total annual expense ratio of 0.99 percent (with no 12b-1 fee) compares very favorably with other funds.

The fund offers all the standard services, such as retirement account availability, automatic withdrawal, and automatic checking account deduction. Its minimum initial investment of $1,000 and minimum subsequent investment of $100 compare favorably with other funds.

Thomas Maguire has managed the fund since 1989. The SAFECO family of funds includes 19 funds and allows shareholders to switch from one fund to another by telephone.

Top Ten Stock Holdings

1. Green Tree Financial
2. Chancellor Media
3. Family Golf Centers
4. Micros Systems
5. United Stationers
6. Avon Products
7. Philip Morris
8. SFX Broadcasting
9. TETRA Technologies
10. Danka Business Systems

Asset mix: common stocks—98%; cash/equivalents—2%
Total net assets: $562 million
Dividend yield: none

Fees

Front-end load	*None*
Redemption fee	*None*
12b-1 fee	*None*
Management fee	0.65%
Other expenses	0.20
Total annual expense	0.85%
Minimum initial investment	$1,000
Minimum subsequent investment	$100

Services

Telephone exchanges	*Yes*
Automatic withdrawal	*Yes*
Automatic checking deduction	*Yes*
Retirement plan/IRA	*Yes*
Instant redemption	*Yes*
Financial statements	*Semiannual*
Income distributions	*Annual*
Capital gains distributions	*Annual*
Portfolio manager: years	9
Number of funds in family	19

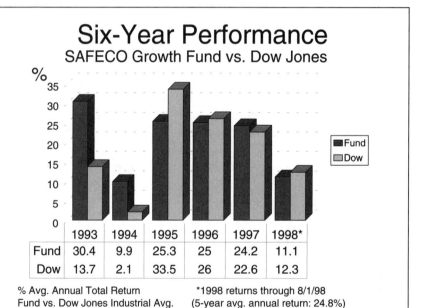

Six-Year Performance
SAFECO Growth Fund vs. Dow Jones

	1993	1994	1995	1996	1997	1998*
Fund	30.4	9.9	25.3	25	24.2	11.1
Dow	13.7	2.1	33.5	26	22.6	12.3

% Avg. Annual Total Return   *1998 returns through 8/1/98
Fund vs. Dow Jones Industrial Avg.   (5-year avg. annual return: 24.8%)

SMALL CAP

14
Franklin Small Cap Growth Fund

Franklin Strategic Funds
777 Mariners Island Boulevard
San Mateo, CA 94404

Fund manager: Edward B. Jamieson
Fund objective: Small-cap stocks
Web site: www.franklin-templeton.com

Toll-free: 800-342-5236
In-state: 415-312-2000
Fax: 415-312-3642

Performance	★ ★ ★ ★ ★
Consistency	★ ★ ★ ★
Fees/Services	★ ★ ★
FRSGX	**12 Points**

Little-known growth stocks of companies with annual revenues of under $1 billion are the focus of the Franklin Small Cap Growth Fund. "In our search for small-capitalization companies that are well positioned for rapid growth of revenues, earnings, or cash flow, we focus on those with competitive advantages such as proprietary products or a unique marketing niche," explains fund manager Edward Jamieson.

Over the past five years, the fund has posted an average annual return of nearly 26 percent. The fund has about 170 stock holdings in all, heavily weighted in technology-related issues. "New developments in technology will lead to significant growth for market leaders well into the next century," says Jamieson.

Leading sectors include electronic technology, 8 percent of assets; semiconductors, 6 percent; technology services, 16 percent; energy, 7 percent; and health-related companies, 9 percent. The fund maintains a fairly conservative trading approach. The annual portfolio turnover ratio is 55 percent.

PERFORMANCE

The fund has enjoyed excellent growth over the last five years. Including dividends and capital gains distributions, the Franklin Small Cap Growth Fund has provided a total return for the last five years (through mid-1998) of 215 percent. A $10,000 investment in 1993 would have grown to about $32,000 five years later. Average annual return: 25.8 percent.

CONSISTENCY

The fund has been very consistent recently, outperforming the Dow Jones Industrial Average in four of the last five years through 1997 (and it was about even with the Dow through the first few months of 1998). Its biggest gain came in 1995, when it moved up 42.2 percent (compared with a 33.5 percent rise in the Dow).

FEES/SERVICES/MANAGEMENT

The Franklin Small Cap Growth Fund has a front-end load of 4.50 percent. The fund's total annual expense ratio of 0.93 percent (including a 0.23 percent 12b-1 fee) compares very favorably with other funds.

The fund offers all the standard services, such as retirement account availability, automatic withdrawal, and automatic checking account deduction. Its minimum initial investment of $100 and minimum subsequent investment of $25 compare very favorably with other funds.

Edward Jamieson has managed the fund since 1992. The Franklin family of funds includes 122 funds and allows shareholders to switch from fund to fund by telephone.

Top Ten Stock Holdings

1. Varco International
2. Komag
3. Affiliated Computer Services
4. Synopsys
5. Integrated Systems
6. Barrett Resources
7. Paging Network
8. CapStar Hotel
9. Norrell
10. Expeditors International of Washington

Asset mix: common stocks—87%; cash/equivalents—13%
Total net assets: $2.8 billion
Dividend yield: 0.33%

Fees

Front-end load	4.50%
Redemption fee	*None*
12b-1 fee	0.23
Management fee	0.48
Other expenses	0.21
Total annual expense	0.92%
Minimum initial investment	$100
Minimum subsequent investment	$25

Services

Telephone exchanges	*Yes*
Automatic withdrawal	*Yes*
Automatic checking deduction	*Yes*
Retirement plan/IRA	*Yes*
Instant redemption	*Yes*
Financial statements	*Semiannual*
Income distributions	*Semiannual*
Capital gains distributions	*Semiannual*
Portfolio manager: years	6
Number of funds in family	122

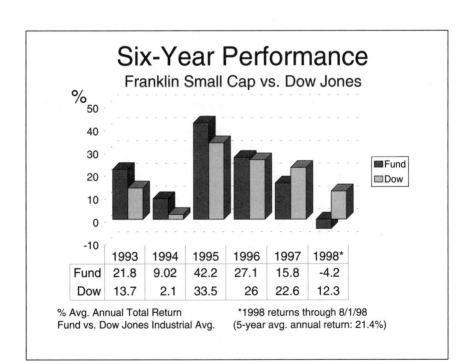

Six-Year Performance
Franklin Small Cap vs. Dow Jones

	1993	1994	1995	1996	1997	1998*
Fund	21.8	9.02	42.2	27.1	15.8	-4.2
Dow	13.7	2.1	33.5	26	22.6	12.3

% Avg. Annual Total Return
Fund vs. Dow Jones Industrial Avg.

*1998 returns through 8/1/98
(5-year avg. annual return: 21.4%)

15
Oak Value Fund

LONG TERM

Oak Funds
3100 Tower Boulevard
Suite 800
Durham, NC 27707

Fund managers: David R. Carr, Jr.,
  and George Brumley
Fund objective: Long-term growth
Web site: www.oakvalue.com

Toll-free: 800-543-8721
In-state: 919-419-1900
Fax: 919-419-1941

Performance	★ ★ ★ ★
Consistency	★ ★ ★
Fees/Services	★ ★ ★ ★ ★
OAKVX	**12 Points**

Good businesses with good management at attractive prices—that's the theme of the Oak Value Fund. In their portfolio selection process, fund managers David Carr and George Brumley visit about 100 companies each year and review the financials of hundreds of other companies on a continuous basis. Their research addresses three main questions: Is this a business we would like to own? What is the true value of the business? Can we buy it at a discount?

Over the past five years, the fund has posted average annual returns of about 25 percent. Most of the fund's holdings are midsize to large-capitalization stocks, such as Coca-Cola, Walt Disney, and Gillette. The fund has only about 25 stock holdings in all. Leading industrial sectors include broadcasting, 11 percent of assets; insurance, 20 percent; media, 15 percent; and consumer products, 10 percent.

The fund managers maintain a conservative buy-and-hold approach. The annual portfolio turnover ratio is 22 percent.

PERFORMANCE

The fund has enjoyed outstanding growth over the last five years. Including dividends and capital gains distributions, the Oak Value Fund has provided a total return for the last five years (through mid-1998) of 202 percent. A $10,000 investment in 1993 would have grown to about $30,000 five years later. Average annual return: 24.7 percent.

CONSISTENCY ★ ★ ★

The fund has been fairly consistent recently, outperforming the Dow Jones Industrial Average in three of the last five years through 1997 (and it led the Dow through the first few months of 1998). Its biggest gain came in 1997, when it moved up 37.7 percent (compared with a 22.6 percent rise in the Dow).

FEES/SERVICES/MANAGEMENT

The Oak Value Fund is a true no-load fund—no fee to buy, no fee to sell. Its total annual expense ratio of 1.54 percent (with no 12b-1 fee) is in line with other funds.

The fund offers all the standard services, such as retirement account availability, automatic withdrawal, and automatic checking account deduction. Its minimum initial investment of $2,500 and minimum subsequent investment of $100 are a little on the high side compared with other funds.

David Carr and George Brumley have managed the fund since 1993. The Oak Value Fund is the only fund offered by Oak Funds.

Top Ten Stock Holdings

1. RLI
2. Berkshire Hathaway
3. E.W. Scripps
4. R.P. Scherer
5. Avon Products
6. Nike
7. Pulitzer Publishing
8. Washington Post
9. AFLAC
10. Walt Disney

Asset mix: common stocks—89%; cash/equivalents—11%
Total net assets: $139.9 million
Dividend yield: none

Fees

Front-end load	*None*
Redemption fee	*None*
12b-1 fee	*None*
Management fee	1.03%
Other expenses	0.51
Total annual expense	1.54%
Minimum initial investment	$2,500
Minimum subsequent investment	$100

Services

Telephone exchanges	*Yes*
Automatic withdrawal	*Yes*
Automatic checking deduction	*Yes*
Retirement plan/IRA	*Yes*
Instant redemption	*Yes*
Financial statements	*Semiannual*
Income distributions	*Semiannual*
Capital gains distributions	*Semiannual*
Portfolio manager: years	5
Number of funds in family	1

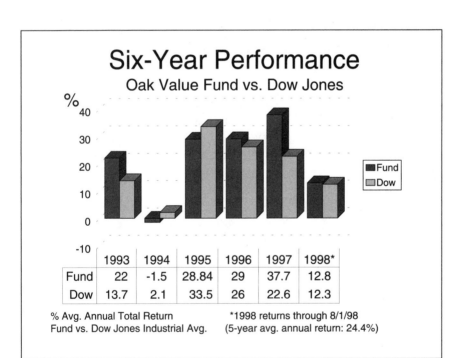

Six-Year Performance
Oak Value Fund vs. Dow Jones

	1993	1994	1995	1996	1997	1998*
Fund	22	-1.5	28.84	29	37.7	12.8
Dow	13.7	2.1	33.5	26	22.6	12.3

% Avg. Annual Total Return   *1998 returns through 8/1/98
Fund vs. Dow Jones Industrial Avg.   (5-year avg. annual return: 24.4%)

16
First Eagle Fund of America

First Eagle Funds
1345 Avenue of the Americas
New York, NY 10105-4300

Fund managers: Harold J. Levy
and David L. Cohen
Fund objective: Long-term growth

Toll-free: 800-451-3623
In-state: 212-698-3000
Fax: 212-299-4315

Performance	★ ★ ★ ★
Consistency	★ ★ ★ ★
Fees/Services	★ ★ ★ ★
FEAFX	**12 Points**

The First Eagle Fund of America focuses on midsize stocks selling at bargain prices that are in the midst of positive change. "We look for potential catalysts which signal corporate change," says fund comanager Harold Levy. "These can be management changes, share repurchases, acquisitions, divestitures, litigation controversies, strategies to enhance value, technological breakthroughs, liquidation of nonperforming assets, or changes in a company's strategy."

The fund has provided outstanding long-term returns. Over the past ten years the fund has grown at an average annual rate of 18.4 percent. A $10,000 investment in the fund ten years ago would now be worth about $55,000.

In all, the fund has about 50 stock holdings. The fund managers take a fairly active trading approach and have an annual portfolio turnover ratio of 98 percent. The fund's holdings are concentrated primarily in five main industrial groups, including banking and financial services, 18 percent of assets; aerospace and defense, 10 percent; industrial products, 13 percent; medical, 11 percent; and technology, 23 percent.

PERFORMANCE

The fund has enjoyed outstanding growth over the last five years. Including dividends and capital gains distributions, the First Eagle Fund has provided a total return for the last five years (through mid-1998) of 196 percent. A $10,000 investment in 1993 would have grown to about $30,000 five years later. Average annual return: 24.3 percent.

CONSISTENCY

The fund has been very consistent recently, outperforming the Dow Jones Industrial Average in four of the last five years through 1997 (and it led the Dow through the first few months of 1998). Its biggest gain came in 1995, when it moved up 36.4 percent (compared with a 33.5 percent rise in the Dow).

FEES/SERVICES/MANAGEMENT

First Eagle is a true no-load fund—no fee to buy or sell. Its annual expense ratio of 1.42 percent (with no 12b-1 fee) compares favorably with other funds. But the fund offers very few of the standard services provided by most fund families. There is no phone switching between the two Eagle Funds, no funds withdrawal plan, and no automatic checking deduction program. Its minimum initial investment of $5,000 is higher than most funds.

Harold Levy has managed the fund since 1987. David Cohen joined as comanager in 1989. The First Eagle family of funds includes only two funds.

Top Ten Stock Holdings

1. BankBoston	6. Aavid Thermal Technologies
2. Tele-Communications	7. Comcast
3. FINOVA Group	8. Storage Technology
4. Ceridian	9. Amgen
5. General Dynamics	10. St. Jude Medical

Asset mix: common stocks—98%; cash/equivalents—2%
Total net assets: $269 million
Dividend yield: none

Fees

Front-end load	*None*
Redemption fee	*None*
12b-1 fee	*None*
Management fee	1.00%
Other expenses	0.42
Total annual expense	1.42%
Minimum initial investment	$5,000
Minimum subsequent investment	$100

Services

Telephone exchanges	*No*
Automatic withdrawal	*No*
Automatic checking deduction	*No*
Retirement plan/IRA	*Yes*
Instant redemption	*No*
Financial statements	*Semiannual*
Income distributions	*Annual*
Capital gains distributions	*Annual*
Portfolio manager: years	11
Number of funds in family	2

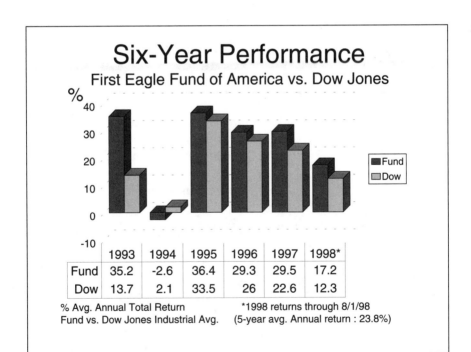

Six-Year Performance
First Eagle Fund of America vs. Dow Jones

	1993	1994	1995	1996	1997	1998*
Fund	35.2	-2.6	36.4	29.3	29.5	17.2
Dow	13.7	2.1	33.5	26	22.6	12.3

% Avg. Annual Total Return
Fund vs. Dow Jones Industrial Avg.

*1998 returns through 8/1/98
(5-year avg. Annual return : 23.8%)

17

Harbor Capital Appreciation Fund

LONG TERM

Harbor Funds
One SeaGate
Toledo, OH 43666

Fund manager: Spiros Segalas
Fund objective: Long-term growth

Toll-free: 800-422-1050
In-state: 419-247-2477
Fax: 419-247-3093

Performance	★ ★ ★ ★
Consistency	★ ★ ★
Fees/Services	★ ★ ★ ★ ★
HACAX	**12 Points**

Big stocks with big profits—that's the focus of the Harbor Capital Appreciation Fund. Among its leading holdings are a number of well-known names, such as Hewlett-Packard, Cisco Systems, Compaq Computer, and General Electric.

Started in 1987, the fund has enjoyed outstanding long-term growth. Over the past ten years the fund has posted an average annual return of 20.5 percent. A $10,000 investment in the fund ten years ago would now be worth about $65,000.

Fund manager Spiros Segalas looks for companies with rapid sales and earnings growth that are likely to benefit from strong marketing competence, commitment to research and development, superior new product flow, and veteran management. The fund invests in both U.S. and foreign blue chip stocks.

Although Segalas keeps an eye on stock values when making investments, he rarely tries to time the market. The fund remains fully invested (95 to 100 percent of its assets are in stocks) almost all the time. Segalas is fairly conservative in his trading activity resulting in an annual portfolio turnover ratio of 74 percent.

The fund has about 60 stock holdings in all. Leading sectors include computer and business equipment, 11 percent of assets; drugs and medicine, 11 percent; retail, 8 percent; semiconductors, 5 percent; electronic instruments, 5 percent; telecommunications, 5 percent; and banks and financial services, 11 percent.

PERFORMANCE

The fund has enjoyed excellent growth over the last five years. Including dividends and capital gains distributions, the Harbor Capital Appreciation Fund has provided a total return for the last five years (through mid-1998) of 190 percent. A $10,000 investment in 1993 would have grown to about $29,000 five years later. Average annual return: 23.7 percent.

CONSISTENCY

The fund has been fairly consistent recently, outperforming the Dow Jones Industrial Average in three of the last five years through 1997 (and it led the Dow through the first few months of 1998). Its biggest gain came in 1995, when it moved up 37.8 percent (compared with a 33.5 percent rise in the Dow).

FEES/SERVICES/MANAGEMENT

Like all Harbor funds, the Capital Appreciation Fund is a true no-load fund—no fee to buy, no fee to sell. The fund's total annual expense ratio of 0.70 percent (with no 12b-1 fee) compares very favorably with other funds.

The fund offers all the standard services, such as retirement account availability, automatic withdrawal, and automatic checking account deduction. Its minimum initial investment of $2,000 and minimum subsequent investment of $500 are a little on the high side compared with most other funds.

Spiros Segalas has managed the fund since 1990. The Harbor family includes nine funds and allows shareholders to switch from fund to fund by telephone.

Top Ten Stock Holdings

1. Pfizer	6. Schlumberger
2. Chase Manhattan	7. Hewlett-Packard
3. General Electric	8. Compaq Computer
4. Walt Disney	9. Cisco Systems
5. Morgan Stanley Dean Witter	10. SmithKline Beecham

Asset mix: common stocks—96%; cash/equivalents—4%
Total net assets: $2.9 billion
Dividend yield: 0.17%

Fees

Front-end load	*None*
Redemption fee	*None*
12b-1 fee	*None*
Management fee	0.60%
Other expenses	0.10
Total annual expense	0.70%
Minimum initial investment	$2,000
Minimum subsequent investment	$500

Services

Telephone exchanges	*Yes*
Automatic withdrawal	*Yes*
Automatic checking deduction	*Yes*
Retirement plan/IRA	*Yes*
Instant redemption	*Yes*
Financial statements	*Semiannual*
Income distributions	*Annual*
Capital gains distributions	*Annual*
Portfolio manager: years	8
Number of funds in family	9

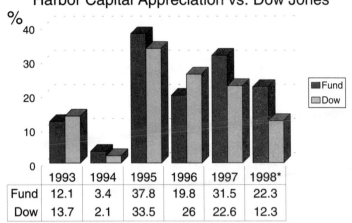

Six-Year Performance
Harbor Capital Appreciation vs. Dow Jones

	1993	1994	1995	1996	1997	1998*
Fund	12.1	3.4	37.8	19.8	31.5	22.3
Dow	13.7	2.1	33.5	26	22.6	12.3

% Avg. Annual Total Return
Fund vs. Dow Jones Industrial Avg.

*1998 returns through 8/1/98
(5-year avg. annual return: 25.3%)

18

American Century Equity Growth Fund

LONG TERM

American Century Investments
P.O. Box 419200
Kansas City, MO 64179-9965

Fund managers: Jeff Tyler
  and Bill Martin
Fund objective: Long-term growth
Web site: www.americancentury.com

Toll-free: 800-345-2021
In-state: 816-531-5575
Fax: 816-340-4753

Performance	★ ★ ★ ★
Consistency	★ ★ ★
Fees/Services	★ ★ ★ ★ ★
BEQGX	**12 Points**

The American Century Equity Growth Fund is a long-term growth fund that invests in major blue chip stocks across a broad range of industrial sectors. Known formerly as the Benham Equity Growth Fund, the fund has posted excellent returns over the past few years.

The fund stays almost 100 percent invested in U.S. stocks at all times. Fund managers Jeff Tyler and Bill Martin make their selections based on the relative price and value of each stock they evaluate. They typically dump stocks that seem overpriced and look for market sectors that seem undervalued relative to the overall market.

The fund has about 150 stock holdings in all. Its leading sectors include banking, 8 percent of total assets; computer-related companies, 8 percent; energy, 8 percent; medical-related businesses, 6 percent; financial services, 10 percent; and communications, 8 percent.

The fund managers are fairly aggressive in their trading approach and have an annual portfolio turnover ratio of 161 percent.

PERFORMANCE

The fund has enjoyed excellent growth over the last five years. Including dividends and capital gains distributions, the American Century Equity Growth Fund has provided a total return for the last five years (through mid-1998) of 188 percent. A $10,000 investment in 1993 would have grown to about $29,000 five years later. Average annual return: 23.5 percent.

CONSISTENCY ★ ★ ★

The fund has been fairly consistent recently, outperforming the Dow Jones Industrial Average in three of the last five years through 1997 (and it led the Dow through the first few months of 1998). Its biggest gain came in 1997, when it jumped 36.1 percent (compared with a 22.6 percent rise in the Dow).

FEES/SERVICES/MANAGEMENT

Like all American Century funds, the Equity Growth Fund is a true no-load fund—no fee to buy, no fee to sell. The fund's low total annual expense ratio of 0.71 percent (with no 12b-1 fee) compares very favorably with other funds.

The fund offers all the standard services, such as retirement account availability, automatic withdrawal, and automatic checking account deduction. Its minimum initial investment of $2,500 and minimum subsequent investment of $50 is in line with most other funds.

Jeff Tyler and Bill Martin have managed the fund since 1991. The American Century family of funds includes more than 20 funds and allows shareholders to switch from fund to fund by telephone.

Top Ten Stock Holdings

1. Ford Motor
2. Morgan Stanley Dean Witter
3. Unilever
4. Chevron
5. First Union
6. Microsoft
7. United Technologies
8. BellSouth
9. Lucent Technologies
10. Schlumberger

Asset mix: common stocks—99%; cash/equivalents—1%
Total net assets: $771 million
Dividend yield: 0.91%

Fees

Front-end load	*None*
Redemption fee	*None*
12b-1 fee	*None*
Management fee	0.70%
Other expenses	0.01
Total annual expense	0.71%
Minimum initial investment	$2,500
Minimum subsequent investment	$50

Services

Telephone exchanges	*Yes*
Automatic withdrawal	*Yes*
Automatic checking deduction	*Yes*
Retirement plan/IRA	*Yes*
Instant redemption	*Yes*
Financial statements	*Semiannual*
Income distributions	*Annual*
Capital gains distributions	*Annual*
Portfolio manager: years	7
Number of funds in family	22

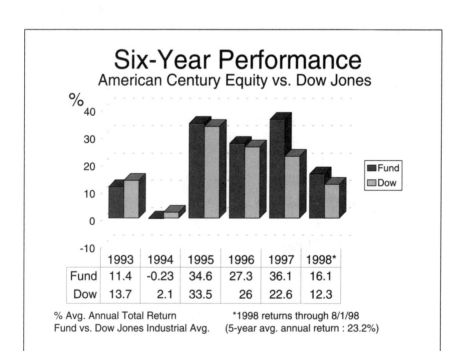

Six-Year Performance
American Century Equity vs. Dow Jones

	1993	1994	1995	1996	1997	1998*
Fund	11.4	-0.23	34.6	27.3	36.1	16.1
Dow	13.7	2.1	33.5	26	22.6	12.3

% Avg. Annual Total Return   *1998 returns through 8/1/98
Fund vs. Dow Jones Industrial Avg.   (5-year avg. annual return : 23.2%)

19
Papp America-Abroad Fund

LONG TERM

Papp Funds
4400 North 32nd Street
Suite 280
Phoenix, AZ 85018

Fund Managers: L. Roy Papp
and Rosellen C. Papp
Fund Objective: Long-term growth
Web site: www.roypapp.com

Toll-Free: 800-421-4004
In-State: 602-956-1115
Fax: 602-956-7053

Performance	★ ★ ★ ★
Consistency	★ ★ ★ ★
Fees/Services	★ ★ ★ ★
PAAFX	**12 Points**

The Papp America-Abroad Fund takes a global approach to the market, primarily through U.S. stocks. While the fund will occasionally invest in a foreign stock, most of its holdings are U.S. companies that derive at least 35 percent of their earnings or sales outside the United States.

"For the most part our investments have been in very large multinational companies which are industry leaders," explains L. Roy Papp, who manages the fund along with his daughter-in-law, Rosellen Papp. Among its leading holdings are Intel, Merck, and Johnson & Johnson. The fund also invests in some smaller companies, such as Arrow Electronics, Viking Office Products, and Steiner Leisure.

The fund has a very conservative buy-and-hold approach and a very low annual portfolio turnover ratio of 12 percent. Its leading industrial sectors include computers and software, 14 percent of assets; industrial services, 15 percent; health care, 11 percent; consumer products, 9 percent; wholesale distributors, 9 percent; electronic equipment, 8 percent; telecommunications, 6 percent; and financial services, 6 percent.

PERFORMANCE

The fund has enjoyed excellent growth over the last five years. Including dividends and capital gains distributions, the Papp America-Abroad Fund has provided a total return for the last five years (through mid-1998) of 182 percent. A $10,000 investment in 1993 would have grown to about $28,000 five years later. Average annual return: 23 percent.

CONSISTENCY

The fund has been very consistent recently, outperforming the Dow Jones Industrial Average in four of the last five years through 1997 (and it was about even with the Dow through the first few months of 1998). Its biggest gain came in 1995, when it moved up 37.1 percent (compared with a 33.5 percent rise in the Dow).

FEES/SERVICES/MANAGEMENT

The fund is a true no-load—no fee to buy, no fee to sell. Its total annual expense ratio of 1.25 percent (with no 12b-1 fee) compares favorably with other funds.

The fund offers just a few of the standard services, including retirement account availability, but does not offer automatic withdrawal or phone switching. Its minimum initial investment of $5,000 and minimum subsequent investment of $1,000 are considerably higher than other funds.

The management team of L. Roy Papp and Rosellen Papp has managed the fund since 1991. The Papp America family of funds includes four funds.

Top Ten Stock Holdings

1. State Street
2. Interpublic Group
3. Viking Office Products
4. Service International
5. Manpower
6. Intel
7. Arrow Electronics
8. Mattel
9. Merck
10. Johnson & Johnson

Asset mix: common stocks—99%; cash/equivalents—1%
Total net assets: $288 million
Dividend yield: 0.07%

Fees

Front-end load	*None*
Redemption fee	*None*
12b-1 fee	*None*
Management fee	1.00%
Other expenses	0.25
Total annual expense	1.25%
Minimum initial investment	$5,000
Minimum subsequent investment	$1,000

Services

Telephone exchanges	*No*
Automatic withdrawal	*No*
Automatic checking deduction	*No*
Retirement plan/IRA	*Yes*
Instant redemption	*No*
Financial statements	*Semiannual*
Income distributions	*Annual*
Capital gains distributions	*Annual*
Portfolio manager: years	7
Number of funds in family	4

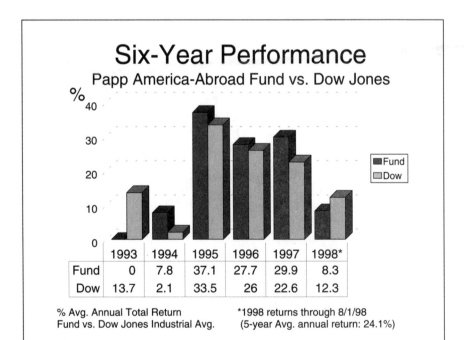

Six-Year Performance
Papp America-Abroad Fund vs. Dow Jones

	1993	1994	1995	1996	1997	1998*
Fund	0	7.8	37.1	27.7	29.9	8.3
Dow	13.7	2.1	33.5	26	22.6	12.3

% Avg. Annual Total Return
Fund vs. Dow Jones Industrial Avg.

*1998 returns through 8/1/98
(5-year Avg. annual return: 24.1%)

20

Dreyfus Appreciation Fund

LONG TERM

Dreyfus Corporation
The Pan Am Building
200 Park Avenue, 7th Floor
New York, NY 10166

Fund manager: Fayez Sarofim
Fund objective: Long-term growth

Toll-free: 800-645-6561
In-state: 516-794-5452
Fax: 212-922-7140

Performance	★ ★ ★
Consistency	★ ★ ★ ★
Fees/Services	★ ★ ★ ★ ★
DGAGX	**12 Points**

The Dreyfus Appreciation Fund is a long-term growth fund that concentrates on large-capitalization, high-quality, multinational companies. "With a long-term time horizon," explains fund manager Fayez Sarofim, "our approach may forsake short-term gains, in which momentum-based strategies and market timers attempt to exploit changes in equity prices related to current market sentiment and technical factors, in favor of long-term, fundamental economic, industry, and company analysis."

The fund stays almost 100 percent invested in stocks all the time. Sarofin does almost no trading within the portfolio. The fund has an annual portfolio turnover ratio of about 5 percent—one of the lowest ratios in the industry.

Over the past ten years, the fund has posted an average annual return of about 18 percent. A $10,000 investment in the fund ten years ago would now be worth about $50,000. Since its inception in 1984, the fund has grown at an average annual rate of about 17 percent.

The fund has about 70 stock holdings in all, primarily in large, well-known, blue chip stocks, such as McDonald's, Coca-Cola, Philip Morris, Microsoft, and General Motors. Leading sectors include health care,

18 percent of total assets; food, beverage, and tobacco, 14 percent; capital goods, 9 percent; energy, 9 percent; automotive, 6 percent; and personal care, 6 percent.

PERFORMANCE

The fund has enjoyed strong growth over the last five years. Including dividends and capital gains distributions, the Dreyfus Appreciation Fund has provided a total return for the last five years (through mid-1998) of 177 percent. A $10,000 investment in 1993 would have grown to about $28,000 five years later. Average annual return: 22.6 percent.

CONSISTENCY

The fund has been fairly consistent recently, outperforming the Dow Jones Industrial Average in three of the last five years through 1997, and it was virtually even with the Dow one other year. (It also led the Dow through the first few months of 1998). Its biggest gain came in 1995, when it jumped 37.9 percent (compared with a 33.5 percent rise in the Dow).

FEES/SERVICES/MANAGEMENT

Like all Dreyfus funds, the Appreciation Fund is a true no-load—no fee to buy, no fee to sell. The fund's total annual expense ratio of 0.96 percent (with no 12b-1 fee) compares very favorably with other funds.

The fund offers all the standard services, such as retirement account availability, automatic withdrawal, and automatic checking account deduction. Its minimum initial investment of $2,500 and minimum subsequent investment of $100 is about in line with most other funds.

Fayez Sarofim has managed the fund since 1990. The Dreyfus family of funds includes more than 100 funds and allows shareholders to switch from fund to fund by telephone.

Top Ten Stock Holdings

1. Pfizer
2. Intel
3. Coca-Cola
4. Philip Morris
5. Merck
6. Johnson & Johnson
7. General Electric
8. Procter & Gamble
9. Citicorp
10. Chase Manhattan

Asset mix: common stocks—99%; cash/equivalents—1%
Total net assets: $1.9 billion
Dividend yield: 0.69%

Fees

Front-end load	*None*
Redemption fee	*None*
12b-1 fee	*None*
Management fee	0.55%
Other expenses	0.41
Total annual expense	0.96%
Minimum initial investment	$2,500
Minimum subsequent investment	$100

Services

Telephone exchanges	*Yes*
Automatic withdrawal	*Yes*
Automatic checking deduction	*Yes*
Retirement plan/IRA	*Yes*
Instant redemption	*Yes*
Financial statements	*Semiannual*
Income distributions	*Annual*
Capital gains distributions	*Annual*
Portfolio manager: years	8
Number of funds in family	117

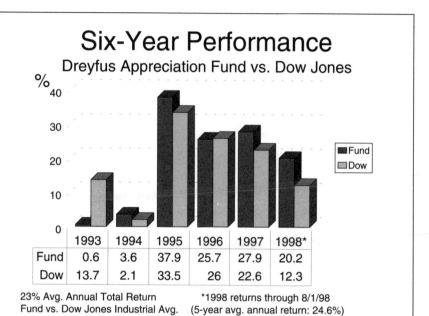

Six-Year Performance
Dreyfus Appreciation Fund vs. Dow Jones

	1993	1994	1995	1996	1997	1998*
Fund	0.6	3.6	37.9	25.7	27.9	20.2
Dow	13.7	2.1	33.5	26	22.6	12.3

23% Avg. Annual Total Return   *1998 returns through 8/1/98
Fund vs. Dow Jones Industrial Avg.   (5-year avg. annual return: 24.6%)

21

Fidelity Select Electronics Portfolio

SECTOR

Fidelity Investments
82 Devonshire Street
Boston, MA 02109

Fund manager: Andy Kaplan
Fund objective: Sector
Web site: www.fidelity.com

Toll-free: 800-544-8888
In-state: 801-534-1910
Fax: 617-476-9753

Performance	★ ★ ★ ★ ★
Consistency	★ ★ ★ ★
Fees/Services	★ ★ ★
FSELX	**12 Points**

The Fidelity Select Electronics Portfolio has been one of the nation's top-performing funds over the past decade, riding the booming high-tech wave. But traditional electronics companies account for just a fraction of the portfolio. The fund, instead, is loaded with computer and office equipment–related stocks.

Despite the makeup of the fund, it's hard to complain about the bottom line. Over the past ten years, the fund has grown about 24 percent per year. A $10,000 investment in the fund ten years ago would now be worth nearly $90,000.

Fund manager Andrew Kaplan, who has been with the fund since 1996, takes a very active trading approach and has a 341 percent annual portfolio turnover ratio.

In all, the fund holds about 100 stocks. Its leading segment is semiconductor manufacturers, which account for 30 percent of the fund's portfolio. Other leading segments include electronic instruments, 20 percent; computers and office equipment, 22 percent; and computer services and software, 7 percent. Industrial machinery and equipment account for about 6 percent of the portfolio.

The fund invests in both large-capitalization stocks, such as Oracle, Compaq, and Intel, and young, emerging growth stocks, such as Atmel, Xilinx, and Microchip Technology.

PERFORMANCE

The fund has enjoyed outstanding growth over the past five years. Including dividends and capital gains distributions, the Fidelity Select Electronics Portfolio has provided a total return for the past five years (through early 1998) of 344 percent. A $10,000 investment in 1993 would have grown to $44,400 five years later. Average annual return: 35 percent.

CONSISTENCY

The fund has been fairly consistent, outperforming the Dow Jones Industrial Average in four of the past five years (and it was about even with the Dow through the first few months of 1998). Its biggest gain came in 1995, when it jumped 69 percent (compared with a 33.5 percent rise in the Dow).

FEES/SERVICES/MANAGEMENT

The fund has a low front-end load of 3 percent and a maximum redemption fee of 0.75 percent if it's sold out within 29 days. Its annual expense ratio of 1.33 percent (with no 12b-1 fee) is about average among all funds.

The fund offers many of the standard services, such as retirement account availability and automatic checking account deduction. Its minimum initial investment of $2,500 and minimum subsequent investment of $250 are a little high compared with other funds.

Andy Kaplan has managed the fund only since 1996 and has been with Fidelity since 1995. The Fidelity family of funds includes more than 230 funds.

Top Ten Stock Holdings

1. Micron Technology
2. Microsoft
3. Seagate Technology
4. Intel
5. Check Point Software

6. EMC
7. Vitesse Semiconductor
8. Gateway 2000
9. Linear Technology
10. Applied Materials

Asset mix: common stocks—91%; cash/equivalents—9 %
Total net assets: $2.3 billion
Dividend yield: none

Fees

Front-end load	3.00%
Redemption fee	0.75
12b-1 fee	*None*
Management fee	0.61
Other expenses	0.72
Total annual expense	1.33%
Minimum initial investment	$2,500
Minimum subsequent investment	$250

Services

Telephone exchanges	*Yes*
Automatic withdrawal	*Yes*
Automatic checking deduction	*Yes*
Retirement plan/IRA	*Yes*
Instant redemption	*Yes*
Financial statements	*Semiannual*
Income distributions	*Semiannual*
Capital gains distributions	*Semiannual*
Portfolio manager: years	2
Number of funds in family	235

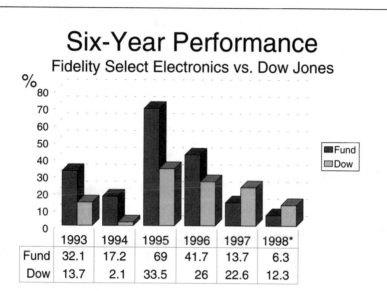

Six-Year Performance
Fidelity Select Electronics vs. Dow Jones

	1993	1994	1995	1996	1997	1998*
Fund	32.1	17.2	69	41.7	13.7	6.3
Dow	13.7	2.1	33.5	26	22.6	12.3

% Avg. Annual Total Return
Fund vs. Dow Jones Industrial Avg.

*1998 returns through 8/1/98
(5-year avg. annual return: 30.1%)

22

Seligman Communications and Information Fund

SECTOR

Seligman Funds
100 Park Avenue
New York, NY 10017

Fund manager: Paul H. Wick
Fund objective: Sector

Toll-free: 800-221-2783
In-state: 212-850-1864
Fax: 212-922-5738

Performance	★ ★ ★ ★ ★
Consistency	★ ★ ★ ★
Fees/Services	★ ★ ★
SLMCX	**12 Points**

The global growth of the communications industry has helped propel the Seligman Communications and Information Fund to an outstanding long-term performance. Over the past ten years, the fund has posted an average annual return of about 25 percent. A $10,000 investment in the fund ten years ago would now be worth about $90,000.

The fund invests in more than just telecommunications stocks. Nearly half the portfolio is invested in computer hardware and software and semiconductors. It also invests in media companies.

Fund manager Paul Wick tries to time his buy and sell decisions carefully. "We try to buy panic and sell euphoria," says Wick. "When the public gets too enthusiastic about a sector, we'll often sell out and move into something else. There's always a lot of volatility with small stocks. We try to recognize the buying opportunities."

Wick is very aggressive in his trading strategy, resulting in a 165 percent annual portfolio turnover ratio. The fund stays almost fully invested in stocks all the time and has about 90 stock holdings in all. Leading sectors include computer hardware and peripherals, 19 percent of assets; computer software, 16 percent; communications infrastructure, 7 percent;

electronic equipment, 16 percent; information services, 8 percent; media companies, 10 percent; and semiconductors, 13 percent.

PERFORMANCE

The fund has enjoyed tremendous growth over the last five years. Including dividends and capital gains distributions, the Seligman Communications and Information Fund has provided a total return for the last five years (through mid-1998) of 302 percent. A $10,000 investment in 1993 would have grown to about $40,000 five years later. Average annual return: 32.1 percent.

CONSISTENCY

The fund has been very consistent recently, outperforming the Dow Jones Industrial Average in four of the last five years through 1997 (and it led the Dow through the first few months of 1998). Its biggest gain came in 1995, when it moved up 43.4 percent (compared with a 33.5 percent rise in the Dow).

FEES/SERVICES/MANAGEMENT

The Seligman Communications and Information Fund has a front-end load of 4.75 percent. Its total annual expense ratio of 1.68 percent (including a 0.25 percent 12b-1 fee) is in line with other funds.

The fund offers all the standard services, such as retirement account availability, automatic withdrawal, and automatic checking account deduction. Its minimum initial investment of $2,500 and minimum subsequent investment of $100 are a little higher than many other funds.

Paul Wick has managed the fund since 1989. The Seligman family of funds includes 40 funds and allows shareholders to switch from fund to fund by telephone.

Top Ten Stock Holdings

1. EMC/Mass	6. Chancellor Media
2. Storage Technology	7. Synopsys
3. CBS	8. Teradyne
4. Network Associates	9. Lattice Semiconductor
5. Parametric Technology	10. Creative Technology

Asset mix: common stocks—95%; cash/equivalents—5%
Total net assets: $3.1 billion
Dividend yield: none

Fees

Front-end load	4.75%
Redemption fee	*None*
12b-1 fee	0.25
Management fee	0.89
Other expenses	0.54
Total annual expense	1.68%
Minimum initial investment	$2,500
Minimum subsequent investment	$100

Services

Telephone exchanges	*Yes*
Automatic withdrawal	*Yes*
Automatic checking deduction	*Yes*
Retirement plan/IRA	*Yes*
Instant redemption	*Yes*
Financial statements	*Semiannual*
Income distributions	*Annual*
Capital gains distributions	*Annual*
Portfolio manager: years	8
Number of funds in family	40

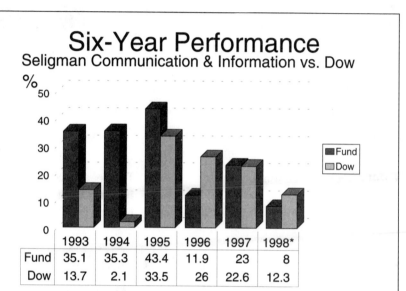

Six-Year Performance
Seligman Communication & Information vs. Dow

	1993	1994	1995	1996	1997	1998*
Fund	35.1	35.3	43.4	11.9	23	8
Dow	13.7	2.1	33.5	26	22.6	12.3

% Avg. Annual Total Return   *1998 returns through 8/1/98
Fund vs. Dow Jones Industrial Avg.   (5-year avg.annual return: 28.1%)

23
Fidelity Select Computers Portfolio

SECTOR

Fidelity Investments
82 Devonshire Street
Boston, MA 02109

Fund manager: Michael Tempero
Fund objective: Sector
Web site: www.fidelity.com

Toll-free: 800-544-8888
In-state: 801-534-1910
Fax: 617-476-9753

Performance	★ ★ ★ ★ ★
Consistency	★ ★ ★ ★
Fees/Services	★ ★ ★
FDCPX	**12 Points**

It should be no surprise, in this age of the computer, that the Fidelity Select Computers Portfolio would be one of the nation's top-performing mutual funds. The fund's success should continue as long as the computer revolution thrives—and that could be for a long time to come. The fund invests mainly in stocks of companies involved in the research, design, manufacturing, and distribution of computers and computer-related products, such as hardware, software, and networking products.

Over the past ten years, the fund has posted average annual returns of about 21 percent. A $10,000 investment in the fund ten years ago would now be worth about $68,000.

The fund invests in stocks of all sizes, from very small, one-product companies to such major manufacturers as IBM and Hewlett-Packard. It takes a different approach with the big companies than with the small, emerging growth stocks. For the larger firms, the fund manager looks at gross profit margins, PE ratios, price-to-cash flow ratios, and price-to-sales ratios. The fund bought IBM and Digital Equipment after their price had plummeted and their gross profit margins had stabilized. For the smaller companies, earnings growth is the major factor, although PE ratios also come into play. The fund also takes advantage of the volatility in the computer sector to scoop up stocks when their price plunges.

The fund will dump a stock if the price gets too high relative to its earnings or if the company's growth is slowing down. But if earnings continue to climb, the fund may hold the stock for years. The fund has a very aggressive trading policy and an annual portfolio turnover ratio of about 190 percent.

The fund holds about 70 stocks. Its leading segments include computer software and services, 8 percent of total assets; computers and office equipment, 51 percent; electronic instruments, 11 percent; and semiconductors, 14 percent.

PERFORMANCE

The fund has enjoyed outstanding growth over the past five years. Including dividends and capital gains distributions, the Fidelity Select Computers Portfolio has provided a total return for the past five years (through early 1998) of 259 percent. A $10,000 investment in 1993 would have grown to $35,900 five years later. Average annual return: 29.2 percent.

CONSISTENCY

Like many sector funds, the Computers Portfolio can be volatile. For instance, while the overall market climbed 22.6 percent in 1997, the Computers Portfolio was down 1.1 percent because the technology sector was in a slump. Otherwise, the fund had outperformed the Dow Jones Industrial Average in the four previous years (and it led the Dow through the first few months of 1998). Its biggest gain came in 1995, when it jumped 51.8 percent (compared with a 33.5 percent rise in the Dow).

FEES/SERVICES/MANAGEMENT

The fund has a low front-end load of 3 percent and a maximum redemption fee of 0.75 percent if it's sold out within 29 days. Its annual expense ratio of 1.48 percent (with no 12b-1 fee) is about average among all funds.

The fund offers many of the standard services, such as retirement account availability and automatic checking account deduction. Its minimum initial investment of $2,500 and minimum subsequent investment of $250 are a little high compared with other funds.

Michael Tempero has managed the fund only since 1997, but he has been with Fidelity since 1993. The Fidelity family of funds includes more than 230 funds.

Top Ten Stock Holdings

1. Dell Computer	6. Sun Microsystems
2. EMC	7. Cisco Systems
3. Quantum	8. Compaq Computer
4. Microsoft	9. Hewlett-Packard
5. Xerox	10. Gateway 2000

Asset mix: common stocks—90%; cash/equivalents—10%
Total net assets: $569 million
Dividend yield: none

Fees

Front-end load	3.00%
Redemption fee	0.75
12b-1 fee	*None*
Management fee	0.61
Other expenses	0.87
Total annual expense	1.48%
Minimum initial investment	$2,500
Minimum subsequent investment	$250

Services

Telephone exchanges	*Yes*
Automatic withdrawal	*Yes*
Automatic checking deduction	*Yes*
Retirement plan/IRA	*Yes*
Instant redemption	*Yes*
Financial statements	*Semiannual*
Income distributions	*Semiannual*
Capital gains distributions	*Semiannual*
Portfolio manager: years	1
Number of funds in family	235

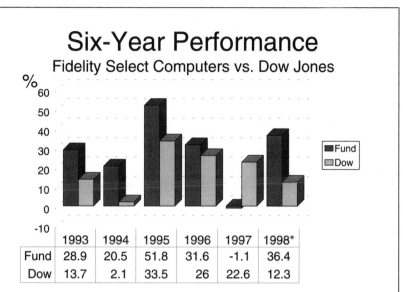

Six-Year Performance
Fidelity Select Computers vs. Dow Jones

	1993	1994	1995	1996	1997	1998*
Fund	28.9	20.5	51.8	31.6	-1.1	36.4
Dow	13.7	2.1	33.5	26	22.6	12.3

% Avg. Annual Total Return
Fund vs. Dow Jones Industrial Avg.

*1998 returns through 8/1/98
(5-year avg. annual return: 30.1%)

24

Fidelity Select Defense and Aerospace Portfolio

SECTOR

Fidelity Investments
82 Devonshire Street
Boston, MA 02109

Fund manager: Peter Saperstone
Fund objective: Sector
Web site: www.fidelity.com

Toll-free: 800-544-8888
In-state: 801-534-1910
Fax: 617-476-9753

Performance	★ ★ ★ ★ ★
Consistency	★ ★ ★ ★
Fees/Services	★ ★ ★
FSDAX	**12 Points**

The end of the cold war in the 1980s sent a chill through the defense and aerospace industry. A cutback in defense spending led to drops in corporate profits and stock prices within the industry. But the sector has rebounded strongly in the past five years, helping push the Fidelity Select Defense and Aerospace Portfolio to exceptional returns.

The fund typically invests at least 80 percent of its assets in stocks of companies within the defense and aerospace industries. In all, the fund has about 40 stock holdings, most of which are well-known blue chip companies, such as Boeing, United Technologies, Lockheed Martin, and Raytheon. The fund also holds a number of foreign-based defense stocks.

While the fund's performance the past five years has been exceptional, its ten-year return is below the market averages. The fund has posted average annual returns of about 16 percent over the past ten years. A $10,000 investment in the fund ten years ago would now be worth about $43,000.

Fund manager Peter Saperstone, who has been with the fund since 1997, takes a very aggressive trading approach. The fund has a 219 percent annual turnover ratio. The leading industrial segments among the fund's holdings include the aerospace and defense industry, 28 percent; defense electronics, 17 percent; electrical equipment, 13 percent; electronics, 8 percent, and autos, tires, and accessories, 5 percent.

With just $50 million in assets under management, the fund is one of Fidelity's smallest funds.

PERFORMANCE

The fund has enjoyed excellent growth over the past five years. Including dividends and capital gains distributions, the Fidelity Defense and Aerospace Portfolio has provided a total return for the past five years (through early 1998) of 227 percent. A $10,000 investment in 1993 would have grown to $32,700 five years later. Average annual return: 26.7 percent.

CONSISTENCY

The fund has been fairly consistent, roughly matching the Dow Jones Industrial Average three of the past five years and beating the market the other two years. (The fund was also ahead of the Dow through the first few months of 1998.) Its biggest gain came in 1995, when it jumped 47.4 percent (compared with a 33.5 percent rise in the Dow).

FEES/SERVICES/MANAGEMENT

The fund has a low front-end load of 3 percent and a maximum redemption fee of 0.75 percent if it's sold out within 29 days. Its annual expense ratio of 1.84 percent (with no 12b-1 fee) is about average among all funds.

The fund offers many of the standard services, such as retirement account availability and automatic checking account deduction. Its minimum initial investment of $2,500 and minimum subsequent investment of $250 are a little high compared with other funds.

Peter Saperstone has managed the fund only since 1997, but he has been with Fidelity since 1995. The Fidelity family of funds includes more than 230 funds.

Top Ten Stock Holdings

1. Remec
2. Maxwell Technologies
3. General Motors Class H
4. Lockheed Martin
5. Northrop Grumman
6. Loral Space & Communications
7. Gulfstream Aerospace
8. Fairchild
9. United Technologies
10. Boeing

Asset mix: common stocks—94%; cash/equivalents—6%
Total net assets: $50 million
Dividend yield: none

Fees

Front-end load	3.00%
Redemption fee	0.75
12b-1 fee	*None*
Management fee	0.61
Other expenses	1.23
Total annual expense	1.84%
Minimum initial investment	$2,500
Minimum subsequent investment	$250

Services

Telephone exchanges	*Yes*
Automatic withdrawal	*Yes*
Automatic checking deduction	*Yes*
Retirement plan/IRA	*Yes*
Instant redemption	*Yes*
Financial statements	*Semiannual*
Income distributions	*Semiannual*
Capital gains distributions	*Semiannual*
Portfolio manager: years	1
Number of funds in family	235

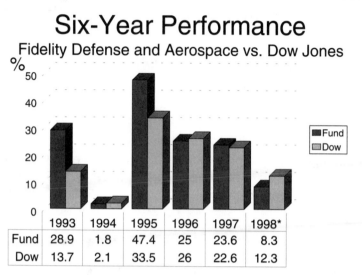

Six-Year Performance
Fidelity Defense and Aerospace vs. Dow Jones

	1993	1994	1995	1996	1997	1998*
Fund	28.9	1.8	47.4	25	23.6	8.3
Dow	13.7	2.1	33.5	26	22.6	12.3

% Avg. Annual Total Return
Fund vs. Dow Jones Industrial Avg.

*1998 returns through 8/1/98
(5-year avg. annual return: 21.7%)

25
Davis Financial Fund

SECTOR

Davis Funds
124 East Marcy Street
Santa Fe, NM 87504-1688

Fund managers: Christopher Davis
  and Ken Feinberg
Fund objective: Sector

Toll-free: 800-279-0279
In-state: 505-820-3101
Fax: 505-820-3002

Performance	★ ★ ★ ★ ★
Consistency	★ ★ ★ ★
Fees/Services	★ ★ ★
RPFGX	**12 Points**

The Davis Financial Fund has benefited from a strong resurgence of the banking and financial industry in recent years.

"We continue to believe financial stocks offer one of the greatest investment opportunities," says fund manager Christopher Davis. "One reason we have always gravitated to financial companies is that they tend to be in nonfaddish businesses with products that don't become obsolete—a particularly attractive attribute for long-term investors. Another reason is that well-managed financial companies generate significant free cash flow that, through the re-purchasing of shares or acquisitions, can benefit shareholders. Looking out over the next two decades, these companies should benefit from powerful demographic and macroeconomic forces as 76 million U.S. baby boomers plan for retirement and enter their peak earning and investing years."

The fund takes a conservative buy-and-hold approach and has an annual portfolio turnover ratio of 26 percent. It has about 70 stock holdings in all. Most are in the financial sector, although the fund does hold some other stocks, such as Nike, SmithKline Beecham, Philip Morris, Intel, and

IBM. Leading sectors include banks, 22 percent of total assets; financial services, 17 percent; insurance companies, 26 percent; and consumer products, 7 percent.

PERFORMANCE

The fund has enjoyed outstanding growth over the last five years. Including dividends and capital gains distributions, the Davis Financial Fund has provided a total return for the last five years (through mid-1998) of 207 percent. A $10,000 investment in 1993 would have grown to about $31,000 five years later. Average annual return: 25.2 percent.

CONSISTENCY

The fund has been very consistent recently, outperforming the Dow Jones Industrial Average in four of the last five years through 1997 (but it trailed the Dow through the first few months of 1998). Its biggest gain came in 1995, when it jumped 50.5 percent (compared with a 33.5 percent rise in the Dow).

FEES/SERVICES/MANAGEMENT

The fund carries a 4.75 percent front-end load. Its total annual expense ratio of 1.15 percent (including a 0.08 percent 12b-1 fee) compares favorably with other funds.

The fund offers all the standard services, such as retirement account availability, automatic withdrawal, and automatic checking account deduction. Its minimum initial investment of $1,000 and minimum subsequent investment of $25 compare favorably with other funds.

Christopher Davis has managed the fund since 1993. He was recently joined by comanager Ken Feinberg. The Davis family of funds includes nine funds and allows shareholders to switch from fund to fund by telephone.

Top Ten Stock Holdings

1. BankAmerica
2. Cincinnati Financial
3. American Express
4. Philip Morris
5. Bank of New York

6. Household International
7. Transatlantic Holdings
8. General Re
9. Masco
10. Citicorp

Asset mix: common stocks—91%; cash/equivalents—9%
Total net assets: $288 million
Dividend yield: 0.42%

Fees

Front-end load	4.75%
Redemption fee	*None*
	(if kept one year)
12b-1 fee	0.08
Management fee	0.75
Other expenses	0.32
Total annual expense	1.15%
Minimum initial investment	$1,000
Minimum subsequent investment	$25

Services

Telephone exchanges	*Yes*
Automatic withdrawal	*Yes*
Automatic checking deduction	*Yes*
Retirement plan/IRA	*Yes*
Instant redemption	*Yes*
Financial statements	*Semiannual*
Income distributions	*Annual*
Capital gains distributions	*Annual*
Portfolio manager: years	5
Number of funds in family	9

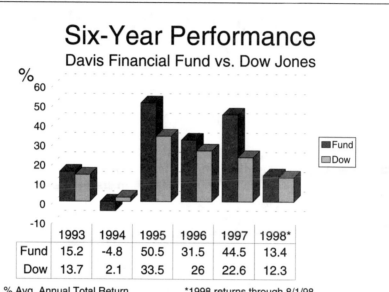

Six-Year Performance
Davis Financial Fund vs. Dow Jones

	1993	1994	1995	1996	1997	1998*
Fund	15.2	-4.8	50.5	31.5	44.5	13.4
Dow	13.7	2.1	33.5	26	22.6	12.3

% Avg. Annual Total Return
Fund vs. Dow Jones Industrial Avg.

*1998 returns through 8/1/98
(5-year avg. annual return: 26.4%)

26

Invesco Strategic Portfolio: Financial Services

SECTOR

Invesco Funds Group
P.O. Box 173706
Denver, CO 80217-3706

Fund managers: Daniel B. Leonard
  and Jeffrey G. Morris
Fund objective: Sector
Web site: www.invesco.com

Toll-free: 800-525-8085
In-state: 303-930-6300
Fax: 303-930-6655

Performance	★ ★ ★ ★
Consistency	★ ★ ★ ★
Fees/Services	★ ★ ★ ★
FSFSX	**12 Points**

Financial service companies have benefited recently from the booming economy, and the Invesco Strategic Financial Services Portfolio has taken advantage of that growth with outstanding returns over the past decade. It has posted an average annual return of 25.5 percent per year over the past ten years. A $10,000 investment in the fund ten years ago would now be worth about $97,000.

As its name implies, the fund specializes in stocks of banks, savings and loans, and other finance-related companies. Among its leading holdings are BankAmerica, Fannie Mae, and Bank of New York. The fund also invests in HMOs, consumer and industrial finance companies, leasing companies, securities brokerage companies, insurance agencies, and real estate stocks and trusts.

The fund managers maintain a fairly active trading policy. The annual portfolio turnover ratio is about 100 percent. Fund comanager Daniel Leonard has also been managing the highly rated Invesco Technology Fund since 1985.

PERFORMANCE

The fund has enjoyed outstanding growth over the last five years. Including dividends and capital gains distributions, the Invesco Strategic Financial Services Portfolio has provided a total return for the last five years (through mid-1998) of 185 percent. A $10,000 investment in 1993 would have grown to about $39,000 five years later. Average annual return: 23.3 percent.

CONSISTENCY

The fund has been very consistent recently, outperforming the Dow Jones Industrial Average in four of the last five years through 1997 (and it was about even with the Dow through the first few months of 1998). Its biggest gain came in 1997, when it jumped 44.8 percent (compared with a 22.6 percent rise in the Dow).

FEES/SERVICES/MANAGEMENT

Like all Invesco funds, the Strategic Financial Services Portfolio is a true no-load fund—no fee to buy, no fee to sell. The fund's total annual expense ratio of 1.30 percent (including a 0.25 percent 12b-1 fee) is in line with other funds.

The fund offers all the standard services, such as retirement account availability, automatic withdrawal, and automatic checking account deduction. Its minimum initial investment of $1,000 and minimum subsequent investment of $50 compare favorably with other funds.

The management team of Daniel Leonard and Jeff Morris has managed the fund since 1996. The Invesco family of funds includes 34 funds and allows shareholders to switch from fund to fund by telephone.

Top Ten Stock Holdings

1. American International Group	6. Compass Bancshares
2. BankAmerica	7. State Street
3. Bank of New York	8. Republic New York
4. Fannie Mae	9. Lincoln National
5. Union Planters	10. Wachovia

Asset mix: common stocks—90%; cash/equivalents—10%
Total net assets: $1.3 billion
Dividend yield: 0.37%

Fees

Front-end load	*None*
Redemption fee	*None*
12b-1 fee	0.25%
Management fee	0.73
Other expenses	0.32
Total annual expense	1.30%
Minimum initial investment	$1,000
Minimum subsequent investment	$50

Services

Telephone exchanges	*Yes*
Automatic withdrawal	*Yes*
Automatic checking deduction	*Yes*
Retirement plan/IRA	*Yes*
Instant redemption	*Yes*
Financial statements	*Semiannual*
Income distributions	*Annual*
Capital gains distributions	*Annual*
Portfolio manager: years	2
Number of funds in family	34

Six-Year Performance
INVESCO Financial Services vs. Dow Jones

	1993	1994	1995	1996	1997	1998*
Fund	18.5	-5.9	39.8	30.3	44.8	15.7
Dow	13.7	2.1	33.5	26	22.6	12.3

% Avg. Annual Total Return
Fund vs. Dow Jones Industrial Avg.

*1998 returns through 8/1/96
(5-year avg. annual return: 24.3%)

Invesco Strategic Portfolio: Technology Fund

SECTOR

Invesco Funds Group
P.O. Box 173706
Denver, CO 80217-3706

Fund managers: Daniel B. Leonard
and Gerard F. Hallaren, Jr.
Fund objective: Sector
Web site: www.invesco.com

Toll-free: 800-525-8085
In-state: 303-930-6300
Fax: 303-930-6655

Performance	★ ★ ★
Consistency	★ ★ ★ ★
Fees/Services	★ ★ ★ ★ ★
FTCHX	**12 Points**

Volatility is always a concern for technology sector funds. A prime example was the 1997 situation when the overall market was up more than 20 percent while many stocks in the technology sector barely moved. The Invesco Strategic Technology Fund was up only 8.9 percent. But over the long term, the technology sector continues to be one of the most promising areas of American industry. "Technology will take us well into the next century," says fund manager Daniel B. Leonard. "We'll all be more wireless and more interactive."

Over the past ten years, the Invesco Strategic Technology Fund has posted an annual average return of 22.4 percent. A $10,000 investment in the fund ten years ago would now be worth about $75,000. The fund stays nearly 100 percent invested in stocks most of the time. Its leading segments include computer systems and services, electronics, medical products and drugs, telecommunications, and financial services.

Leonard's strategy is to focus on companies with strong earnings and sales growth. "We like companies with accelerating sales. When they begin to slow down, that probably means the stock price will slow down, too." Leonard maintains an aggressive trading policy, resulting in an annual portfolio turnover ratio of 237 percent.

PERFORMANCE

The fund has enjoyed strong growth over the last five years. Including dividends and capital gains distributions, the Invesco Strategic Technology Fund has provided a total return for the last five years (through mid-1998) of 180 percent. A $10,000 investment in 1993 would have grown to about $28,000 five years later. Average annual return: 22.9 percent.

CONSISTENCY

The fund has been fairly consistent recently, outperforming the Dow Jones Industrial Average in four of the last five years through 1997 (and it led the Dow through the first few months of 1998). Its biggest gain came in 1995, when it jumped 45.8 percent (compared with a 33.5 percent rise in the Dow).

FEES/SERVICES/MANAGEMENT

Like all Invesco funds, the Strategic Technology Fund is a true no-load fund—no fee to buy, no fee to sell. The fund's total annual expense ratio of 1.34 percent (including a 0.25 percent 12b-1 fee) is in line with other funds.

The fund offers all the standard services, such as retirement account availability, automatic withdrawal, and automatic checking account deduction. Its minimum initial investment of $1,000 and minimum subsequent investment of $50 compare favorably with other funds.

Daniel Leonard has managed the fund since 1985 (and was later joined by Gerard Hallaren as comanager). The Invesco family of funds includes 34 funds and allows shareholders to switch from fund to fund by telephone.

Top Ten Stock Holdings

1. IBM	6. American Express
2. Schlumberger	7. Texas Instruments
3. International Game Technology	8. Tandy
4. Hewlett-Packard	9. Lexmark International
5. Intel	10. Western Atlas

Asset mix: common stocks—98%; cash/equivalents—2%
Total net assets: $1.02 billion
Dividend yield: 0.37%

Fees

Front-end load	*None*
Redemption fee	*None*
12b-1 fee	0.25%
Management fee	0.70
Other expenses	0.39
Total annual expense	1.34%
Minimum initial investment	$1,000
Minimum subsequent investment	$50

Services

Telephone exchanges	*Yes*
Automatic withdrawal	*Yes*
Automatic checking deduction	*Yes*
Retirement plan/IRA	*Yes*
Instant redemption	*Yes*
Financial statements	*Semiannual*
Income distributions	*Annual*
Capital gains distributions	*Annual*
Portfolio manager: years	13
Number of funds in family	34

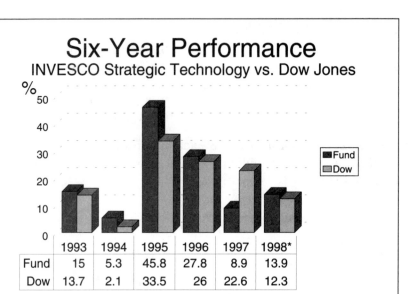

Six-Year Performance
INVESCO Strategic Technology vs. Dow Jones

	1993	1994	1995	1996	1997	1998*
Fund	15	5.3	45.8	27.8	8.9	13.9
Dow	13.7	2.1	33.5	26	22.6	12.3

% Avg. Annual Total Return   *1998 returns through 8/1/96
Fund vs. Dow Jones Industrial Avg.   (5-year avg. annual return: 20.8%)

SMALL CAP

28
MFS Emerging Growth Fund

MFS Funds Distributors, Inc.
500 Boylston Street
Boston, MA 02116

Fund manager: John W. Ballen
Fund objective: Small-cap stocks
Web site: www.mfs.com

Toll-free: 800-225-2606
In-state: 617-954-5000
Fax: 617-954-6617

Performance	★ ★ ★ ★ ★
Consistency	★ ★ ★
Fees/Services	★ ★ ★
MFEGX	**11 Points**

The MFS Emerging Growth Fund is a huge fund that specializes in small stocks. That's no easy task for manager John Ballen. With more than $9 billion in assets to invest (including both "A" shares and "B" shares), Ballen has had to spread the money across a broad universe of stocks. The fund has nearly 600 stock holdings in all.

Ballen's success with the fund continues to attract new investment dollars, which keeps Ballen and his staff constantly on the prowl for good new prospects. Ballen has tried to stay true to the mission of the fund, which is to "invest primarily (at least 80 percent of assets under normal circumstances) in stocks of small and medium-sized companies that are early in their life cycle but which have the potential to become major enterprises."

Once Ballen uncovers a solid prospect, he likes to hold for the long term. The fund's annual portfolio turnover ratio is a very conservative 22 percent. The fund is broadly diversified across industry groups. The leading sectors include technology, 39 percent; retailing, 9 percent; leisure, 14 percent; and health care, 11 percent.

PERFORMANCE

The fund has enjoyed exceptional growth over the last five years. Including dividends and capital gains distributions, the MFS Emerging Growth Fund has provided a total return for the last five years (through mid-1998) of 214 percent. A $10,000 investment in 1993 would have grown to about $31,000 five years later. Average annual return: 25.7 percent.

CONSISTENCY

The fund has been fairly consistent recently, outperforming the Dow Jones Industrial Average three of the last five years through 1997 (and it led the Dow through the first few months of 1998). Its biggest gain came in 1995, when it moved up 40.1 percent (compared with a 33.5 percent rise in the Dow).

FEES/SERVICES/MANAGEMENT

The MFS Emerging Growth Fund has a front-end load of 5.75 percent. Its total annual expense ratio of 1.22 percent (including a 0.25 percent 12b-1 fee) compares favorably with other funds.

The fund offers all the standard services, such as retirement account availability, automatic withdrawal, and automatic checking account deduction. Its minimum initial investment of $1,000 and minimum subsequent investment of $50 compare favorably with other funds.

John Ballen has managed the fund since 1986. The MFS family of funds includes 50 funds and allows shareholders to switch from fund to fund by telephone.

Top Ten Stock Holdings

1. Cendant	6. United Healthcare
2. Computer Associates	7. BMC Software
3. Tyco International	8. Compuware
4. Cisco Systems	9. Cadence Design Systems
5. Oracle	10. Microsoft

Asset mix: common stocks—98%; cash/equivalents—2%
Total net assets: $5.1 billion
Dividend yield: none

Fees

Front-end load	5.75%
Redemption fee	*None*
12b-1 fee	0.25
Management fee	0.73
Other expenses	0.24
Total annual expense	1.22%
Minimum initial investment	$1,000
Minimum subsequent investment	$50

Services

Telephone exchanges	*Yes*
Automatic withdrawal	*Yes*
Automatic checking deduction	*Yes*
Retirement plan/IRA	*Yes*
Instant redemption	*Yes*
Financial statements	*Semiannual*
Income distributions	*Annual*
Capital gains distributions	*Annual*
Portfolio manager: years	12
Number of funds in family	50

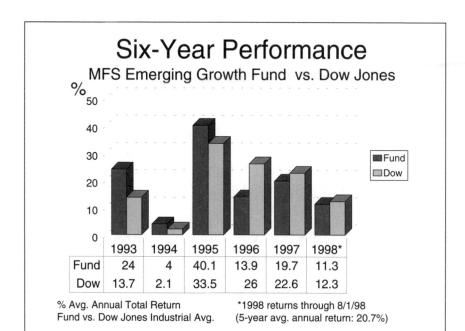

Six-Year Performance
MFS Emerging Growth Fund vs. Dow Jones

	1993	1994	1995	1996	1997	1998*
Fund	24	4	40.1	13.9	19.7	11.3
Dow	13.7	2.1	33.5	26	22.6	12.3

% Avg. Annual Total Return
Fund vs. Dow Jones Industrial Avg.

*1998 returns through 8/1/98
(5-year avg. annual return: 20.7%)

29

GAM Global Fund

INTERNATIONAL

Global Asset Management Funds
135 East 57th Street
25th Floor
New York, NY 10022

Fund manager: John R. Horseman
Fund objective: International equity
Web site: www.usinfo.gam.com

Toll-free: 800-426-4685
In-state: 212-407-4700
Fax: 212-407-4684

Performance	★ ★ ★ ★ ★
Consistency	★ ★ ★
Fees/Services	★ ★ ★
GAGLX	**11 Points**

The GAM Global Fund invests in a broad range of U.S. blue chip growth stocks, along with a smattering of stocks from Europe and Asia. Over the past ten years, the fund has posted an average annual return of about 17 percent. A $10,000 investment in the fund ten years ago would now be worth about $48,000.

The fund has about 40 stock holdings spread across a wide range of industries. Leading sectors include health and personal care, 13 percent of total assets; business and public services, 12 percent; banking, 12 percent; electronics, 8 percent; and transportation, 7 percent.

About 64 percent of the fund's stock portfolio is in U.S. stocks. Other leading areas include Japan, 9 percent; United Kingdom, 7 percent; France, 4 percent; and Hong Kong, 4 percent.

Fund manager John Horseman maintains a fairly active trading policy. The annual portfolio turnover ratio is 107 percent.

PERFORMANCE

The fund has enjoyed exceptional growth over the last five years. Including dividends and capital gains distributions, the GAM Global Fund has provided a total return for the last five years (through mid-1998) of 208 percent. A $10,000 investment in 1993 would have grown to about $31,000 five years later. Average annual return: 25.2 percent.

CONSISTENCY

The fund has been fairly consistent recently, outperforming the Dow Jones Industrial Average in three of the last five years through 1997 (and it led the Dow through the first few months of 1998). Its biggest gain came in 1993, when it moved up 75.3 percent.

FEES/SERVICES/MANAGEMENT

The GAM Global Fund has a front-end load of 5 percent. The fund's total annual expense ratio of 1.83 percent (including a 0.30 percent 12b-1 fee) is very high compared with other funds.

The fund offers all the standard services, such as retirement account availability, automatic withdrawal, and automatic checking account deduction. Its minimum initial investment of $5,000 and minimum subsequent investment of $500 are high compared with other funds.

John Horseman has managed the fund since 1990. The GAM family of funds includes eight funds and allows shareholders to switch from fund to fund by telephone.

Top Ten Stock Holdings

1. Merrill Lynch	6. Intel
2. US Airways Group	7. Novartis
3. NationsBank	8. Barclays
4. Microsoft	9. HSBC Holdings (HKD)
5. Delta Airlines	10. Honda Motor

Asset mix: common stocks—83%; adjustable rate index notes—4%; bond/currency warrants—2%; cash/equivalents—11%
Total net assets: $3.8 million
Dividend yield: 0.28%

Fees

Front-end load	5.00%
Redemption fee	*None*
12b-1 fee	0.30
Management fee	1.00
Other expenses	0.53
Total annual expense	1.83%
Minimum initial investment	$5,000
Minimum subsequent investment	$500

Services

Telephone exchanges	*Yes*
Automatic withdrawal	*Yes*
Automatic checking deduction	*Yes*
Retirement plan/IRA	*Yes*
Instant redemption	*Yes*
Financial statements	*Semiannual*
Income distributions	*Annual*
Capital gains distributions	*Annual*
Portfolio manager: years	8
Number of funds in family	8

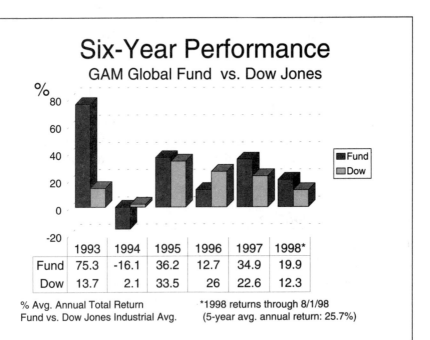

Six-Year Performance
GAM Global Fund vs. Dow Jones

	1993	1994	1995	1996	1997	1998*
Fund	75.3	-16.1	36.2	12.7	34.9	19.9
Dow	13.7	2.1	33.5	26	22.6	12.3

% Avg. Annual Total Return
Fund vs. Dow Jones Industrial Avg.

*1998 returns through 8/1/98
(5-year avg. annual return: 25.7%)

30
Morgan Stanley Dean Witter European Growth Fund

Dean Witter Funds
Two World Trade Center
New York, NY 10048

Fund manager: Jeremy Lodwick
Fund objective: International equity
Web site: www.deanwitter.com/intercapital

Toll-free: 800-869-3863
In-state: 212-392-2550
Fax: 212-392-7204

Performance	★ ★ ★ ★ ★
Consistency	★ ★ ★
Fees/Services	★ ★ ★
EUGAX	**11 Points**

While Asia has been mired in one of its biggest recessions in years, Europe has been going through an economic resurgence. The strong European market has helped make the Morgan Stanley Dean Witter European Growth Fund one of the nation's top-performing funds the past few years. Over the past five years, the fund has posted an average annual return of 25.2 percent.

The fund invests in a broad cross section of stocks from throughout Europe. Its heaviest concentration is in the United Kingdom, which accounts for about one-third of its total assets. Also well represented in the portfolio are Germany, the Netherlands, Spain, Sweden, Switzerland, and Italy. Most of the stocks in the fund are well-established blue chips such as Glaxo Wellcome, Bayer, British Telecommunications, and BASF.

Fund manager Jeremy Lodwick maintains a fairly conservative trading approach, resulting in a 44 percent annual portfolio turnover ratio. Leading sectors include financial stocks, 15 percent of assets; business and consumer services, 16 percent; health-related companies, 12 percent; consumer staples, 11 percent; industrial cyclicals, 14 percent; and retail businesses, 10 percent.

PERFORMANCE

The fund has enjoyed outstanding growth over the last five years. Including dividends and capital gains distributions, the European Growth Fund has provided a total return for the last five years (through mid-1998) of 207 percent. A $10,000 investment in 1993 would have grown to about $31,000 five years later. Average annual return: 25.2 percent.

CONSISTENCY

The fund has been fairly consistent recently, outperforming the Dow Jones Industrial Average in three of the last five years through 1997 (and it led the Dow through the first few months of 1998). Its biggest gain came in 1993, when it jumped 38.3 percent (compared with a 13.7 percent rise in the Dow).

FEES/SERVICES/MANAGEMENT

The fund's "A" shares carry a 5.25 percent front-end load and a 1.45 percent annual expense ratio, which is in line with other funds. The fund is also available in "B" shares that have a 5 percent redemption fee and a slightly higher annual expense ratio of 2.06 percent.

The fund offers all the standard services, such as retirement account availability, automatic withdrawal, and automatic checking account deduction. Its minimum initial investment of $1,000 and minimum subsequent investment of $100 compare favorably with other funds.

Jeremy Lodwick has managed the fund since 1994. The Dean Witter family of funds includes more than 60 funds and allows shareholders to switch from fund to fund by telephone.

Top Ten Stock Holdings

1. Phillips Electronics
2. Accor
3. AXA-UAP
4. Alcatel Alstholm
5. Ericsson
6. Nestlé
7. British Telecommunications
8. Glaxo Wellcome
9. Credit Suisse Group
10. Aegon

Asset mix: common stocks—90%; corporate bonds—2%; cash/equivalents—8%
Total net assets: $1.7 billion
Dividend yield: 0.74%

Fees

Front-end load	5.25%
Redemption fee	*None*
12b-1 fee	0.25
Management fee	0.97
Other expenses	0.23
Total annual expense	1.45%
Minimum initial investment	$1,000
Minimum subsequent investment	$100

Services

Telephone exchanges	*Yes*
Automatic withdrawal	*Yes*
Automatic checking deduction	*Yes*
Retirement plan/IRA	*Yes*
Instant redemption	*Yes*
Financial statements	*Semiannual*
Income distributions	*Annual*
Capital gains distributions	*Annual*
Portfolio manager: years	4
Number of funds in family	62

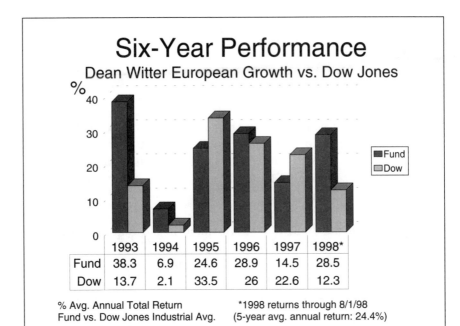

Six-Year Performance
Dean Witter European Growth vs. Dow Jones

%	1993	1994	1995	1996	1997	1998*
Fund	38.3	6.9	24.6	28.9	14.5	28.5
Dow	13.7	2.1	33.5	26	22.6	12.3

% Avg. Annual Total Return
Fund vs. Dow Jones Industrial Avg.

*1998 returns through 8/1/98
(5-year avg. annual return: 24.4%)

31

Enterprise Growth Portfolio

LONG TERM

Enterprise Funds
3343 Peachtree Road, N.E. Suite 450
Atlanta, GA 30326-1022

Fund manager: Ronald E. Canakaris
Fund objective: Long-term growth
Web site: www.enterprisegroup.com

Toll-free: 800-368-3527
In-state: 404-261-1116
Fax: 404-261-1118

Performance	★ ★ ★ ★ ★
Consistency	★ ★ ★
Fees/Services	★ ★ ★
ENGRX	**11 Points**

Since 1980, when Ronald Canakaris began his tenure managing the Enterprise Growth Portfolio, the fund has enjoyed outstanding long-term returns. The fund invests in an all-star portfolio of the nation's top companies, such as Microsoft, Bristol-Myers Squibb, Procter & Gamble, Gillette, Coca-Cola, and Intel.

Over the past ten years, the fund has posted an average annual return of about 19 percent. A $10,000 investment in the fund ten years ago would now be worth nearly $60,000. Canakaris takes a pure buy-and-hold approach, staying fully invested in stocks while maintaining the fund at a very low 30 percent annual turnover ratio. Canakaris looks for companies with strong earnings growth that are positioned to benefit from the expansion of global markets.

The fund has only about 35 stock holdings, primarily in fast-growth industries. Leading sectors include computer-related companies, 21 percent of assets; pharmaceuticals, 17 percent; food and beverages, 7 percent; consumer nondurables, 10 percent; retail businesses, 5 percent; and hotels and restaurants, 6 percent.

PERFORMANCE

The fund has enjoyed exceptional growth over the last five years. Including dividends and capital gains distributions, the Enterprise Growth Portfolio has provided a total return for the last five years (through mid-1998) of 205 percent. A $10,000 investment in 1993 would have grown to about $30,000 five years later. Average annual return: 25 percent.

CONSISTENCY

The fund has been fairly consistent recently, outperforming the Dow Jones Industrial Average in three of the last five years through 1997 (and it led the Dow through the first few months of 1998). Its biggest gain came in 1995, when it jumped 40 percent (compared with a 33.5 percent rise in the Dow).

FEES/SERVICES/MANAGEMENT

The Enterprise Growth Portfolio charges a 4.75 percent front-end load. Its 1.53 percent annual expense ratio (including a 0.45 percent 12b-1 fee) is in line with other funds.

The fund offers all the standard services, such as retirement account availability, automatic withdrawal, and automatic checking account deduction. Its minimum initial investment of $1,000 and minimum subsequent investment of $50 compare favorably with other funds.

Ronald Canakaris has managed the fund since 1980. The Enterprise fund family includes 13 funds and allows shareholders to switch from fund to fund by telephone.

Top Ten Stock Holdings

1. Johnson & Johnson
2. Microsoft
3. Bristol-Myers Squibb
4. Proctor & Gamble
5. Gillette
6. Coca-Cola
7. Intel
8. Eli Lilly
9. Cisco Systems
10. McDonald's

Asset mix: common stocks—96%; cash/equivalents—4%
Total net assets: $423 million
Dividend yield: none

Fees

Front-end load	4.75%
Redemption fee	*None*
12b-1 fee	0.45
Management fee	0.75
Other expenses	0.33
Total annual expense	1.53%
Minimum initial investment	$1,000
Minimum subsequent investment	$50

Services

Telephone exchanges	*Yes*
Automatic withdrawal	*Yes*
Automatic checking deduction	*Yes*
Retirement plan/IRA	*Yes*
Instant redemption	*Yes*
Financial statements	*Semiannual*
Income distributions	*Annual*
Capital gains distributions	*Annual*
Portfolio manager: years	18
Number of funds in family	3

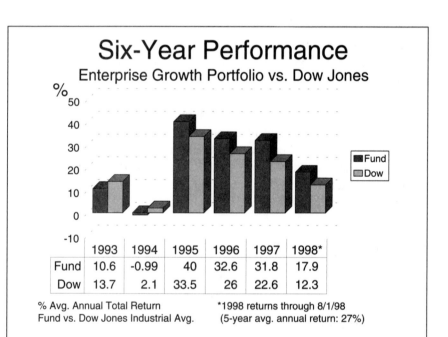

Six-Year Performance
Enterprise Growth Portfolio vs. Dow Jones

	1993	1994	1995	1996	1997	1998*
Fund	10.6	-0.99	40	32.6	31.8	17.9
Dow	13.7	2.1	33.5	26	22.6	12.3

% Avg. Annual Total Return
Fund vs. Dow Jones Industrial Avg.

*1998 returns through 8/1/98
(5-year avg. annual return: 27%)

GROWTH

32
SAFECO Equity Fund

SAFECO Funds
P.O. Box 34890
Seattle, WA 98124-1890

Fund manager: Richard Meagley
Fund objective: Growth and income
Web site: www.safecofunds.com

Toll-free: 800-624-5711
In-state: 206-545-7319
Fax: 206-548-7150

Performance	★ ★ ★ ★
Consistency	★ ★ ★
Fees/Services	★ ★ ★ ★
SAFQX	**11 Points**

The SAFECO Equity Fund invests in a diverse cross section of about 50 blue chip growth stocks, such as Johnson & Johnson, Kimberly-Clark, and Walt Disney. Over the past ten years, the fund has posted average annual returns of about 19 percent. A $10,000 investment in the fund ten years ago would now be worth about $60,000.

In selecting stocks for the portfolio, fund manager Rich Meagley looks for the top-performing companies in the fastest-growing industrial sectors. "We are less interested in companies with less predictable earnings—mainly technology and HMOs," explains Meagley.

Meagley takes a conservative buy-and-hold approach. The fund has an annual portfolio turnover ratio of 34 percent. Leading industrial sectors include health care and medical services, 13 percent of assets; computers, 10 percent; retail businesses, 8 percent; oil, 8 percent; banks, insurance, and financial services, 14 percent; telecommunications, 5 percent.

PERFORMANCE

The fund has enjoyed exceptional growth over the last five years. Including dividends and capital gains distributions, the SAFECO Equity Fund has provided a total return for the last five years (through mid-1998) of 198 percent. A $10,000 investment in 1993 would have grown to about $30,000 five years later. Average annual return: 24.4 percent.

CONSISTENCY

The fund has been fairly consistent recently, outperforming the Dow Jones Industrial Average in three of the last five years through 1997 (and it led the Dow through the first few months of 1998). Its biggest gain came in 1993, when it moved up 30.4 percent (compared with a 13.7 percent rise in the Dow).

FEES/SERVICES/MANAGEMENT

Like all SAFECO funds, the Equity Fund is a true no-load—no fee to buy, no fee to sell. Its total annual expense ratio of 0.73 percent (with no 12b-1 fee) compares very favorably with other funds.

The fund offers all the standard services, such as retirement account availability, automatic withdrawal, and automatic checking account deduction. Its minimum initial investment of $1,000 and minimum subsequent investment of $100 compare favorably with other funds.

Richard Meagley has managed the fund only since 1995. The SAFECO family of funds includes 19 funds and allows shareholders to switch from fund to fund by telephone.

Top Ten Stock Holdings

1. Chase Manhattan
2. Kimberly-Clark
3. American Stores
4. Hartford Financial Services Group
5. Burlington Northern Santa Fe
6. American Home Products
7. Anheuser-Busch
8. Allied Signal
9. Fannie Mae
10. Texaco

Asset mix: common stocks—97%; cash/equivalents—3%
Total net assets: $1.7 billion
Dividend yield: 0.97%

Fees

Front-end load	*None*
Redemption fee	*None*
12b-1 fee	*None*
Management fee	0.52%
Other expenses	0.21
Total annual expense	0.73%
Minimum initial investment	$1,000
Minimum subsequent investment	$100

Services

Telephone exchanges	*Yes*
Automatic withdrawal	*Yes*
Automatic checking deduction	*Yes*
Retirement plan/IRA	*Yes*
Instant redemption	*Yes*
Financial statements	*Semiannual*
Income distributions	*Annual*
Capital gains distributions	*Annual*
Portfolio manager: years	3
Number of funds in family	19

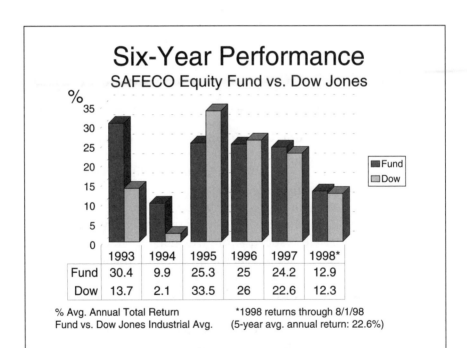

Six-Year Performance
SAFECO Equity Fund vs. Dow Jones

	1993	1994	1995	1996	1997	1998*
Fund	30.4	9.9	25.3	25	24.2	12.9
Dow	13.7	2.1	33.5	26	22.6	12.3

% Avg. Annual Total Return
Fund vs. Dow Jones Industrial Avg.

*1998 returns through 8/1/98
(5-year avg. annual return: 22.6%)

33

T. Rowe Price Mid-Cap Growth Fund

LONG TERM

T. Rowe Price Funds
100 East Pratt Street
Baltimore, MD 21202

Fund manager: Brian W. H. Berghuis
Fund objective: Long-term growth
Web site: www.troweprice.com

Toll-free: 800-225-5132
In-state: 410-547-2000
Fax: 410-347-1572

Performance	★ ★ ★ ★
Consistency	★ ★
Fees/Services	★ ★ ★ ★ ★
RPMGX	**11 Points**

The T. Rowe Price Mid-Cap Growth Fund invests in emerging stocks in fast-growing industries. "Several of the criteria we focus on," explains fund manager Brian Berghuis, "include the growth in the company's industry sector; the growth rate we foresee for the company over the next several years; the strength of a company's business model (competitive advantages such as brand names, low-cost production, and patent positions); management we respect; strong financial characteristics such as good cash flow and healthy balance sheets; and, finally, reasonable valuations."

Over the past five years, the fund has posted an average annual return of about 24 percent.

The fund stays almost fully invested in stocks most of the time. Berghuis maintains a fairly conservative trading approach resulting in an annual turnover ratio of 38 percent.

The fund has about 100 stock holdings in all. Most of the stocks in the fund have market capitalizations of $300 million to $5 billion. With few exceptions, they are little-known companies, such as Warnaco Group, Tri-Mass, and ACE Limited.

The fund is fairly diverse across industry sectors. Its leading sectors are business services, 28 percent of assets; consumer-related companies, 18 percent; industrial firms, 10 percent; health care, 10 percent; technology, 7 percent; financial services, 9 percent; and energy, 7 percent.

PERFORMANCE

The fund has enjoyed outstanding growth over the last five years. Including dividends and capital gains distributions, the T. Rowe Price Mid-Cap Growth Fund has provided a total return for the last five years (through mid-1998) of 193 percent. A $10,000 investment in 1993 would have grown to about $29,000 five years later. Average annual return: 24 percent.

CONSISTENCY

The fund has been inconsistent recently, outperforming the Dow Jones Industrial Average only two of the last five years through 1997 (but it led the Dow through the first few months of 1998). Its biggest gain came in 1995, when it moved up 41 percent (compared with a 33.5 percent rise in the Dow).

FEES/SERVICES/MANAGEMENT

Like all T. Rowe Price funds, the Mid-Cap Growth Fund is a true no-load fund—no fee to buy, no fee to sell. Its total annual expense ratio of 1.04 percent (with no 12b-1 fee) compares favorably with other funds.

The fund offers all the standard services, such as retirement account availability, automatic withdrawal, and automatic checking account deduction. Its minimum initial investment of $2,500 and minimum subsequent investment of $100 are a little on the high side compared with other funds.

Brian W.H. Berghuis has managed the fund since 1992. The T. Rowe Price family of funds includes 70 funds and allows shareholders to switch from fund to fund by telephone.

Top Ten Stock Holdings

1. Warnaco Group	6. Affiliated Computer Services
2. JP Foodservice	7. Danaher
3. Biogen	8. Royal Carribbean Cruises
4. Suiza Foods	9. Culligan Water Technologies
5. TriMass	10. Outdoor Systems

Asset mix: common stocks—92%; cash/equivalents—8%
Total net assets: $2.3 billion
Dividend yield: none

Fees

Front-end load	*None*
Redemption fee	*None*
12b-1 fee	*None*
Management fee	0.69%
Other expenses	0.35
Total annual expense	1.04%
Minimum initial investment	$2,500
Minimum subsequent investment	$100

Services

Telephone exchanges	*Yes*
Automatic withdrawal	*Yes*
Automatic checking deduction	*Yes*
Retirement plan/IRA	*Yes*
Instant redemption	*Yes*
Financial statements	*Semiannual*
Income distributions	*Annual*
Capital gains distributions	*Annual*
Portfolio manager: years	6
Number of funds in family	70

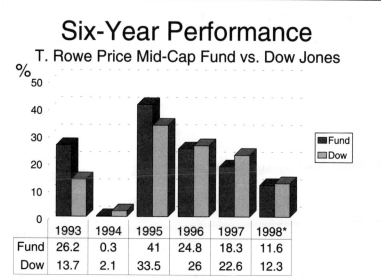

Six-Year Performance
T. Rowe Price Mid-Cap Fund vs. Dow Jones

	1993	1994	1995	1996	1997	1998*
Fund	26.2	0.3	41	24.8	18.3	11.6
Dow	13.7	2.1	33.5	26	22.6	12.3

% Avg. Annual Total Return   *1998 returns through 8/1/98
Fund vs. Dow Jones Industrial Avg. (5-year avg. annual return: 21.9%)

34
Founders Growth Fund

LONG TERM

Founders Funds
2930 East Third Avenue
Denver, CO 80206-5002

Fund manager: Edward Keely
Fund objective: Long-term growth
Web site: www.founders.com

Toll-free: 800-525-2440
In-state: 303-394-4404
Fax: 303-331-9862

Performance	★ ★ ★
Consistency	★ ★ ★
Fees/Services	★ ★ ★ ★ ★
FRGRX	**11 Points**

The Founders Growth Fund invests in solid, well-established companies with a track record of consistent growth. The fund's diverse selection of midcap and large-cap stocks include such blue chips as Gillette, Procter and Gamble, General Electric, Coca-Cola, and Microsoft. "As we research individual companies, we pay special attention to business fundamentals, innovative management, increased productivity, and high recurring income," explains fund manager Edward Keely. "We will continue to rely on our bottom-up, company-by-company research methods to seek companies that may see growth in almost any market condition."

The fund has enjoyed a stellar performance for many years. Over the past ten years, the fund has posted an average annual return of 19.5 percent. A $10,000 investment in the fund ten years ago would now be worth about $60,000.

In all, the fund has about 80 stock holdings across a broad spectrum of industries. Foreign stocks make up about 5 percent of the portfolio. Leading industrial sectors include computer products and services, 16 percent of assets; banking and financial services, 15 percent; pharmaceuticals, 10 percent; and consumer products, 11 percent. Keely maintains a fairly aggressive trading policy; the annual portfolio turnover ratio is 134 percent.

PERFORMANCE

The fund has enjoyed strong growth over the last five years. Including dividends and capital gains distributions, the Founders Growth Fund has provided a total return for the last five years (through mid-1998) of 180 percent. A $10,000 investment in 1993 would have grown to about $28,000 five years later. Average annual return: 22.8 percent.

CONSISTENCY

The fund has been fairly consistent recently, outperforming the Dow Jones Industrial Average in three of the last five years through 1997 (and it led the Dow through the first few months of 1998). Its biggest gain came in 1995, when it moved up 45.6 percent (compared with a 33.5 percent rise in the Dow).

FEES/SERVICES/MANAGEMENT

Like all Founders funds, the Growth Fund is a true no-load—no fee to buy, no fee to sell. The fund's total annual expense ratio of 1.20 percent (including a 0.25 percent 12b-1 fee) compares favorably with other funds.

The fund offers all the standard services, such as retirement account availability, automatic withdrawal, and automatic checking account deduction. Its minimum initial investment of $1,000 and minimum subsequent investment of $100 is in line with other funds.

Edward Keely has managed the fund since 1993. Founders Funds include 11 funds and allow shareholders to switch from fund to fund by telephone.

Top Ten Stock Holdings

1. Eli Lilly
2. General Electric
3. Microsoft
4. Pfizer
5. Sunbeam

6. MCI Communications
7. Fiserv
8. Maytag
9. Bristol-Myers Squibb
10. Procter & Gamble

Asset mix: common stocks—87%; cash/equivalents—13%
Total net assets: $1.76 billion
Dividend yield: 0.31%

Fees

Front-end load	*None*
Redemption fee	*None*
12b-1 fee	0.25%
Management fee	0.71
Other expenses	0.24
Total annual expense	1.20%
Minimum initial investment	$1,000
Minimum subsequent investment	$100

Services

Telephone exchanges	*Yes*
Automatic withdrawal	*Yes*
Automatic checking deduction	*Yes*
Retirement plan/IRA	*Yes*
Instant redemption	*Yes*
Financial statements	*Semiannual*
Income distributions	*Annual*
Capital gains distributions	*Annual*
Portfolio manager: years	5
Number of funds in family	11

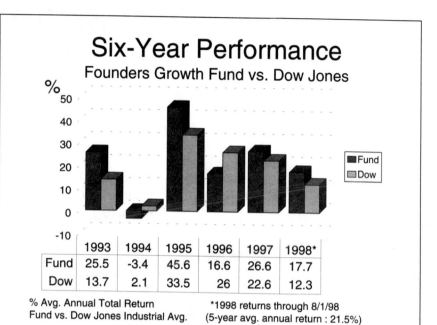

Six-Year Performance
Founders Growth Fund vs. Dow Jones

	1993	1994	1995	1996	1997	1998*
Fund	25.5	-3.4	45.6	16.6	26.6	17.7
Dow	13.7	2.1	33.5	26	22.6	12.3

% Avg. Annual Total Return   *1998 returns through 8/1/98
Fund vs. Dow Jones Industrial Avg.   (5-year avg. annual return : 21.5%)

35

Vanguard Growth and Income Portfolio

GROWTH

Vanguard Group
P.O. Box 2600
Valley Forge, PA 19482

Fund manager: John Nagorniak
Fund objective: Growth and income
Web site: www.vanguard.com

Toll-free: 800-635-1511
In-state: 610-669-1000
Fax: 610-640-1371

Performance	★ ★ ★
Consistency	★ ★ ★
Fees/Services	★ ★ ★ ★ ★
VQNPX	**11 Points**

The Vanguard Growth and Income Portfolio invests in a diverse array of dividend-paying blue chip growth companies, such as Merck, Dow Chemical, and Ford Motor. In selecting his portfolio, fund manager John Nagorniak looks for undervalued stocks, using three basic types of measures. He uses fundamental momentum measures to identify companies whose business prospects are relatively strong; he uses relative value measures to quantify the attractiveness of a stock's price in relation to such financial measures as value, sales, or earnings; and he uses future cash flow to identify likely favorable payoffs in terms of future earnings and dividends for an investment made today.

Over the past ten years, the fund has posted an average annual return of about 19 percent. A $10,000 investment in the fund ten years ago would now be worth about $57,000.

Nagorniak stays almost 100 percent invested in stocks under normal circumstances. He maintains a fairly active trading policy; the annual portfolio turnover ratio is 75 percent.

The fund has about 110 stock holdings spread across a broad range of industries. Leading sectors include financial services, 20 percent of total assets; health care, 10 percent; utilities, 10 percent; technology, 9 percent; materials and processing, 8 percent; and consumer products, 16 percent.

PERFORMANCE

The fund has enjoyed strong growth over the last five years. Including dividends and capital gains distributions, the Vanguard Growth and Income Fund has provided a total return for the last five years (through mid-1998) of 175 percent. A $10,000 investment in 1993 would have grown to about $27,500 five years later. Average annual return: 22.4 percent.

CONSISTENCY

The fund has been fairly consistent recently, outperforming the Dow Jones Industrial Average in three of the last five years through 1997 (and it led the Dow through the first few months of 1998). Its biggest gain came in 1995, when it moved up 35.9 percent (compared with a 33.5 percent rise in the Dow).

FEES/SERVICES/MANAGEMENT

Like all Vanguard funds, the Growth and Income Fund is a true no-load—no fee to buy, no fee to sell. Its total annual expense ratio of just 0.38 percent (with no 12b-1 fee) compares very favorably with other funds.

The fund offers all the standard services, such as retirement account availability, automatic withdrawal, and automatic checking account deduction. Its minimum initial investment of $3,000 and minimum subsequent investment of $100 are a little higher than most funds.

John Nagorniak has managed the fund since 1986. The Vanguard fund family includes 95 funds and allows shareholders to switch from fund to fund by telephone.

Top Ten Stock Holdings

1. American International Group
2. Merck
3. Ford Motor
4. Dayton Hudson
5. Bell Atlantic
6. Morgan Stanley Dean Witter
7. Dow Chemical
8. Compaq Computer
9. AirTouch Communications
10. Tyco International

Asset mix: common stocks—96%; cash/equivalents—4%
Total net assets: $2.1 billion
Dividend yield: 1.31%

Fees

Front-end load	*None*
Redemption fee	*None*
12b-1 fee	*None*
Management fee	0.24%
Other expenses	0.14
Total annual expense	0.38%
Minimum initial investment	$3,000
Minimum subsequent investment	$100

Services

Telephone exchanges	*Yes*
Automatic withdrawal	*Yes*
Automatic checking deduction	*Yes*
Retirement plan/IRA	*Yes*
Instant redemption	*Yes*
Financial statements	*Semiannual*
Income distributions	*Semiannual*
Capital gains distributions	*Annual*
Portfolio manager: years	12
Number of funds in family	95

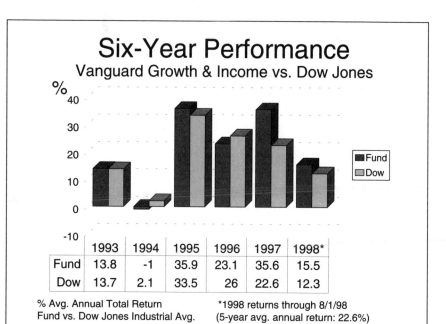

Six-Year Performance
Vanguard Growth & Income vs. Dow Jones

	1993	1994	1995	1996	1997	1998*
Fund	13.8	-1	35.9	23.1	35.6	15.5
Dow	13.7	2.1	33.5	26	22.6	12.3

% Avg. Annual Total Return
Fund vs. Dow Jones Industrial Avg.

*1998 returns through 8/1/98
(5-year avg. annual return: 22.6%)

36

Vanguard International Equity Index Fund European Portfolio

INTERNATIONAL

Vanguard Group
P.O. Box 2600
Valley Forge, PA 19482

Fund manager: George U. Sauter
Fund objective: International equity
Web site: www.vanguard.com

Toll-free: 800-635-1511
In-state: 610-669-1000
Fax: 610-640-1371

Performance	★ ★ ★
Consistency	★ ★ ★
Fees/Services	★ ★ ★ ★ ★
VEURX	**11 Points**

The Vanguard International Equity Index Fund European Portfolio invests in a broad selection of more than 550 European stocks intended to mirror the overall European market. The fund has investments in 14 countries, including Austria, Belgium, Denmark, Finland, France, Germany, Ireland, Italy, the Netherlands, Norway, Spain, Sweden, Switzerland, and the United Kingdom.

Fund manager George Sauter takes a very conservative buy-and-hold approach that results in an annual portfolio turnover ratio of just 4 percent. The fund stays nearly 100 percent invested in stocks all the time.

The fund has benefited in recent years from a strong European economy. Over the past five years, the fund has posted an average annual return of about 22 percent. That growth should continue as long as the European markets remain strong. In terms of geographical weighting, about a third of the fund's assets are invested in stocks from the United Kingdom. Other leading regions include Germany, 16 percent; France, 12 percent; Switzerland, 10 percent; and the Netherlands, 9 percent.

The fund invests across a very diverse range of industries. Nearly every industrial sector is represented. Most of its holdings are well-established blue chip stocks.

PERFORMANCE

The fund has enjoyed strong growth over the last five years. Including dividends and capital gains distributions, the Vanguard International Equity Index Fund European Portfolio has provided a total return for the last five years (through mid-1998) of 175 percent. A $10,000 investment in 1993 would have grown to about $27,500 five years later. Average annual return: 22.4 percent.

CONSISTENCY

Because it is an international fund, it does not move in sync with the U.S. market. It has outperformed the Dow Jones Industrial Average in two of the last five years through 1997 and was nearly even with the Dow two other years (and it led the Dow through the first few months of 1998). Its biggest gain came in 1997, when it moved up 24.2 percent (compared with a 22.6 percent rise in the Dow).

FEES/SERVICES/MANAGEMENT

Like all Vanguard funds, the International Equity Index Fund European Portfolio is a true no-load fund—no fee to buy, no fee to sell. Its total annual expense ratio of 0.31 percent (with no 12b-1 fee) compares very favorably with other funds.

The fund offers all the standard services, such as retirement account availability, automatic withdrawal, and automatic checking account deduction. Its minimum initial investment of $3,000 and minimum subsequent investment of $100 are a little higher than most funds.

George Sauter has managed the fund since 1990. The Vanguard Group includes 95 funds and allows shareholders to switch from fund to fund by telephone.

Top Ten Stock Holdings

1. Royal Dutch Petroleum
2. Novartis
3. Glaxo Wellcome
4. British Petroleum
5. Roche Holding

6. Lloyds TSB Group
7. Allianz
8. Nestlé
9. SmithKline Beecham
10. British Telecommunications

Asset mix: common stocks—98%; cash/equivalents—2%
Total net assets: $2.4 billion
Dividend yield: 1.52%

Fees

Front-end load	*None*
Redemption fee	*None*
12b-1 fee	*None*
Management fee	0.22%
Other expenses	0.09
Total annual expense	0.31%
Minimum initial investment	$3,000
Minimum subsequent investment	$100

Services

Telephone exchanges	*Yes*
Automatic withdrawal	*Yes*
Automatic checking deduction	*Yes*
Retirement plan/IRA	*Yes*
Instant redemption	*Yes*
Financial statements	*Semiannual*
Income distributions	*Annual*
Capital gains distributions	*Annual*
Portfolio manager: years	8
Number of funds in family	95

Six-Year Performance
Vanguard International Equity Index vs. Dow

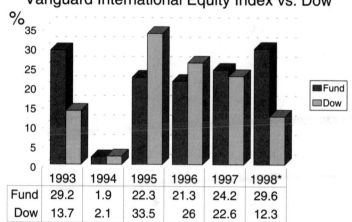

	1993	1994	1995	1996	1997	1998*
Fund	29.2	1.9	22.3	21.3	24.2	29.6
Dow	13.7	2.1	33.5	26	22.6	12.3

% Avg. Annual Total Return   *1998 returns through 8/1/98
Fund vs. Dow Jones Industrial Avg.   (5-year avg.annual return : 23.6%)

37
Janus Worldwide Fund

INTERNATIONAL

Janus Investment Funds
100 Fillmore Street
Denver, CO 80206-4928

Fund manager: Helen Young Hayes
Fund objective: International equity
Web site: www.janus.com

Toll-free: 800-525-8983
In-state: 303-333-3863
Fax: 303-394-7659

Performance	★ ★ ★
Consistency	★ ★ ★
Fees/Services	★ ★ ★ ★ ★
JAWWX	**11 Points**

The Janus Worldwide Fund is one of the world's most diversified mutual funds with stock holdings in more than 70 industrial sectors throughout 25 countries.

Janus Worldwide invests primarily in stocks of mid-capitalization to large-capitalization companies that have shown steady earnings and revenue growth. U.S. stocks account for only about 20 percent of the fund's assets. The largest concentration of holdings is in Europe and makes up just over 50 percent of the fund's assets. Asian stocks account for about 20 percent. The fund also has some minor stock holdings in South America and South Africa. It also holds some foreign currency contracts.

The fund, which opened in 1991, has posted an average annual return of about 22 percent over the past five years. Fund manager Helen Young Hayes, who has been with the fund since it opened, takes a fairly conservative trading approach. The annual portfolio turnover ratio is 79 percent. The fund usually stays almost fully invested in stocks.

The Worldwide Fund has about 200 stock holdings across a broad range of industries. Its leading industrial sectors include computer software and services, 8 percent of assets; medical, 8 percent; diversified holding companies, 11 percent; banks, 8 percent; and chemicals, 6 percent.

PERFORMANCE

The fund has enjoyed strong growth over the last five years. Including dividends and capital gains distributions, the Janus Worldwide Fund has provided a total return for the last five years (through mid-1998) of 173 percent. A $10,000 investment in 1993 would have grown to about $27,000 five years later. Average annual return: 22.2 percent.

CONSISTENCY

The fund has been fairly consistent recently, outperforming the Dow Jones Industrial Average in three of the last five years through 1997 (and it led the Dow through the first few months of 1998). Its biggest gain came in 1993, when it moved up 28.4 percent.

FEES/SERVICES/MANAGEMENT

The Janus Worldwide Fund is a true no-load—no fee to buy, no fee to sell. The fund's total annual expense ratio of just 0.96 percent (with no 12b-1 fee) compares very favorably with other funds.

The fund offers all the standard services, such as retirement account availability, automatic withdrawal, and automatic checking account deduction. Its minimum initial investment of $2,500 is a little higher than most other funds, but its minimum subsequent investment of $100 compares favorably with other funds.

Helen Young Hayes has managed the fund since 1991. The Janus family of funds includes 16 funds and allows shareholders to switch from fund to fund by telephone.

Top Ten Stock Holdings

1. Rentokil Initial
2. Microsoft
3. Siebe
4. Akzo Nobel
5. Cisco Systems

6. Novartis
7. Tyco International
8. Monsanto
9. Union Bank Switzerland
10. Parametric Technology

Asset mix: common stocks—97%; cash/equivalents—3%
Total net assets: $10.6 billion
Dividend yield: 0.44%

Fees

Front-end load	*None*
Redemption fee	*None*
12b-1 fee	*None*
Management fee	0.65%
Other expenses	0.31
Total annual expense	0.96%
Minimum initial investment	$2,500
Minimum subsequent investment	$100

Services

Telephone exchanges	*Yes*
Automatic withdrawal	*Yes*
Automatic checking deduction	*Yes*
Retirement plan/IRA	*Yes*
Instant redemption	*Yes*
Financial statements	*Semiannual*
Income distributions	*Annual*
Capital gains distributions	*Annual*
Portfolio manager: years	7
Number of funds in family	16

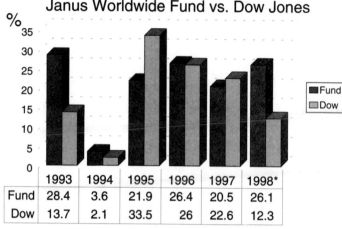

Six-Year Performance
Janus Worldwide Fund vs. Dow Jones

	1993	1994	1995	1996	1997	1998*
Fund	28.4	3.6	21.9	26.4	20.5	26.1
Dow	13.7	2.1	33.5	26	22.6	12.3

% Avg. Annual Total Return   *1998 returns through 8/1/98
Fund vs. Dow Jones Industrial Avg.   (5-year avg. annual return: 23.7%)

38

Selected American Shares

GROWTH

Selected Funds
P.O. Box 1688
Santa Fe, NM 87504-1688

Fund manager: Christopher Davis
Fund objective: Growth and income

Toll-free: 800-243-1575
In-state: 505-983-4335
Fax: 505-820-3002

Performance	★ ★ ★
Consistency	★ ★ ★
Fees/Services	★ ★ ★ ★ ★
SLASX	**11 Points**

The Selected American Shares Fund invests primarily in dividend-paying blue chip stocks, such as American Express, McDonald's, and IBM. "The kinds of businesses we want to own have characteristics such as first-class management, high returns on capital, a lean expense structure, a dominant or growing share in a growing market, products or services that do not become obsolete, a strong balance sheet, and successful international operations," says fund manager Christopher Davis. "We base stock valuations on the return we would expect to earn if we bought the entire business, and we focus on the owners' cash earnings relative to the purchase price."

Over the past ten years, the fund has posted an average annual return of about 19 percent. A $10,000 investment in the fund ten years ago would now be worth about $55,000.

The fund stays almost 100 percent invested in stocks under normal circumstances. Davis takes a conservative buy-and-hold approach. The annual portfolio turnover ratio is 29 percent. The fund has about 60 stock holdings in all. Leading industrial sectors include banks, 13 percent; energy, 10 percent; insurance, 13 percent; pharmaceutical and health care, 6 percent; real estate, 6 percent; and technology, 9 percent.

PERFORMANCE

The fund has enjoyed strong growth over the last five years. Including dividends and capital gains distributions, the Selected American Shares Fund has provided a total return for the last five years (through mid-1998) of 173 percent. A $10,000 investment in 1993 would have grown to about $27,000 five years later. Average annual return: 22.2 percent.

CONSISTENCY

The fund has been fairly consistent recently, outperforming the Dow Jones Industrial Average in three of the last five years through 1997 (but it trailed the Dow through the first few months of 1998). Its biggest gain came in 1995, when it moved up 38.1 percent (compared with a 33.5 percent rise in the Dow).

FEES/SERVICES/MANAGEMENT

Like all Selected funds, the American Shares Fund is a true no-load—no fee to buy, no fee to sell. Its total annual expense ratio of 0.96 percent (with no 12b-1 fee) compares very favorably with other funds.

The fund offers all the standard services, such as retirement account availability, automatic withdrawal, and automatic checking account deduction. Its minimum initial investment of $1,000 and minimum subsequent investment of $100 compare favorably with other funds.

Christopher Davis has managed the fund since 1993. The Selected fund family includes four funds and allows shareholders to switch from fund to fund by telephone.

Top Ten Stock Holdings

1. American Express	6. IBM
2. Wells Fargo	7. General Re
3. Travelers Group	8. McDonald's
4. Morgan Stanley Dean Witter	9. Halliburton
5. Hewlett-Packard	10. BankAmerica

Asset mix: common stocks—97%; cash/equivalents—3%
Total net assets: $2.2 billion
Dividend yield: 0.63%

Fees

Front-end load	*None*
Redemption fee	*None*
12b-1 fee	0.25%
Management fee	0.59
Other expenses	0.12
Total annual expense	0.96%
Minimum initial investment	$1,000
Minimum subsequent investment	$100

Services

Telephone exchanges	*Yes*
Automatic withdrawal	*Yes*
Automatic checking deduction	*Yes*
Retirement plan/IRA	*Yes*
Instant redemption	*Yes*
Financial statements	*Semiannual*
Income distributions	*Annual*
Capital gains distributions	*Annual*
Portfolio manager: years	5
Number of funds in family	4

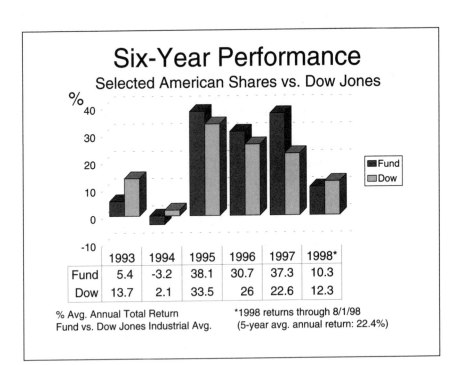

Six-Year Performance
Selected American Shares vs. Dow Jones

	1993	1994	1995	1996	1997	1998*
Fund	5.4	-3.2	38.1	30.7	37.3	10.3
Dow	13.7	2.1	33.5	26	22.6	12.3

% Avg. Annual Total Return
Fund vs. Dow Jones Industrial Avg.

*1998 returns through 8/1/98
(5-year avg. annual return: 22.4%)

SMALL CAP

39

SSgA Small Cap Fund

SSgA Funds
2 International Place
Boston, MA 02110

Fund manager: Jeffrey Adams
Fund objective: Small-cap stocks

Toll-free: 800-647-7327
In-state: 253-798-9500
Fax: 253-593-1603

Performance	★ ★ ★
Consistency	★ ★ ★
Fees/Services	★ ★ ★ ★ ★
SVSCX	**11 Points**

A few well-known names are in the SSgA Small Cap Fund—B.F. Goodrich, Dean Foods, and Adolph Coors—but most are lesser-known small-cap and mid-cap emerging growth stocks. The fund is loaded with such emerging growth stocks as Alpharma, Safeskin, Pillowtex, and Computer Task Group. Most of the stocks in the fund have market capitalizations ranging from $50 million to $3 billion.

Over the past five years, the fund has posted an average annual return of about 22 percent. The fund stays almost 100 percent invested in stocks most of the time. Fund manager Jeff Adams maintains a fairly active trading strategy. The annual portfolio turnover ratio is 144 percent.

The fund has about 200 stock holdings in all, spread across a diverse range of industries. Leading sectors include technology, 16 percent of assets; financial services, 12 percent; capital goods, 7 percent; consumer basics, 16 percent; consumer durables, 5 percent; consumer services, 5 percent; and consumer nondurables, 10 percent.

PERFORMANCE

The fund has enjoyed strong growth over the last five years. Including dividends and capital gains distributions, the SSgA Small Cap Fund has provided a total return for the last five years (through mid-1998) of 173 percent. A $10,000 investment in 1993 would have grown to about $27,000 five years later. Average annual return: 22.2 percent.

CONSISTENCY

The fund has been fairly consistent recently, outperforming the Dow Jones Industrial Average in three of the last five years through 1997 (and it kept pace with the Dow through the first few months of 1998). Its biggest gain came in 1995, when it moved up 41.8 percent (compared with a 33.5 percent rise in the Dow).

FEES/SERVICES/MANAGEMENT

Like all SSgA funds, the Small Cap Fund is a true no-load—no fee to buy, no fee to sell. Its total annual expense ratio of 1 percent (with a 0.25 percent 12b-1 fee) compares favorably with other funds.

The fund offers many of the standard services, such as retirement account availability and automatic checking account deduction; however, an automatic withdrawal plan is unavailable. Its minimum initial investment of $1,000 and minimum subsequent investment of $100 compare favorably with other funds.

Jeffrey Adams has managed the fund since 1994. The SSgA family of funds includes 12 funds and allows shareholders to switch from fund to fund by telephone.

Top Ten Stock Holdings

1. Best Buy
2. Southdown
3. Rexall Sundown
4. Texas Industries
5. Cliffs Drilling
6. Pier 1 Imports
7. Systems & Computer Technology
8. FIRSTPLUS Financial Group
9. Broderbund Software
10. Medicis Pharmaceutical

Asset mix: common stocks—97%; cash/equivalents—3%
Total net assets: $282 million
Dividend yield: 0.17%

Fees

Front-end load	*None*
Redemption fee	*None*
12b-1 fee	0.25%
Management fee	0.75
Other expenses	0.00
Total annual expense	1.00%
Minimum initial investment	$1,000
Minimum subsequent investment	$100

Services

Telephone exchanges	*Yes*
Automatic withdrawal	*No*
Automatic checking deduction	*Yes*
Retirement plan/IRA	*Yes*
Instant redemption	*Yes*
Financial statements	*Semiannual*
Income distributions	*Annual*
Capital gains distributions	*Annual*
Portfolio manager: years	4
Number of funds in family	12

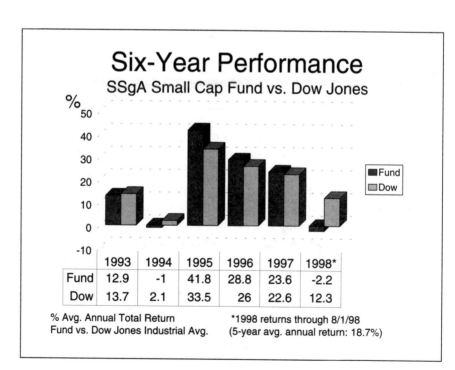

Six-Year Performance
SSgA Small Cap Fund vs. Dow Jones

	1993	1994	1995	1996	1997	1998*
Fund	12.9	-1	41.8	28.8	23.6	-2.2
Dow	13.7	2.1	33.5	26	22.6	12.3

% Avg. Annual Total Return
Fund vs. Dow Jones Industrial Avg.

*1998 returns through 8/1/98
(5-year avg. annual return: 18.7%)

40

Dreyfus Disciplined Stock Fund

GROWTH

Dreyfus Corporation
The Pan Am Building
200 Park Avenue, 7th floor
New York, NY 10166

Fund manager: Bert J. Mullins
Fund objective: Growth and income

Toll-free: 800-645-6561
In-state: 516-794-5452
Fax: 212-922-7140

Performance	★ ★ ★
Consistency	★ ★ ★
Fees/Services	★ ★ ★ ★ ★
DDSTX	**11 Points**

The Dreyfus Disciplined Stock Fund takes a very conservative approach, investing in major blue chip companies—most of which pay dividends—such as General Electric, Procter & Gamble, Exxon, and Ameritech.

Fund manager Bert Mullins says he adheres to a disciplined investment process that emphasizes stocks that are undervalued or have improving earnings momentum. The fund stays fully invested in the stock market at all times, spreading its assets across a wide range of industries. That investment approach has resulted in excellent long-term returns. Over the past ten years, the fund has posted an average annual return of nearly 20 percent. A $10,000 investment in the fund ten years ago would now be worth about $60,000.

Mullins, who has been with the fund since 1987, takes a fairly conservative trading approach. The annual portfolio turnover ratio is 69 percent. The fund has about 200 stock holdings in all. Leading sectors include consumer staples, 11 percent of total assets; basic industries, 4 percent; energy, 9 percent; financial-related companies, 16 percent; utilities, 8 percent; and technology, 25 percent.

PERFORMANCE

The fund has enjoyed strong growth over the last five years. Including dividends and capital gains distributions, the Dreyfus Disciplined Stock Fund has provided a total return for the last five years (through mid-1998) of 172 percent. A $10,000 investment in 1993 would have grown to about $27,000 five years later. Average annual return: 22.2 percent.

CONSISTENCY

The fund has been fairly consistent recently, outperforming the Dow Jones Industrial Average in three of the last five years through 1997 (and it led the Dow through the first few months of 1998). Its biggest gain came in 1995, when it jumped 36.9 percent (compared with a 33.5 percent rise in the Dow).

FEES/SERVICES/MANAGEMENT

Like all Dreyfus funds, the Disciplined Stock Fund is a true no-load—no fee to buy, no fee to sell. The fund's total annual expense ratio of 1 percent (including a 0.10 percent 12b-1 fee) compares very favorably with other funds.

The fund offers all the standard services, such as retirement account availability, automatic withdrawal, and automatic checking account deduction. Its minimum initial investment of $2,500 and minimum subsequent investment of $100 are about in line with most other funds.

Bert Mullins has managed the fund since 1987. The Dreyfus family of funds includes more than 100 funds and allows shareholders to switch from fund to fund by telephone.

Top Ten Stock Holdings

1. General Electric	6. IBM
2. Microsoft	7. Eli Lilly
3. Intel	8. BankAmerica
4. Procter & Gamble	9. Coca-Cola
5. Exxon	10. Chase Manhattan

Asset mix: common stocks—99%; cash/equivalents—1%
Total net assets: $1.6 billion
Dividend yield: 0.60%

Fees

Front-end load	*None*
Redemption fee	*None*
12b-1 fee	0.10%
Management fee	0.90
Other expenses	0.00
Total annual expense	1.00%
Minimum initial investment	$2,500
Minimum subsequent investment	$100

Services

Telephone exchanges	*Yes*
Automatic withdrawal	*Yes*
Automatic checking deduction	*Yes*
Retirement plan/IRA	*Yes*
Instant redemption	*Yes*
Financial statements	*Semiannual*
Income distributions	*Annual*
Capital gains distributions	*Annual*
Portfolio manager: years	11
Number of funds in family	117

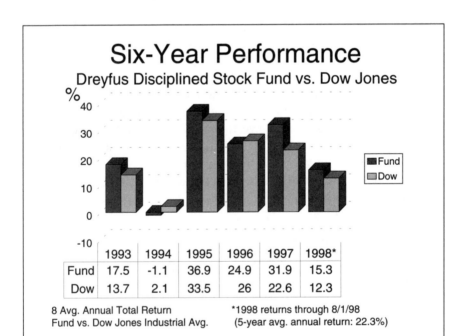

Six-Year Performance
Dreyfus Disciplined Stock Fund vs. Dow Jones

	1993	1994	1995	1996	1997	1998*
Fund	17.5	-1.1	36.9	24.9	31.9	15.3
Dow	13.7	2.1	33.5	26	22.6	12.3

8 Avg. Annual Total Return
Fund vs. Dow Jones Industrial Avg.

*1998 returns through 8/1/98
(5-year avg. annual return: 22.3%)

AGGRESSIVE

PBHG Growth Fund

PBHG Funds
680 East Swedesford Road
Wayne, PA 19087-1658

Fund manager: Gary L. Pilgrim
Fund objective: Aggressive growth

Toll-free: 800-433-0051
In-state: 610-989-1000
Fax: 610-989-6088

Performance	★ ★ ★
Consistency	★ ★ ★
Fees/Services	★ ★ ★ ★ ★
PBHGX	**11 Points**

For a ten-year period through 1995, the PBHG Growth Fund was the best in America. Then the emerging growth stock fund hit a bump in the road. Or, more accurately, a mountain. In 1996, when the overall market was up over 20 percent, the fund climbed just 9.8 percent. In 1997, with the Standard & Poor's 500-stock index climbing more than 30 percent, the PBHG Fund lost 3.4 percent.

Fund manager Gary Pilgrim seems to have lost his golden touch. Part of the problem is that the emerging growth stock sector of the market was down through parts of 1996 and 1997, but other growth funds managed to survive the lull much better than Pilgrim's PBHG Growth Fund. With his years of experience, Pilgrim will probably turn the fund around, but, to say the least, the legend has lost some of its luster.

Pilgrim has managed the fund since its inception in 1985. In analyzing emerging growth stocks for his fund, Pilgrim runs through the usual screens and formulas, and he may even pay a visit to a promising young company to look it over. But for the most part, Pilgrim doesn't try to read too much between the lines. Fast growth—past and present—is the biggest factor that catches his eye. "Twenty-five years in this business has taught me that a good company is a company that is doing good," says Pilgrim. "The world pays for results."

Pilgrim cofounded Pilgrim Baxter and Associates in 1982 after serving as a portfolio manager and analyst for 15 years with Philadelphia National Bank. His PBHG Growth Fund invests almost exclusively in small to midsize growth stocks. Pilgrim prefers stocks in the range of $250 million to $1 billion in market capitalization. He will hold onto the $1 billion-plus stocks if they're still on a fast-growth track, but once they hit $2 billion, he unloads them. "What we try to do is identify and hold onto the really high-growth stocks as long as it makes sense to do so. We'd like to hold them for four or five years, but that's pretty rare. Most growth companies go through stages of very rapid growth and then, for various reasons, they slow down. That growth phase may be nine months or it may be three years. When they start to slow down, that's when we weed them out of the portfolio."

The fund has about 100 stock holdings in all. Its leading industrial sectors include technology, 27 percent of assets; health, 13 percent; consumer products, 15 percent; energy, 9 percent; business and consumer services, 23 percent; and financial services, 5 percent.

PERFORMANCE

The fund has enjoyed strong growth over the last five years. Including dividends and capital gains distributions, the PBHG Growth Fund has provided a total return for the last five years (through mid-1998) of 175 percent. A $10,000 investment in 1993 would have grown to about $28,000 five years later. Average annual return: 22.5 percent.

CONSISTENCY

The fund has been fairly consistent recently, outperforming the Dow Jones Industrial Average in three of the last five years through 1997 (and it was about even with the Dow through the first few months of 1998). Its biggest gain came in 1995, with a 50.4 percent jump (compared with a 33.5 percent rise in the Dow).

FEES/SERVICES/MANAGEMENT　　★　★　★　★　★

The PBHG Growth Fund is a true no-load—no fee to buy, no fee to sell. Its total annual expense ratio of 1.25 percent (with no 12b-1 fee) compares favorably with other funds.

The fund offers all the standard services, such as retirement account availability, automatic withdrawal, and automatic checking account deduction. Its minimum initial investment of $2,500 is a little higher than most funds, but its minimum subsequent investment of one dollar compares favorably with other funds.

Gary Pilgrim has managed the fund since 1985. PBHG Funds include 13 funds and allow shareholders to switch from fund to fund by telephone.

Top Ten Stock Holdings

1. Citrix Systems
2. Saville Systems
3. General Nutrition
4. Total Renal Care Holdings
5. CBT Group
6. Apollo Group
7. Whole Foods Market
8. Concord EFS
9. Cambridge Technology Partners
10. Proffitt's

Asset mix: common stocks—95%; cash/equivalents—5%.
Total net assets: $5.5 billion
Dividend yield: none

Fees

Front-end load	*None*
Redemption fee	*None*
12b-1 fee	*None*
Management fee	0.85%
Other expenses	0.40
Total annual expense	1.25%
Minimum initial investment	$2,500
Minimum subsequent investment	$1

Services

Telephone exchanges	*Yes*
Automatic withdrawal	*Yes*
Automatic checking deduction	*Yes*
Retirement plan/IRA	*Yes*
Instant redemption	*Yes*
Financial statements	*Semiannual*
Income distributions	*Annual*
Capital gains distributions	*Annual*
Portfolio manager: years	13
Number of funds in family	13

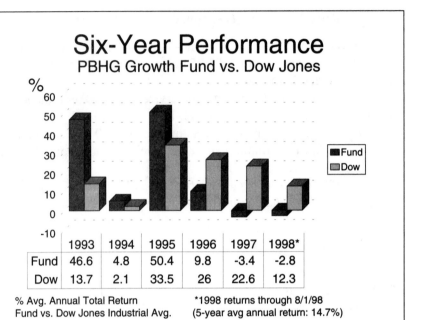

Six-Year Performance
PBHG Growth Fund vs. Dow Jones

	1993	1994	1995	1996	1997	1998*
Fund	46.6	4.8	50.4	9.8	-3.4	-2.8
Dow	13.7	2.1	33.5	26	22.6	12.3

% Avg. Annual Total Return   *1998 returns through 8/1/98
Fund vs. Dow Jones Industrial Avg.   (5-year avg annual return: 14.7%)

AGGRESSIVE

42

Kaufmann Fund

Kaufmann Fund, Inc.
20 Academy Street
Norwalk, CT 06850-4832

Fund managers: Hans P. Utsch
and Lawrence Auriana
Fund objective: Aggressive growth
Web site: www.kaufmann.com

Toll-free: 800-666-9181
In-state: 212-922-0123
Fax: 212-661-2266

Performance	★ ★ ★
Consistency	★ ★ ★
Fees/Services	★ ★ ★ ★ ★
KAUFX	**11 Points**

After years of outstanding performance, the Kaufmann Fund finally struggled through some tough times—particularly during the high-tech slump of 1997. The fund managed only a 12.6 percent gain that year while the Dow Jones Industrial Average climbed 22.6 percent. But over the past ten years, the fund has been one of the nation's best. It has posted an average annual return over the past decade of about 25 percent. A $10,000 investment in the fund ten years ago would now be worth about $95,000.

Because of the success of the fund, it continues to attract new investment dollars. Its assets have climbed to over $6 billion, which poses a real challenge for fund managers Lawrence Auriana and Hans Utsch. Trying to move nimbly through the market becomes increasingly difficult the larger a fund becomes—particularly an aggressive growth fund.

One way Auriana and Utsch have tried to keep the fund on track is by investing in larger companies. "We like companies that have proprietary products or unique services that appeal to a substantial market," says Auriana. "We want companies that can grow at 20 percent per year or more for the next three to five years."

Auriana and Utsch look well beyond the numbers to sift out winning stocks for their portfolio. "Management is the most important criterion," says Auriana. "Every day we meet with the management of two to six companies. It can be risky meeting with management if you're not as experienced at it as we are. Management of these young companies are, almost without exception, terrific salespeople, and they're trying to sell you on their companies."

Auriana has enough experience in the business that he can usually cut through the hype to figure out which managers really have something to offer. "We already know a lot about these businesses—usually we know more than they expect us to know. In most cases, we've already met with their competitors and their suppliers, and we've followed their industries for years. We can usually tell if their estimates are overly optimistic."

Although strong management, fast growth, and solid cash flow attract Auriana to a stock, changes in those factors will prompt him to sell. "If there is some fundamental change in the business or the dynamics of the industry, if the company is not living up to its plan, or if it can't implement its business model, then we'll sell the stock."

A drop in earnings will often be the catalyst for the fund to sell its position, but exceptions do occur. "Sometimes we may already know the earnings are going to drop for that quarter, but we also know the long-term prospects are still good. Then we'll hold onto the stock, although we may also take a short position in the stock to hedge against a temporary drop in the price." The managers take a surprisingly conservative approach in their trading policy and have an annual portfolio turnover ratio of just 72 percent.

The fund managers like to ride their winners and sell their losers, but Auriana says they are not true momentum players. "Sometimes we'll buy a stock if a bad earnings quarter knocks the price down to what we consider to be a bargain level. A momentum player wouldn't do that." The fund stays fully invested in stocks at almost all times. It has about 400 stock holdings, many of which are in technology-related industries. Its leading sectors include medical-related companies, 25 percent of assets; computer technology businesses, 17 percent; service companies, 11 percent; and retail, 13 percent.

PERFORMANCE

The fund has enjoyed solid growth over the last five years. Including dividends and capital gains distributions, the Kaufmann Fund has provided a total return for the last five years (through mid-1998) of 166 percent. A $10,000 investment in 1993 would have grown to about $27,000 five years later. Average annual return: 21.7 percent.

CONSISTENCY

The fund has been fairly consistent, outperforming the Dow Jones Industrial Average in three of the last five years through 1997 (and it was about even with the Dow through the first few months of 1998). Its biggest gain came in 1995 with a 36.9 percent rise compared with a 33.5 percent rise in the Dow).

FEES/SERVICES/MANAGEMENT

The Kaufmann Fund is a no-load fund—no fee to buy, no fee to sell (if held at least one year). The fund's total annual expense ratio of 1.93 percent (including a 0.32 percent 12b-1 fee) is a little higher than most funds.

The fund offers all the standard services, such as retirement account availability, automatic withdrawal, and automatic checking account deduction. Its minimum initial investment of $1,500 and minimum subsequent investment of $100 are in line with other funds.

Hans P. Utsch and Lawrence Auriana have managed the fund since 1985. The Kaufmann Fund is the only fund the company offers.

Top Ten Stock Holdings

1. Cendant
2. Steris
3. HEALTHSOUTH
4. Lincare Holdings
5. Viking Office Products
6. Blyth Industries
7. Network Associates
8. Access Health
9. PSS World Medical
10. Central Garden & Pet

Asset mix: common stocks—91%; warrants—1%; cash/equivalents—8%
Total net assets: $6 billion
Dividend yield: none

Fees

Front-end load	*None*
Redemption fee	0.20%
12b-1 fee	0.32
Management fee	1.50
Other expenses	0.11
Total annual expense	1.93%
Minimum initial investment	$1,500
Minimum subsequent investment	$100

Services

Telephone exchanges	*Yes*
Automatic withdrawal	*Yes*
Automatic checking deduction	*Yes*
Retirement plan/IRA	*Yes*
Instant redemption	*Yes*
Financial statements	*Semiannual*
Income distributions	*Annual*
Capital gains distributions	*Annual*
Portfolio manager: years	13
Number of funds in family	1

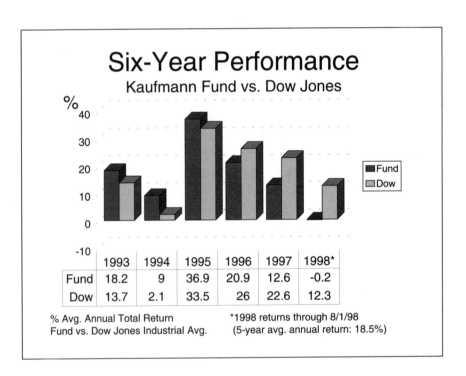

Six-Year Performance
Kaufmann Fund vs. Dow Jones

	1993	1994	1995	1996	1997	1998*
Fund	18.2	9	36.9	20.9	12.6	-0.2
Dow	13.7	2.1	33.5	26	22.6	12.3

% Avg. Annual Total Return
Fund vs. Dow Jones Industrial Avg.

*1998 returns through 8/1/98
(5-year avg. annual return: 18.5%)

AGGRESSIVE

43

Invesco Dynamics Fund

Invesco Funds Group
P.O. Box 173706
Denver, CO 80217-3706

Fund managers: Timothy J. Miller and Thomas Wald
Fund objective: Aggressive growth
Web site: www.invesco.com

Toll-free: 800-525-8085
In-state: 303-930-6300
Fax: 303-930-6655

Performance	★ ★ ★
Consistency	★ ★ ★
Fees/Services	★ ★ ★ ★ ★
FIDYX	**11 Points**

The Invesco Dynamics Fund is a diversified aggressive growth fund that invests primarily in emerging growth stocks such as PeopleSoft, Tellabs, and Lucent Technologies. Introduced in 1967, the fund also has some larger holdings, such as Motorola, Compaq, and Intel. In addition to U.S. stocks, the fund also keeps a few foreign stocks in the portfolio. Over the past ten years, the fund has provided an average return of nearly 19 percent per year. A $10,000 investment in the fund ten years ago would now be worth about $55,000.

The fund's basic strategy is to buy and sell stocks based on such market factors as price movements of the stock, indicated investor interest, current information about the company, and general market and monetary conditions. As much as 25 percent of the portfolio may be in foreign stock holdings. Fund managers Timothy Miller and Thomas Wald maintain an aggressive trading strategy, resulting in an annual portfolio turnover ratio of about 200 percent.

The fund has about 85 stock holdings in all. In terms of industrial sectors, the fund is most heavily weighted in computer-related stocks, which make up 11 percent of its assets. Other leading segments include health-care-related stocks, 10 percent; oil and gas, 8 percent, retail, 10 percent; and communications equipment, 4 percent.

PERFORMANCE

The fund has enjoyed strong growth over the last five years. Including dividends and capital gains distributions, the Invesco Dynamics Fund has provided a total return for the last five years (through mid-1998) of 164 percent. A $10,000 investment in 1993 would have grown to about $26,000 five years later. Average annual return: 21.6 percent.

CONSISTENCY

The fund has been fairly consistent recently, outperforming the Dow Jones Industrial Average in three of the last five years through 1997 (and it led the Dow through the first few months of 1998). Its biggest gain came in 1995, when it jumped 37.6 percent (compared with a 33.5 percent rise in the Dow).

FEES/SERVICES/MANAGEMENT

Like all Invesco funds, the Dynamics Fund is a true no-load—no fee to buy, no fee to sell. The fund's total annual expense ratio of 1.16 percent (including a 0.25 percent 12b-1 fee) compares favorably with other funds.

The fund offers all the standard services, such as retirement account availability, automatic withdrawal, and automatic checking account deduction. Its minimum initial investment of $1,000 and minimum subsequent investment of $50 compare favorably with other funds.

Timothy Miller has been a manager of the fund since 1993. Thomas Wald was later added as a comanager. The Invesco family of funds includes 34 funds and allows shareholders to switch from fund to fund by telephone.

Top Ten Stock Holdings

1. Maxim Integrated Products
2. Budget Group
3. Teleport Communications Group
4. Tandy
5. Eaton
6. PeopleSoft
7. Watson Pharmaceuticals
8. HBO
9. I2 Technologies
10. Tellabs

Asset mix: common stocks—95%; cash/equivalents—5%
Total net assets: $1.1 billion
Dividend yield: none

Fees

Front-end load	*None*
Redemption fee	*None*
12b-1 fee	0.25%
Management fee	0.56
Other expenses	0.35
Total annual expense	1.16%
Minimum initial investment	$1,000
Minimum subsequent investment	$50

Services

Telephone exchanges	*Yes*
Automatic withdrawal	*Yes*
Automatic checking deduction	*Yes*
Retirement plan/IRA	*Yes*
Instant redemption	*Yes*
Financial statements	*Semiannual*
Income distributions	*Annual*
Capital gains distributions	*Annual*
Portfolio manager: years	6
Number of funds in family	34

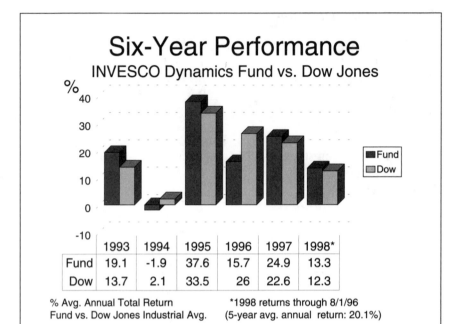

Six-Year Performance
INVESCO Dynamics Fund vs. Dow Jones

	1993	1994	1995	1996	1997	1998*
Fund	19.1	-1.9	37.6	15.7	24.9	13.3
Dow	13.7	2.1	33.5	26	22.6	12.3

% Avg. Annual Total Return   *1998 returns through 8/1/96
Fund vs. Dow Jones Industrial Avg.   (5-year avg. annual return: 20.1%)

44
Strong Schafer Value Fund

Strong Funds
P.O. Box 2936
Milwaukee, WI 53201-2936

Fund manager: David K. Schafer
Fund objective: Long-term growth
Web site: www.strong-funds.com

Toll-free: 800-368-1030
In-state: 414-359-3400
Fax: 414-359-3947

Performance	★ ★ ★
Consistency	★ ★ ★
Fees/Services	★ ★ ★ ★ ★
SCHVX	**11 Points**

David Schafer, manager of the Strong Schafer Value Fund, looks for bargains in the blue chip market. "Simply stated," he says, "we are looking for above-average growth at a discounted price." Schafer focuses on finding stocks with low PE ratios that may have been beaten down by the market but are poised for a rebound.

While there are plenty of well-known names in the portfolio, such as Ford Motor, Chase Manhattan, Borg-Warner, and AT&T, you won't see any fast-growth companies such as Microsoft or Gillette. Many of the stocks in the portfolio have lagged the market in the recent past.

Schafer takes a conservative long-term approach; the annual portfolio turnover ratio is 23 percent. "When we buy a stock that we think is a bargain, we're content to wait for the market to realize its value," says Schafer. "That means we generally hold stocks for the long term, and keep our portfolio turnover very low." Schafer stays almost 100 percent invested in stocks under normal circumstances.

The fund is well diversified with stocks from a broad range of sectors. "We try to maintain an equal weighting of every stock in the portfolio," says Shafer. "That way we don't let our natural enthusiasm for a particular stock influence our diversification strategy. And we tend to remain fully invested because we believe that trying to time the market will decrease rather than increase our return over time."

The fund has about 60 stock holdings in all. Leading sectors include oil and minerals, 16 percent; insurance, 8 percent; automotive, 12 percent; banks, 10 percent; and electronic equipment and distribution, 7 percent.

PERFORMANCE

The fund has enjoyed strong growth over the last five years. Including dividends and capital gains distributions, the Strong Schafer Value Fund has provided a total return for the last five years (through mid-1998) of 161 percent. A $10,000 investment in 1993 would have grown to about $26,000 five years later. Average annual return: 21.2 percent.

CONSISTENCY

The fund has been fairly consistent recently, outperforming the Dow Jones Industrial Average in three of the last five years through 1997 (and it led the Dow through the first few months of 1998). Its biggest gain came in 1995, when it moved up 27.3 percent (compared with a 33.5 percent rise in the Dow).

FEES/SERVICES/MANAGEMENT

Like all Strong funds, the Schafer Value Fund is a true no-load—no fee to buy, no fee to sell. Its total annual expense ratio of 1.22 percent (with no 12b-1 fee) compares favorably with other funds.

The fund offers all the standard services, such as retirement account availability, automatic withdrawal, and automatic checking account deduction. Its minimum initial investment of $2,500 and minimum subsequent investment of $50 is a little on the high side compared with other funds.

David Schafer has managed the fund since 1985. The Strong family of funds includes 21 funds and allows shareholders to switch from fund to fund by telephone.

Top Ten Stock Holdings

1. Owens-Corning
2. Kansas City Southern Industries
3. Ford Motor
4. R&B Falcon
5. Diamond Offshore Drilling
6. New Holland
7. Chase Manhattan
8. National Bank of Canada
9. Borg-Warner Automotive
10. Repsol

Asset mix: common stocks—99%; cash/equivalents—1%
Total net assets: $1.8 billion
Dividend yield: 0.49%

Fees

Front-end load	*None*
Redemption fee	*None*
12b-1 fee	*None*
Management fee	1.00%
Other expenses	0.22
Total annual expense	1.22%
Minimum initial investment	$2,500
Minimum subsequent investment	$50

Services

Telephone exchanges	*Yes*
Automatic withdrawal	*Yes*
Automatic checking deduction	*Yes*
Retirement plan/IRA	*Yes*
Instant redemption	*Yes*
Financial statements	*Semiannual*
Income distributions	*Annual*
Capital gains distributions	*Annual*
Portfolio manager: years	13
Number of funds in family	21

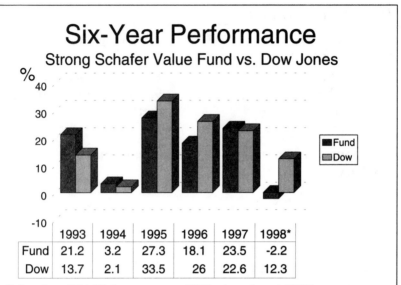

Six-Year Performance
Strong Schafer Value Fund vs. Dow Jones

	1993	1994	1995	1996	1997	1998*
Fund	21.2	3.2	27.3	18.1	23.5	-2.2
Dow	13.7	2.1	33.5	26	22.6	12.3

% Avg. Annual Total Return   *1998 returns through 8/1/98
Fund vs. Dow Jones Industrial Avg.   (5-year avg. annual return: 17.1%)

SECTOR

45

Fidelity Select Health Care Portfolio

Fidelity Investments
82 Devonshire Street
Boston, MA 02109

Fund manager: Beso Sikharulidze
Fund objective: Sector
Web site: www.fidelity.com

Toll-free: 800-544-8888
In-state: 801-534-1910
Fax: 617-476-9753

Performance	★ ★ ★ ★ ★
Consistency	★ ★ ★
Fees/Services	★ ★ ★
FSPHX	**11 Points**

Health care stocks have been among the most profitable in American industry, helping propel the Fidelity Select Health Care Portfolio to outstanding returns for the past ten years.

The fund, which invests at least 80 percent of its assets in health care stocks, has dramatically outperformed the overall market in recent years. Over the past ten years, the fund has posted average annual returns of about 24 percent. A $10,000 investment in the fund ten years ago would now be worth about $86,000.

The fund has about 70 stock holdings in all. Most are in major drug and medical manufacturing companies, such as American Home Products, Bristol-Myers Squibb, Warner Lambert, and Medtronic. The fund also invests in a number of foreign medical operations, such as Glaxo Wellcome, Yamanouchi Pharmaceutical, and Elan.

Fund manager Beso Sikharulidze takes a fairly modest approach in managing the fund; 59 percent is the annual turnover ratio. The leading industrial segments among the fund's holdings include drugs and pharmaceuticals, 55 percent; medical equipment and supplies, 27 percent; and medical facilities management, 8 percent.

PERFORMANCE

The fund has enjoyed outstanding growth over the past five years. Including dividends and capital gains distributions, the Fidelity Select Health Care Portfolio has provided a total return for the past five years (through early 1998) of 266 percent. A $10,000 investment in 1993 would have grown to $36,600 five years later. Average annual return: 29.6 percent.

CONSISTENCY

The fund has been fairly consistent, outpacing the Dow Jones Industrial Average in three of the past five years (and again through the first few months of 1998). Its biggest gain came in 1995, when it jumped 45.9 percent (compared with a 33.5 percent rise in the Dow).

FEES/SERVICES/MANAGEMENT

The fund has a low front-end load of 3 percent and a maximum redemption fee of 0.75 percent if it's sold out within 29 days. Its annual expense ratio of 1.33 percent (with no 12b-1 fee) is about average among all funds.

The fund offers many of the standard services, such as retirement account availability and automatic checking account deduction. Its minimum initial investment of $2,500 and minimum subsequent investment of $250 are a little high compared with other funds.

Beso Sikharulidze has managed the fund only since 1997, but he has been with Fidelity since 1992. The Fidelity family of funds includes more than 230 funds.

Top Ten Stock Holdings

1. American Home Products	6. Eli Lilly
2. Warner-Lambert	7. Johnson & Johnson
3. Schering-Plough	8. Abbott Laboratories
4. Bristol-Myers Squibb	9. Medtronic
5. Merck	10. Baxter International

Asset mix: common stocks—90%; cash/equivalents—10%
Total net assets: $1.63 billion
Dividend yield: 0.18%

Fees

Front-end load	*None*
Redemption fee (max)	0.75%
12b-1 fee	*None*
Management fee	0.60
Other expenses	0.73
Total annual expense	1.33%
Minimum initial investment	$2,500
Minimum subsequent investment	$250

Services

Telephone exchanges	*Yes*
Automatic withdrawal	*Yes*
Automatic checking deduction	*Yes*
Retirement plan/IRA	*Yes*
Instant redemption	*Yes*
Financial statements	*Semiannual*
Income distributions	*Semiannual*
Capital gains distributions	*Semiannual*
Portfolio manager: years	1
Number of funds in family	235

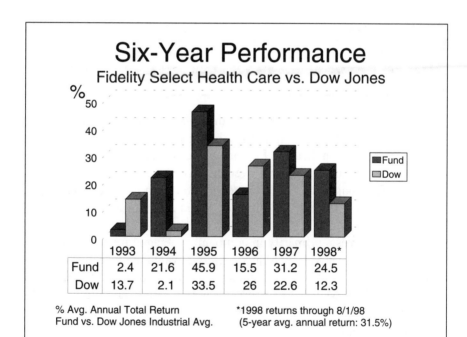

Six-Year Performance
Fidelity Select Health Care vs. Dow Jones

	1993	1994	1995	1996	1997	1998*
Fund	2.4	21.6	45.9	15.5	31.2	24.5
Dow	13.7	2.1	33.5	26	22.6	12.3

% Avg. Annual Total Return
Fund vs. Dow Jones Industrial Avg.

*1998 returns through 8/1/98
(5-year avg. annual return: 31.5%)

46

Fidelity Select Brokerage and Investment Portfolio

SECTOR

Fidelity Investments
82 Devonshire Street
Boston, MA 02109

Fund manager: Peter Fruzzetti
Fund objective: Sector
Web site: www.fidelity.com

Toll-free: 800-544-8888
In-state: 801-534-1910
Fax: 617-476-9753

Performance	★ ★ ★ ★ ★
Consistency	★ ★ ★
Fees/Services	★ ★ ★
FSLBX	**11 Points**

No business has benefited more from the booming stock market than the brokerage industry. Strong profits among brokerage and investment companies have propelled the Fidelity Select Brokerage and Investment Portfolio to outstanding growth over the past decade. Over the past ten years, the fund has posted an average annual return of about 23 percent. A $10,000 investment in the fund ten years ago would now be worth about $80,000.

The fund invests primarily in companies engaged in stock and commodity brokerage, investment banking, tax-advantaged investment or investment sales, and investment management firms or related investment advisory services. Many of its approximately 60 stock holdings are well-known blue chip companies, such as BankAmerica, Morgan Stanley, Charles Schwab, and Franklin Resources.

The fund stays about 90 percent or more invested in stocks most of the time. Fund manager Peter Fruzzetti takes a conservative buy-and-hold approach that results in a 16 percent annual portfolio turnover ratio. Leading industrial sectors include brokerage companies, 50 percent of assets; banks, 12 percent; insurance companies, 14 percent; and investment management firms, 9 percent.

PERFORMANCE

The fund has enjoyed exceptional growth over the last five years. Including dividends and capital gains distributions, Fidelity's Brokerage and Investment Portfolio has provided a total return for the last five years (through mid-1998) of 242 percent. A $10,000 investment in 1993 would have grown to about $34,000 five years later. Average annual return: 27.9 percent.

CONSISTENCY

The fund has been fairly consistent recently, outperforming the Dow Jones Industrial Average in three of the last five years through 1997 (and it led the Dow through the first few months of 1998). Its biggest gain came in 1997, when it moved up 62.3 percent (compared with a 22.6 percent rise in the Dow).

FEES/SERVICES/MANAGEMENT

The Brokerage and Investment Portfolio has a front-end load of 3 percent. Its total annual expense ratio of 1.94 percent (with no 12b-1 fee) is somewhat higher than other funds.

The fund offers all the standard services, such as retirement account availability, automatic withdrawal, and automatic checking account deduction. Its minimum initial investment of $2,500 and minimum subsequent investment of $250 is a little higher than most other funds.

Peter Fruzzetti joined Fidelity in 1993 and has managed the fund since 1996. The Fidelity family of funds includes 235 funds and allows shareholders to switch from fund to fund by telephone.

Top Ten Stock Holdings

1. Lehman Brothers Holdings
2. Travelers Group
3. Bear Stearns
4. Merrill Lynch
5. PaineWebber Group
6. A.G. Edwards
7. Morgan Stanley Dean Witter
8. Equitable Companies
9. Franklin Resources
10. Bankers Trust

Asset mix: common stocks—90%; cash/equivalents—10%
Total net assets: $648 million
Dividend yield: 0.20%

Fees

Front-end load	3.00%
Redemption fee	0.75
12b-1 fee	*None*
Management fee	0.62
Other expenses	1.32
Total annual expense	1.94%
Minimum initial investment	$2,500
Minimum subsequent investment	$250

Services

Telephone exchanges	*Yes*
Automatic withdrawal	*Yes*
Automatic checking deduction	*Yes*
Retirement plan/IRA	*Yes*
Instant redemption	*Yes*
Financial statements	*Semiannual*
Income distributions	*Semiannual*
Capital gains distributions	*Semiannual*
Portfolio manager: years	2
Number of funds in family	235

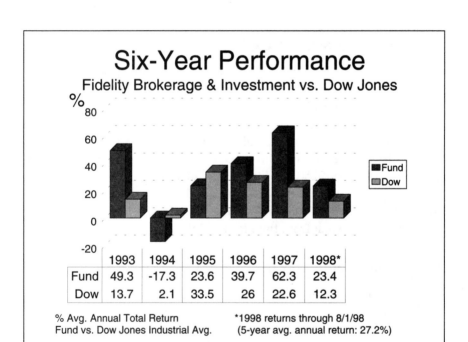

Six-Year Performance
Fidelity Brokerage & Investment vs. Dow Jones

	1993	1994	1995	1996	1997	1998*
Fund	49.3	-17.3	23.6	39.7	62.3	23.4
Dow	13.7	2.1	33.5	26	22.6	12.3

% Avg. Annual Total Return
Fund vs. Dow Jones Industrial Avg.

*1998 returns through 8/1/98
(5-year avg. annual return: 27.2%)

47

Alliance Technology Fund

Alliance Funds Group
1345 Avenue of the Americas
New York, NY 10105

Fund managers: Peter Anastos
and Gerald Malone
Fund objective: Sector
Web site: www.alliancecapital.com

Toll-free: 800-221-5672
In-state: 201-319-4000
Fax: 201-319-4139

Performance	★ ★ ★ ★ ★
Consistency	★ ★ ★
Fees/Services	★ ★ ★
ALTFX	**11 Points**

Founded in 1982, the Alliance Technology Fund is one of the oldest and most successful of all technology funds. Over the past ten years, it has posted an average annual return of about 19 percent. A $10,000 investment in the fund ten years ago would now be worth about $58,000.

The fund's aim is to invest in the fastest-growing, leading-edge technology stocks when they are reasonably priced. The fund can be volatile in the short term, but the growth prospects in the technology area continue to be alluring for the long term.

Fund managers Gerald Malone and Peter Anastos point out that the worldwide demand for technology products continues to snowball. For instance, technology spending as a percentage of gross domestic product in the United States is approaching ten percent, its level in the late 1970s. "We see similar dynamics in international markets and, in many cases, an even more rapid acceptance and deployment of technology in these economies," says Malone.

The fund has about 50 stock holdings in all. The leading sectors include computer hardware, 12 percent of total assets; computer services, 9 percent; computer software, 17 percent; networking software, 12 percent; semiconductor components, 18 percent; and communications equipment, 9 percent. The fund managers maintain a fairly conservative trading approach that results in an annual portfolio turnover ratio of 51 percent.

PERFORMANCE

The fund has enjoyed outstanding growth over the last five years. Including dividends and capital gains distributions, the Alliance Technology Fund has provided a total return for the last five years (through mid-1998) of 223 percent. A $10,000 investment in 1993 would have grown to about $32,000 five years later. Average annual return: 26.4 percent.

CONSISTENCY

The fund can be very volatile. It was up 28.5 percent in 1994 when the Dow Jones Industrial Average was up only 2.1 percent. It was up only 4.5 percent in 1997 when the Dow was up 22.6 percent. Through the first quarter of 1998, it was up a whopping 24.9 percent. It has outperformed the Dow in three of the past five years.

FEES/SERVICES/MANAGEMENT

The Alliance Technology Fund has a front-end load of 4.25 percent. Its annual expense ratio of 1.67 percent (including a 0.30 percent 12b-1 fee) is in line with other funds.

The fund offers all the standard services, such as retirement account availability, automatic withdrawal, and automatic checking account deduction. Its minimum initial investment of $250 and minimum subsequent investment of $50 compare very favorably with other funds.

Peter Anastos and Gerald Malone have managed the fund since 1992. The Alliance Funds Group includes more than 50 funds and allows shareholders to switch from fund to fund by telephone.

Top Ten Stock Holdings

1. Cisco Systems
2. Dell Computer
3. Compaq Computer
4. Altera
5. Oracle

6. Bay Networks
7. Intel
8. HBO
9. Microsoft
10. Applied Materials

Asset mix: common stocks—91%; cash/equivalents—9%
Total net assets: $598 million
Dividend yield: none

Fees

Front-end load	4.25%
Redemption fee	*None*
12b-1 fee	0.30
Management fee	1.04
Other expenses	0.33
Total annual expense	1.67%
Minimum initial investment	$250
Minimum subsequent investment	$50

Services

Telephone exchanges	*Yes*
Automatic withdrawal	*Yes*
Automatic checking deduction	*Yes*
Retirement plan/IRA	*Yes*
Instant redemption	*Yes*
Financial statements	*Semiannual*
Income distributions	*Annual*
Capital gains distributions	*Annual*
Portfolio manager: years	6
Number of funds in family	53

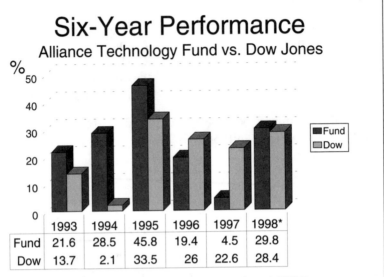

Six-Year Performance
Alliance Technology Fund vs. Dow Jones

	1993	1994	1995	1996	1997	1998*
Fund	21.6	28.5	45.8	19.4	4.5	29.8
Dow	13.7	2.1	33.5	26	22.6	28.4

% Avg. Annual Total Return
Fund vs. Dow Jones Industrial Avg.

*1998 returns through 8/1/98
(5-year avg. annual return: 28.4%)

48

Fidelity Select Energy Service Portfolio

Fidelity Investments
82 Devonshire Street
Boston, MA 02109

Fund manager: Jim Catudal
Fund objective: Sector
Web site: www.fidelity.com

Toll-free: 800-544-8888
In-state: 801-534-1910
Fax: 617-476-9753

Performance	★ ★ ★ ★ ★
Consistency	★ ★ ★ ★
Fees/Services	★ ★
FSESX	**11 Points**

The oil and gas industry has gone through a major surge in business in recent years as the world continues its search for new sources of fuel to power the booming industrial economy (not to mention the surging fleet of gas-guzzling sport utility vehicles now crowding the nation's highways). That growing demand has helped push the Fidelity Select Energy Service Portfolio to exceptional growth in recent years. The fund has posted an average annual return of more than 25 percent the past five years. It's up 15 percent per year over the past ten years.

The fund invests in energy-related companies such as those that provide services and equipment to the conventional areas of oil, gas, electricity, and coal as well as to newer sources of energy such as nuclear, geothermal, oil shale, and solar power. The fund can be very volatile. In 1991, for instance, it was down 23 percent. But it's also had some stellar years: it was up more than 40 percent for three consecutive years from 1995 through 1997.

The fund has about 80 stock holdings in all. Leading sectors include oil and gas services, 40 percent of assets; drilling, 25 percent; and oil field equipment, 11 percent. The fund stays nearly 100 percent invested in stocks under normal circumstances. Fund manager Jim Catudal takes an aggressive buy-and-sell approach. The annual turnover ratio is 167 percent.

PERFORMANCE

The fund has enjoyed tremendous growth over the past five years. Including dividends and capital gains distributions, the Fidelity Select Energy Service Portfolio has provided a total return for the past five years (through early 1998) of 211 percent. A $10,000 investment in 1993 would have grown to about $31,000 five years later. Average annual return: 25.5 percent.

CONSISTENCY

The fund has been very consistent, outpacing the Dow Jones Industrial Average in four of the past five years (but it trailed the Dow through the first few months of 1998). Its biggest gain came in 1997, when it jumped 51.9 percent (compared with a 22.6 percent gain for the Dow).

FEES/SERVICES/MANAGEMENT

The fund has a low front-end load of 3 percent and a maximum redemption fee of 0.75 percent if it's sold out within 29 days. Its annual expense ratio of 1.47 percent (with no 12b-1 fee) is in line with similar funds.

The fund offers many of the standard services, such as retirement account availability and automatic checking account deduction. Its minimum initial investment of $2,500 and minimum subsequent investment of $250 are a little high compared with other funds.

Jim Catudal has managed the fund only since 1998. The Fidelity fund family includes more than 230 funds.

Top Ten Stock Holdings

1. Cooper Cameron
2. Transocean Offshore
3. Schlumberger
4. Halliburton
5. R&B Falcon

6. Noble Drilling
7. Coflexip ADS
8. Diamond Offshore Drilling
9. Western Atlas
10. Baker Hughes

Asset mix: common stocks—97%; cash/equivalents—3%
Total net assets: $1.1 billion
Dividend yield: none

Fees

Front-end load	3.00%
Redemption fee	0.75
12b-1 fee	*None*
Management fee	0.60
Other expenses	0.87
Total annual expense	1.47%
Minimum initial investment	$2,500
Minimum subsequent investment	$250

Services

Telephone exchanges	*Yes*
Automatic withdrawal	*Yes*
Automatic checking deduction	*Yes*
Retirement plan/IRA	*Yes*
Instant redemption	*Yes*
Financial statements	*Semiannual*
Income distributions	*Semiannual*
Capital gains distributions	*Semiannual*
Portfolio manager: years	0
Number of funds in family	235

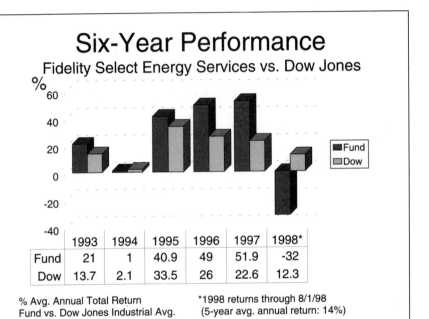

Six-Year Performance
Fidelity Select Energy Services vs. Dow Jones

	1993	1994	1995	1996	1997	1998*
Fund	21	1	40.9	49	51.9	-32
Dow	13.7	2.1	33.5	26	22.6	12.3

% Avg. Annual Total Return   *1998 returns through 8/1/98
Fund vs. Dow Jones Industrial Avg.   (5-year avg. annual return: 14%)

SECTOR

Fidelity Select Financial Services Portfolio

Fidelity Investments
82 Devonshire Street
Boston, MA 02109

Fund manager: Robert Ewing
Fund objective: Sector
Web site: www.fidelity.com

Toll-free: 800-544-8888
In-state: 801-534-1910
Fax: 617-476-9753

Performance	★ ★ ★ ★ ★
Consistency	★ ★ ★ ★
Fees/Services	★ ★
FIDSX	**11 Points**

The Fidelity Select Financial Services Portfolio has enjoyed outstanding returns in recent years investing in banks, insurance companies, and other financial services–related institutions. Companies that are involved specifically in financial services make up only about 12 percent of the portfolio. Banks account for 42 percent, personal credit institutions (such as Beneficial Corp. and Household International) account for 22 percent, federally sponsored credit agencies (such as the FHLMC) make up 8 percent, and insurance companies account for 8 percent.

Over the past ten years, the fund has posted an average annual return of about 22.5 percent. A $10,000 investment in the fund ten years ago would now be worth about $76,000. The fund should continue to perform well as long as interest rates remain low.

The fund manager maintains a fairly active trading policy; the annual portfolio turnover ratio is 80 percent. In all the fund has about 35 stock holdings.

PERFORMANCE

The fund has enjoyed outstanding growth over the past five years. Including dividends and capital gains distributions, the Fidelity Select Financial Services Portfolio has provided a total return for the past five years (through early 1998) of 209 percent. A $10,000 investment in 1993 would have grown to about $31,000 five years later. Average annual return: 25.3 percent.

CONSISTENCY

The fund has been very consistent, outpacing the Dow Jones Industrial Average in four of the past five years (and again through the first few months of 1998). Its biggest gains came in 1995, when it moved up 47.3 percent (compared with a 33.5 percent gain for the Dow).

FEES/SERVICES/MANAGEMENT

The fund has a low front-end load of 3 percent and a maximum redemption fee of 0.75 percent if it's sold out within 29 days. Its annual expense ratio of 1.45 percent (with no 12b-1 fee) is about average among all funds.

The fund offers many of the standard services, such as retirement account availability and automatic checking account deduction. Its minimum initial investment of $2,500 and minimum subsequent investment of $250 are a little high compared with other funds.

Fund manager Robert Ewing was just assigned to the fund in 1998. The Fidelity fund family includes more than 230 funds.

Top Ten Stock Holdings

1. NationsBank
2. Citicorp
3. Banc One
4. American International Group
5. BankAmerica
6. American Express
7. Bank of New York
8. U.S. Bancorp
9. Travelers Group
10. MBNA

Asset mix: common stocks—85%; cash/equivalents—15%
Total net assets: $548.7 million
Dividend yield: 0.52%

Fees

Front-end load	3.00%
Redemption fee	0.75
12b-1 fee	*None*
Management fee	0.61
Other expenses	0.84
Total annual expense	1.45%
Minimum initial investment	$2,500
Minimum subsequent investment	$250

Services

Telephone exchanges	*Yes*
Automatic withdrawal	*Yes*
Automatic checking deduction	*Yes*
Retirement plan/IRA	*Yes*
Instant redemption	*Yes*
Financial statements	*Semiannual*
Income distributions	*Semiannual*
Capital gains distributions	*Semiannual*
Portfolio manager: years	0
Number of funds in family	235

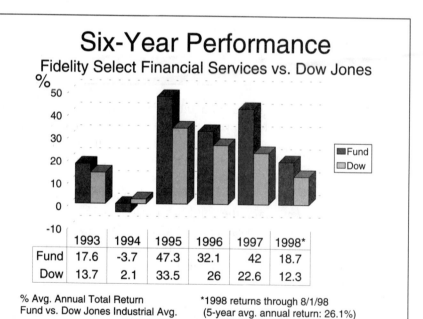

Six-Year Performance
Fidelity Select Financial Services vs. Dow Jones

	1993	1994	1995	1996	1997	1998*
Fund	17.6	-3.7	47.3	32.1	42	18.7
Dow	13.7	2.1	33.5	26	22.6	12.3

% Avg. Annual Total Return
Fund vs. Dow Jones Industrial Avg.

*1998 returns through 8/1/98
(5-year avg. annual return: 26.1%)

50

MFS Capital Opportunities Fund

AGGRESSIVE

MFS Funds Distributors, Inc.
500 Boylston Street
Boston, MA 02116

Fund manager: John F. Brennan, Jr.
Fund objective: Aggressive growth
Fax: 617-954-6617

Toll-free: 800-225-2606
In-state: 617-954-5000
Web site: www.mfs.com

Performance	★ ★ ★ ★
Consistency	★ ★ ★
Fees/Services	★ ★ ★
MCOFX	**10 Points**

Formerly called the MFS Value Fund, the MFS Capital Opportunities Fund continues to pursue a "value" investing approach, buying stocks of restructured companies, those emerging from bankruptcy, and companies with strong growth potential that are trading at a low price relative to the market. Fund manager John Brennan tries to cash in on the hard-luck, down-and-out corporate castoffs that he believes are headed for a turnaround.

Over the past ten years, the fund has posted an 18 percent average annual return. A $10,000 investment in the fund ten years ago would now be worth about $50,000. The fund invests primarily in midcap to large-cap stocks such as Tyco International, Raytheon, Rite Aid, and Cellular Communications.

Brennan takes a fairly active trading approach that results in an annual portfolio turnover ratio of 112 percent. In all, the fund has about 80 stock holdings, including a fair representation of foreign stocks. Foreign stocks generally account for 10 to 25 percent of total assets.

The fund is well diversified across a broad range of industry sectors. Leading sectors include leisure, 13 percent; technology, 12 percent; retailing, 12 percent; and health care, 12 percent. The fund stays almost fully invested in stocks most of the time.

PERFORMANCE

The fund has enjoyed outstanding growth over the last five years. Including dividends and capital gains distributions, the MFS Capital Opportunities Fund has provided a total return for the last five years (through mid-1998) of 190 percent. A $10,000 investment in 1993 would have grown to about $29,000 five years later. Average annual return: 23.7 percent.

CONSISTENCY

The fund has been fairly consistent recently, outperforming the Dow Jones Industrial Average in three of the last five years through 1997 (and it led the Dow through the first few months of 1998). Its biggest gain came in 1995, when it moved up 44.2 percent (compared with a 33.5 percent rise in the Dow).

FEES/SERVICES/MANAGEMENT

The fund has a front-end load of 5.75 percent. Its total annual expense ratio of 1.30 percent (including a 0.25 12b-1 fee) compares favorably with other funds.

The fund offers all the standard services, such as retirement account availability, automatic withdrawal, and automatic checking account deduction. Its minimum initial investment of $1,000 and minimum subsequent investment of $50 compare favorably with other funds.

John Brennan, Jr., has managed the fund since 1991. The MFS family of funds includes 50 funds and allows shareholders to switch from fund to fund by telephone.

Top Ten Stock Holdings

1. Tyco International
2. Fred Meyer
3. American Radio Systems
4. Cellular Communication
5. Sanofi
6. Raytheon
7. United Healthcare
8. Canadian National
9. Alcatel Alsthom
10. Rite Aid

Asset mix: common stocks—92%; cash/equivalents—8%
Total net assets: $624 million
Dividend yield: 0.14%

Fees

Front-end load	5.75%
Redemption fee	*None*
12b-1 fee	0.25
Management fee	0.75
Other expenses	0.30
Total annual expense	1.30%
Minimum initial investment	$1,000
Minimum subsequent investment	$50

Services

Telephone exchanges	*Yes*
Automatic withdrawal	*Yes*
Automatic checking deduction	*Yes*
Retirement plan/IRA	*Yes*
Instant redemption	*Yes*
Financial statements	*Semiannual*
Income distributions	*Annual*
Capital gains distributions	*Annual*
Portfolio manager: years	7
Number of funds in family	50

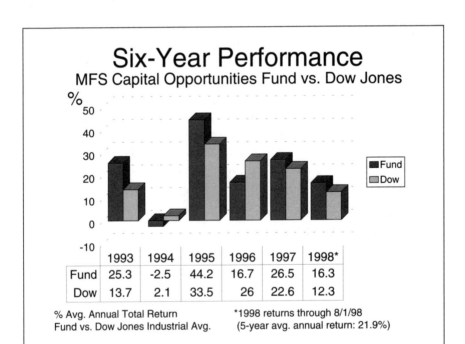

Six-Year Performance
MFS Capital Opportunities Fund vs. Dow Jones

	1993	1994	1995	1996	1997	1998*
Fund	25.3	-2.5	44.2	16.7	26.5	16.3
Dow	13.7	2.1	33.5	26	22.6	12.3

% Avg. Annual Total Return
Fund vs. Dow Jones Industrial Avg.

*1998 returns through 8/1/98
(5-year avg. annual return: 21.9%)

AGGRESSIVE

51

American Century Income and Growth Fund

American Century Investments
P.O. Box 419200
Kansas City, MO 64179-9965

Fund managers: John Schniedwind
and Kurt Borgwardt
Fund objective: Aggressive growth
Web site: www.americancentury.com

Toll-free: 800-345-2021
In-state: 816-531-5575
Fax: 816-340-4753

Performance	★ ★ ★ ★
Consistency	★ ★ ★
Fees/Services	★ ★ ★
BIGRX	**10 Points**

The American Century Income and Growth Fund invests in a wide range of blue chip stocks—primarily those that pay dividends—selected from a pool of about 2,500 large-cap and midcap stocks.

Fund managers John Schniedwind and Kurt Borgwardt evaluate the stocks from their vast pool, selecting the ones that appear to be underpriced based on each company's earnings growth, business fundamentals or intrinsic value. The fund has about 200 stock holdings in all. Its primary focus is to provide dividend income and capital appreciation. The fund stays nearly 100 percent invested in stocks (all U.S. issues) all the time.

The fund's performance closely mirrors the overall market because it is broadly diversified across many industries. Leading sectors include automotive, 5 percent of total assets; banking, 8 percent; communications services, 7 percent; computer products and services, 8 percent; energy production, 8 percent; financial services and insurance, 10 percent; medically related companies, 9 percent; and utilities, 6 percent.

The fund managers maintain a fairly active trading approach resulting in an annual portfolio turnover ratio of 102 percent.

PERFORMANCE

The fund has enjoyed outstanding growth over the last five years. Including dividends and capital gains distributions, the American Century Income and Growth Fund has provided a total return for the last five years (through mid-1998) of 177 percent. A $10,000 investment in 1993 would have grown to about $28,000 five years later. Average annual return: 23.2 percent.

CONSISTENCY

While the fund has trailed the Dow Jones Industrial Average in three of the last five years (through 1997), it was always within 3 percent of the market average. Because of its diversification, it tends to move in a pattern similar to the overall market. Its biggest gain came in 1995, when it jumped 36.9 percent (compared with a 33.5 percent rise in the Dow).

FEES/SERVICES/MANAGEMENT

Like all American Century funds, the Income and Growth Fund is a true no-load—no fee to buy, no fee to sell. The fund's low total annual expense ratio of 0.71 percent (with no 12b-1 fee) compares very favorably with other funds.

The fund offers all the standard services, such as retirement account availability, automatic withdrawal, and automatic checking account deduction. Its minimum initial investment of $2,500 and minimum subsequent investment of $50 is in line with most other funds.

John Schniedwind and Kurt Borgwardt have managed the fund only since 1996. The American Century family of funds includes more than 20 funds and allows shareholders to switch from fund to fund by telephone.

Top Ten Stock Holdings

1. Ford Motor
2. Unilever
3. United Technologies
4. Microsoft
5. Merck
6. Ameritech
7. Atlantic Richfield
8. Morgan Stanley Dean Witter
9. First Union
10. Chevron

Asset mix: common stocks—97%; cash/equivalents—3%
Total net assets: $1.8 billion
Dividend yield: 1.17%

Fees

Front-end load	*None*
Redemption fee	*None*
12b-1 fee	*None*
Management fee	0.70%
Other expenses	<u>0.01</u>
Total annual expense	0.71%
Minimum initial investment	$2,500
Minimum subsequent investment	$50

Services

Telephone exchanges	*Yes*
Automatic withdrawal	*Yes*
Automatic checking deduction	*Yes*
Retirement plan/IRA	*Yes*
Instant redemption	*Yes*
Financial statements	*Semiannual*
Income distributions	*Annual*
Capital gains distributions	*Annual*
Portfolio manager: years	2
Number of funds in family	22

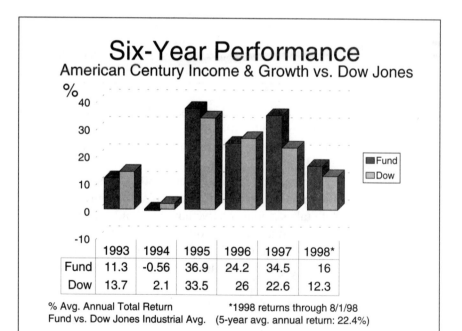

Six-Year Performance
American Century Income & Growth vs. Dow Jones

	1993	1994	1995	1996	1997	1998*
Fund	11.3	-0.56	36.9	24.2	34.5	16
Dow	13.7	2.1	33.5	26	22.6	12.3

% Avg. Annual Total Return   *1998 returns through 8/1/98
Fund vs. Dow Jones Industrial Avg.   (5-year avg. annual return: 22.4%)

52
Nationwide Fund

GROWTH

Nationwide Funds
One Nationwide Plaza
Columbus, OH 43216-2220

Fund manager: Charles S. Bath
Fund objective: Growth and income

Toll-free: 800-848-0920
In-state: 614-249-7885
Fax: 614-249-4007

Performance	★ ★ ★ ★
Consistency	★ ★ ★
Fees/Services	★ ★ ★
MUIFX	**10 Points**

Started in 1933, the Nationwide Fund has posted 21 consecutive years of positive returns. It is one of the few funds ever to achieve that record. The fund invests in solid blue chip growth companies, such as Warner-Lambert, Texaco, and IBM.

Fund manager Charles Bath normally keeps 50 to 60 stock holdings in the portfolio, with about 40 percent of the fund's assets invested in the top ten holdings. Bath takes a conservative buy-and-hold approach resulting in a very low 15 percent annual portfolio turnover ratio.

Over the past ten years, the fund has posted an average annual return of about 19 percent. A $10,000 investment in the fund ten years ago would now be worth about $56,000.

The fund stays almost 100 percent invested in stocks and is well-diversified across industry groups. Leading sectors include financial services and insurance, 19 percent; drugs and hospital supplies, 20 percent; printing and publishing, 10 percent; food and beverages, 8 percent; and chemicals, 7 percent.

PERFORMANCE

The fund has enjoyed outstanding growth over the last five years. Including dividends and capital gains distributions, the Nationwide Fund has provided a total return for the last five years (through mid-1998) of 189 percent. A $10,000 investment in 1993 would have grown to about $29,000 five years later. Average annual return: 23.7 percent.

CONSISTENCY

The fund has trailed the Dow Jones Industrial Average in four of the past five years but never by more than a few percentage points. (It led the Dow through the first few months of 1998.) Its biggest gain came in 1997, when it moved up 39.6 percent. The fund has proven through 21 straight years of positive performance that while it may not always beat the market, it has a knack for keeping its investors in the black.

FEES/SERVICES/MANAGEMENT

The Nationwide Fund has a front-end load of 5.50 percent. Its total annual expense ratio of 1 percent (including a 0.25 percent 12b-1 fee) compares favorably with other funds.

The fund offers all the standard services, such as retirement account availability, automatic withdrawal, and automatic checking account deduction. Its minimum initial investment of $1,000 and minimum subsequent investment of $100 compare favorably with other funds.

Charles Bath has managed the fund since 1985. Nationwide Funds includes six funds and allows shareholders to switch from fund to fund by telephone.

Top Ten Stock Holdings

1. Warner-Lambert
2. Schering-Plough
3. Mellon Bank
4. Black & Decker
5. Texaco
6. New York Times
7. Chubb
8. Fannie Mae
9. Avon Products
10. IBM

Asset mix: common stocks—99%; cash/equivalents—1%
Total net assets: $2 billion
Dividend yield: 0.99%

Fees

Front-end load	5.50%
Redemption fee	*None*
12b-1 fee	0.25
Management fee	0.60
Other expenses	0.15
Total annual expense	1.00%
Minimum initial investment	$1,000
Minimum subsequent investment	$100

Services

Telephone exchanges	*Yes*
Automatic withdrawal	*Yes*
Automatic checking deduction	*Yes*
Retirement plan/IRA	*Yes*
Instant redemption	*Yes*
Financial statements	*Semiannual*
Income distributions	*Quarterly*
Capital gains distributions	*Annual*
Portfolio manager: years	13
Number of funds in family	6

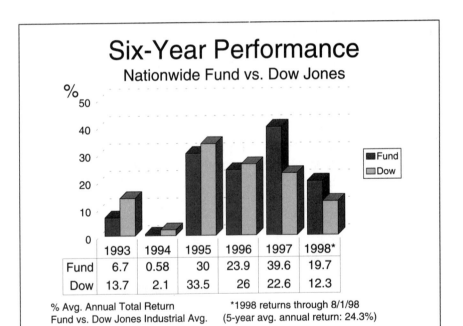

Six-Year Performance
Nationwide Fund vs. Dow Jones

	1993	1994	1995	1996	1997	1998*
Fund	6.7	0.58	30	23.9	39.6	19.7
Dow	13.7	2.1	33.5	26	22.6	12.3

% Avg. Annual Total Return
Fund vs. Dow Jones Industrial Avg.

*1998 returns through 8/1/98
(5-year avg. annual return: 24.3%)

53

Pioneer Europe Fund

Pioneer Funds
60 State Street
Boston, MA 02109-4275

Fund manager: Patrick M. Smith
Fund objective: International Equity
Web site: www.pioneerfunds.com

Toll-free: 800-225-6292
In-state: 617-742-7825
Fax: 617-422-4275

Performance	★ ★ ★ ★
Consistency	★ ★ ★
Fees/Services	★ ★ ★
PEURX	**10 Points**

The Pioneer Europe Fund invests in a broad range of European growth stocks. Nearly every major market in Europe is represented in the fund's holdings. With a strong European economy, the fund has enjoyed outstanding performance the past few years. It has posted an annual average return of nearly 24 percent over the past five years.

Fund manager Patrick Smith takes a fairly conservative buy-and-hold approach. The annual portfolio turnover ratio is 32 percent. Most of the fund's assets are invested in the United Kingdom (20 percent of assets), Germany (14 percent), France (11 percent), Switzerland (9 percent), Italy (9 percent), the Netherlands (8 percent), and Spain (7 percent). The fund also has investments in Sweden, Finland, Denmark, Belgium, Austria, Portugal, Norway, Poland, and the Czech Republic.

The fund's leading industrial sectors include financial services, 20 percent of assets; consumer cyclicals, 20 percent; capital goods, 16 percent; consumer staples, 12 percent; and health care, 9 percent.

PERFORMANCE

The Pioneer Europe Fund has enjoyed outstanding growth over the last five years. Including dividends and capital gains distributions, it has provided a total return for the last five years (through mid-1998) of 189 percent. A $10,000 investment in 1993 would have grown to about $29,000 five years later. Average annual return: 23.7 percent.

CONSISTENCY

The fund has been fairly consistent recently, outperforming the Dow Jones Industrial Average in three of the last five years through 1997 (and it led the Dow through the first few months of 1998). Its biggest gain came in 1996, when it moved up 27 percent.

FEES/SERVICES/MANAGEMENT

The fund has a front-end load of 5.75 percent. Its total annual expense ratio of 1.77 percent (including a 0.25 percent 12b-1 fee) compares favorably with other funds.

The fund offers all the standard services, such as retirement account availability, automatic withdrawal, and automatic checking account deduction. Its minimum initial investment of $1,000 and minimum subsequent investment of $50 compare favorably with other funds.

Patrick Smith has managed the fund since 1994. The Pioneer family of funds includes 20 funds and allows shareholders to switch from fund to fund by telephone.

Top Ten Stock Holdings

1. Raiso Group
2. MobilCom
3. Biora
4. Siebe
5. Kwik-Fit Holdings
6. TT Group
7. Gehe
8. Hugo Boss
9. Getronics
10. Henkel KFaA

Asset mix: common stocks—95%; cash/equivalents—5%
Total net assets: $215 million
Dividend yield: none

Fees

Front-end load	5.75%
Redemption fee	*None*
12b-1 fee	0.25
Management fee	1.00
Other expenses	0.52
Total annual expense	1.77%
Minimum initial investment	$1,000
Minimum subsequent investment	$50

Services

Telephone exchanges	*Yes*
Automatic withdrawal	*Yes*
Automatic checking deduction	*Yes*
Retirement plan/IRA	*Yes*
Instant redemption	*Yes*
Financial statements	*Semiannual*
Income distributions	*Annual*
Capital gains distributions	*Annual*
Portfolio manager: years	4
Number of funds in family	20

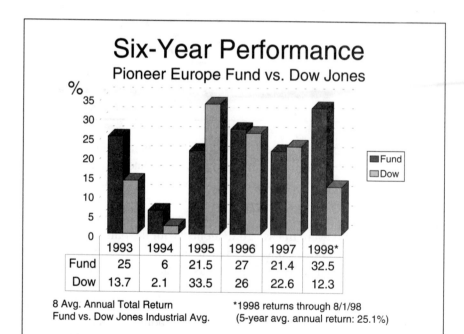

Six-Year Performance
Pioneer Europe Fund vs. Dow Jones

	1993	1994	1995	1996	1997	1998*
Fund	25	6	21.5	27	21.4	32.5
Dow	13.7	2.1	33.5	26	22.6	12.3

8 Avg. Annual Total Return
Fund vs. Dow Jones Industrial Avg.

*1998 returns through 8/1/98
(5-year avg. annual return: 25.1%)

54

Enterprise Growth and Income Portfolio

GROWTH

Enterprise Funds
3343 Peachtree Road, N.E., Suite 450
Atlanta, GA 30326-1022

Fund manager: James Coughlin
Fund objective: Growth and income
Web site: www.enterprisegroup.com

Toll-free: 800-368-3527
In-state: 404-261-1116
Fax: 404-261-1118

Performance	★ ★ ★
Consistency	★ ★ ★ ★
Fees/Services	★ ★ ★
EGNAX	**10 Points**

The Enterprise Growth and Income Portfolio invests in a diverse range of dividend-paying growth stocks that provide both income and long-term stock price appreciation. In addition to stocks, the fund puts a fair share of its assets into cash equivalents, such as commercial paper, short-term government securities, and repurchase agreements. Recently, about 20 percent of its assets were in cash equivalents (with the balance in stocks).

Fund manager James Coughlin says he likes to buy "good companies at attractive prices—usually during periods of market uncertainty or temporary setbacks."

Coughlin's conservative buy-and-hold approach results in a very low 18 percent annual turnover ratio. The fund has about 30 stock holdings in all. Its leading industrial sectors include computer hardware, 14 percent of total assets; computer software, 8 percent; machinery, 7 percent; electrical equipment, 8 percent; aerospace, 6 percent; and banking, 6 percent.

PERFORMANCE

The fund has enjoyed strong growth over the last five years. Including dividends and capital gains distributions, the Enterprise Growth and Income Portfolio has provided a total return for the last five years (through mid-1998) of 179 percent. A $10,000 investment in 1993 would have grown to about $28,000 five years later. Average annual return: 22.8 percent.

CONSISTENCY

The fund has been very consistent recently, outperforming the Dow Jones Industrial Average in four of the last five years through 1997 (and it was about even with the Dow through the first few months of 1998). Its biggest gain came in 1995, when it jumped 36.2 percent (compared with a 33.5 percent rise in the Dow).

FEES/SERVICES/MANAGEMENT

The Enterprise Growth and Income Portfolio charges a 4.75 percent front-end load. Its 1.50 percent annual expense ratio (including a 0.45 percent 12b-1 fee) is in line with other funds.

The fund offers all the standard services, such as retirement account availability, automatic withdrawal, and automatic checking account deduction. Its minimum initial investment of $1,000 and minimum subsequent investment of $50 compare favorably with other funds.

James Coughlin has managed the fund since 1991. The Enterprise family of funds includes 13 funds and allows shareholders to switch from fund to fund by telephone.

Top Ten Stock Holdings

1. EMC	6. Allied Signal
2. Emerson Electric	7. SunAmerica
3. IBM	8. duPont (EI) de Nemours
4. Snap-On	9. Lockheed Martin
5. Computer Associates	10. Chase Manhattan

Asset mix: common stocks—82%; cash/equivalents—18%
Total net assets: $16 million
Dividend yield: 0.40%

Fees

Front-end load	4.75%
Redemption fee	*None*
12b-1 fee	0.45
Management fee	0.75
Other expenses	0.30
Total annual expense	1.50%
Minimum initial investment	$1,000
Minimum subsequent investment	$50

Services

Telephone exchanges	*Yes*
Automatic withdrawal	*Yes*
Automatic checking deduction	*Yes*
Retirement plan/IRA	*Yes*
Instant redemption	*Yes*
Financial statements	*Semiannual*
Income distributions	*Annual*
Capital gains distributions	*Annual*
Portfolio manager: years	7
Number of funds in family	13

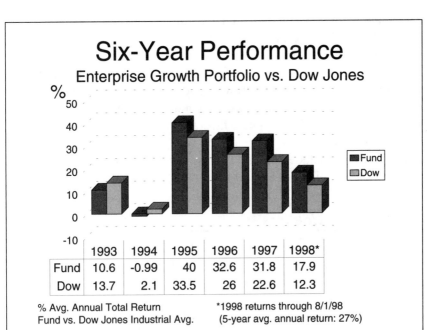

Six-Year Performance
Enterprise Growth Portfolio vs. Dow Jones

	1993	1994	1995	1996	1997	1998*
Fund	10.6	-0.99	40	32.6	31.8	17.9
Dow	13.7	2.1	33.5	26	22.6	12.3

% Avg. Annual Total Return
Fund vs. Dow Jones Industrial Avg.

*1998 returns through 8/1/98
(5-year avg. annual return: 27%)

AGGRESSIVE

Stein Roe Capital Opportunities Fund

Stein Roe Mutual Funds
P.O. Box 8900
Boston, MA 02205-0593

Fund managers: Gloria Santella
and Eric Maddix
Fund objective: Aggressive growth
Web site: www.steinroe.com

Toll-free: 800-338-2550
In-state: 312-368-7800
Fax: 312-368-5632

Performance	★ ★ ★
Consistency	★ ★
Fees/Services	★ ★ ★ ★ ★
SRFCX	**10 Points**

Fast-rising stars in booming industries—that's the theme of the Stein Roe Capital Opportunities Fund. The fund is loaded with stocks from such fast-growth sectors as healthcare, technology, and business services. But rapid growth isn't the only quality fund managers Gloria Santella and Eric Maddix look for in a stock. They also like companies with veteran management, a strong balance sheet, and the ability to exploit market opportunities with successful products or services.

Over the past ten years, the fund has posted an average annual return of about 15 percent. A $10,000 investment in the fund ten years ago would now be worth about $46,000. But fasten your seat belt: the Stein Roe Capital Opportunities Fund has had some wild swings. Down 29 percent in 1990, it roared back with a 62.8 percent gain in 1991; dead even in 1994, it jumped 50.7 percent in 1995. In 1997, when the Dow Jones Industrial Average was up over 20 percent, the Capital Opportunities Fund managed a paltry 6 percent gain.

The fund stays almost fully invested in stocks most of the time. It has about 50 stock holdings in all. The fund managers have taken a conservative trading approach recently; the annual portfolio turnover ratio is 22 percent.

The leading industrial sectors include business services, 20 percent of assets; health care, 18 percent; technology, 13 percent; leisure and entertainment, 13 percent; and industrial products, 9 percent.

PERFORMANCE

The fund has enjoyed strong growth over the last five years. Including dividends and capital gains distributions, the Stein Roe Capital Opportunities Fund has provided a total return for the last five years (through mid-1998) of 174 percent. A $10,000 investment in 1993 would have grown to about $27,000 five years later. Average annual return: 22.3 percent.

CONSISTENCY

The fund has been fairly inconsistent recently, outperforming the Dow Jones Industrial Average in only two of the last five years through 1997 (and it led the Dow through the first few months of 1998). Its biggest gain came in 1995, when it moved up 50.7 percent (compared with a 33.5 percent rise in the Dow).

FEES/SERVICES/MANAGEMENT

Like all Stein Roe funds, the Capital Opportunities Fund is a true no-load—no fee to buy, no fee to sell. Its total annual expense ratio of 1.17 percent (with no 12b-1 fee) compares favorably with other funds.

The fund offers all the standard services, such as retirement account availability, automatic withdrawal, and automatic checking account deduction. Its minimum initial investment of $2,500 and minimum subsequent investment of $100 are a little higher than many other funds.

Gloria Santella and Eric Maddix have managed the fund since 1991. The Stein Roe family of funds includes 18 funds and allows shareholders to switch from fund to fund by telephone.

Top Ten Stock Holdings

1. Paychex
2. Carnival
3. HBO
4. Clear Channel Communications
5. MSC Industrial Direct
6. Cendant
7. CBT Group
8. Tellabs
9. Omnicare
10. Papa John's International

Asset mix: common stocks—93%; cash/equivalents—7%
Total net assets: $1 billion
Dividend yield: none

Fees

Front-end load	*None*
Redemption fee	*None*
12b-1 fee	*None*
Management fee	0.85%
Other expenses	0.32
Total annual expense	1.17%
Minimum initial investment	$2,500
Minimum subsequent investment	$100

Services

Telephone exchanges	*Yes*
Automatic withdrawal	*Yes*
Automatic checking deduction	*Yes*
Retirement plan/IRA	*Yes*
Instant redemption	*Yes*
Financial statements	*Semiannual*
Income distributions	*Annual*
Capital gains distributions	*Annual*
Portfolio manager: years	7
Number of funds in family	18

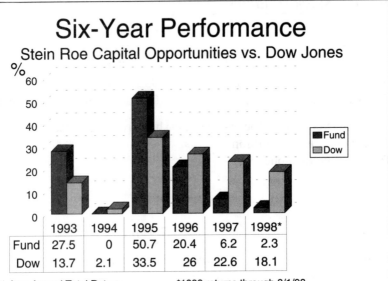

Six-Year Performance
Stein Roe Capital Opportunities vs. Dow Jones

	1993	1994	1995	1996	1997	1998*
Fund	27.5	0	50.7	20.4	6.2	2.3
Dow	13.7	2.1	33.5	26	22.6	18.1

% Avg. Annual Total Return   *1998 returns through 8/1/98
Fund vs. Dow Jones Industrial Avg.   (5-year avg. annual return: 18.1%)

LONG TERM

Davis New York Venture Fund

Davis Funds
124 East Marcy Street
Santa Fe, NM 87504-1688

Fund manager: Christopher Davis
Fund objective: Long-term growth

Toll-free: 800-279-0279
In-state: 505-820-3101
Fax: 505-820-3002

Performance	★ ★ ★
Consistency	★ ★ ★ ★
Fees/Services	★ ★ ★
NYVTX	**10 Points**

Davis New York Venture Fund manager Christopher Davis looks for stocks of good companies that have been battered by the market. "Strong businesses become great investments when they are purchased at opportunistic prices," says Davis. "That is why we generally buy companies when they are under a cloud, that is, when some short-term disappointment has created an opportunity to buy growth at a value price, particularly at a low valuation relative to the market."

Over the past ten years, the fund has posted an average annual return of about 21 percent. A $10,000 investment in the fund ten years ago would now be worth about $65,000.

Davis uses extensive research to uncover top stock prospects, and then holds for the long term. The fund has a very low annual portfolio turnover ratio of just 24 percent and stays almost fully invested in stocks all the time. It is invested in a broad selection of well-established blue chip stocks, such as IBM, Banc One, Nike, Johnson & Johnson, and McDonald's. It has about 100 stock holdings in all.

The fund is heavily weighted in financial service–related stocks, such as banks, brokerages, and insurance companies, which account for about

30 percent of total assets. Other leading sectors include medically–related companies, 5 percent; technology, 12 percent; consumer products, 5 percent; and transportation, 12 percent.

PERFORMANCE

The fund has enjoyed excellent growth over the last five years. Including dividends and capital gains distributions, the Davis New York Venture Fund has provided a total return for the last five years (through mid-1998) of 169 percent. A $10,000 investment in 1993 would have grown to about $27,000 five years later. Average annual return: 21.8 percent.

CONSISTENCY

The fund has been very consistent recently, outperforming the Dow Jones Industrial Average in three of the last five years through 1997 (and it led the Dow through the first few months of 1998). Its biggest gain came in 1995, when it jumped 40.6 percent (compared with a 33.5 percent rise in the Dow).

FEES/SERVICES/MANAGEMENT

The fund carries a 4.75 percent front-end load. Its total annual expense ratio of 0.89 percent (including a 0.20 percent 12b-1 fee) compares very favorably with other funds.

The fund offers all the standard services, such as retirement account availability, automatic withdrawal, and automatic checking account deduction. Its minimum initial investment of $1,000 and minimum subsequent investment of $25 compare favorably with other funds.

Fund founder Shelby Davis recently retired, leaving the fund to his son Christopher Davis, who has been a fund manager with Davis Funds since 1989. The Davis family of funds includes nine funds and allows shareholders to switch from fund to fund by telephone.

Top Ten Stock Holdings

1. McDonald's
2. General Re
3. Hewlett-Packard
4. Wells Fargo
5. Citicorp

6. IBM
7. BankAmerica
8. American Express
9. Texas Instruments
10. Morgan Stanley Dean Witter

Asset mix: common stocks—89%; cash/equivalents—11%
Total net assets: $4.7 billion
Dividend yield: 0.91%

Fees

Front-end load	4.75%
Redemption fee	*None*
(after the first year)	
12b-1 fee	0.20
Management fee	0.57
Other expenses	0.12
Total annual expense	0.89%
Minimum initial investment	$1,000
Minimum subsequent investment	$25

Services

Telephone exchanges	*Yes*
Automatic withdrawal	*Yes*
Automatic checking deduction	*Yes*
Retirement plan/IRA	*Yes*
Instant redemption	*Yes*
Financial statements	*Semiannual*
Income distributions	*Annual*
Capital gains distributions	*Annual*
Portfolio manager: years	3
Number of funds in family	9

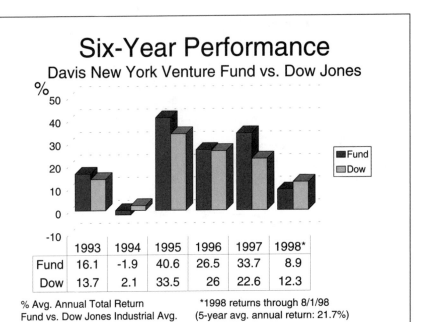

Six-Year Performance
Davis New York Venture Fund vs. Dow Jones

	1993	1994	1995	1996	1997	1998*
Fund	16.1	-1.9	40.6	26.5	33.7	8.9
Dow	13.7	2.1	33.5	26	22.6	12.3

% Avg. Annual Total Return   *1998 returns through 8/1/98
Fund vs. Dow Jones Industrial Avg.   (5-year avg. annual return: 21.7%)

LONG TERM

57
T. Rowe Price New America Growth Fund

T. Rowe Price Funds
100 East Pratt Street
Baltimore, MD 21202

Fund manager: John LaPorte
Fund objective: Long-term growth
Web site: www.troweprice.com

Toll-free: 800-225-5132
In-state: 410-547-2000
Fax: 410-347-1572

Performance	★ ★ ★
Consistency	★ ★
Fees/Services	★ ★ ★ ★ ★
PRWAX	**10 Points**

The U.S. economy is moving increasingly to the service sector, a development that is playing right into the hands of the T. Rowe Price New America Growth Fund. The fund invests primarily in stocks of service-related companies such as First Data, Franklin Resources, and AirTouch Communications. Over the past ten years, the fund has had an average annual return of about 19 percent. A $10,000 investment in the fund ten years ago would now be worth about $57,000.

In selecting stocks for the portfolio, fund manager John LaPorte looks for solid, growing companies with a good balance sheet, strong management, and significant market share in their key sector. The stocks in the portfolio vary in size from small, emerging growth companies to large blue chips.

LaPorte is fairly modest in his trading strategy. The annual portfolio turnover ratio is 43 percent. The fund stays almost fully invested in stocks most of the time. Among the types of stocks LaPorte invests in are health care, computer processing, retailers, restaurant chains, insurance and financial services, media, entertainment, energy services, and environmental services. Business services account for about 44 percent of total assets; consumer services make up 32 percent, and financial services account for 20 percent. The fund has about 70 stock holdings in all.

PERFORMANCE

The fund has enjoyed strong growth over the last five years. Including dividends and capital gains distributions, the T. Rowe Price New America Growth Fund has provided a total return for the last five years (through mid-1998) of 163 percent. A $10,000 investment in 1993 would have grown to about $26,000 five years later. Average annual return: 21.4 percent.

CONSISTENCY

The fund has been inconsistent recently, outperforming the Dow Jones Industrial Average in only two of the last five years through 1997 (but it led the Dow through the first few months of 1998). Its biggest gain came in 1995, when it moved up 44.3 percent (compared with a 33.5 percent rise in the Dow).

FEES/SERVICES/MANAGEMENT

Like all T. Rowe Price funds, the New America Growth Fund is a true no-load—no fee to buy, no fee to sell. Its total annual expense ratio of 1.01 percent (with no 12b-1 fee) compares favorably with other funds.

The fund offers all the standard services, such as retirement account availability, automatic withdrawal, and automatic checking account deduction. Its minimum initial investment of $2,500 and minimum subsequent investment of $100 are a little on the high side compared with other funds.

John LaPorte has managed the fund since 1985. The T. Rowe Price family of funds includes 70 funds and allows shareholders to switch from fund to fund by telephone.

Top Ten Stock Holdings

1. Cendant
2. Franklin Resources
3. Service International
4. Comcast Special
5. UNUM

6. USA Waste Services
7. AirTouch Communications
8. Cardinal Health
9. ACE
10. FHLMC

Asset mix: common stocks—95%; cash/equivalents—5%
Total net assets: $2.1 billion
Dividend yield: none

Fees

Front-end load	*None*
Redemption fee	*None*
12b-1 fee	*None*
Management fee	0.68%
Other expenses	0.33
Total annual expense	1.01%
Minimum initial investment	$2,500
Minimum subsequent investment	$100

Services

Telephone exchanges	*Yes*
Automatic withdrawal	*Yes*
Automatic checking deduction	*Yes*
Retirement plan/IRA	*Yes*
Instant redemption	*Yes*
Financial statements	*Semiannual*
Income distributions	*Annual*
Capital gains distributions	*Annual*
Portfolio manager: years	13
Number of funds in family	70

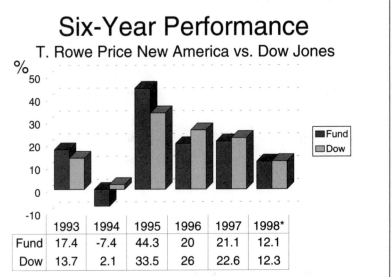

Six-Year Performance
T. Rowe Price New America vs. Dow Jones

	1993	1994	1995	1996	1997	1998*
Fund	17.4	-7.4	44.3	20	21.1	12.1
Dow	13.7	2.1	33.5	26	22.6	12.3

% Avg. Annual Total Return   *1998 returns through 8/1/98
Fund vs. Dow Jones Industrial Avg.   (5-year avg. annual return: 19.9%)

AGGRESSIVE

58

American Century–Twentieth Century Ultra Fund

American Century Investments
P.O. Box 419200
Kansas City, MO 64179-9965

Fund managers: James Stowers III and Bruce Wimberly
Fund objective: Aggressive growth
Web site: www.americancentury.com

Toll-free: 800-345-2021
In-state: 816-531-5575
Fax: 816-340-4753

Performance	★ ★ ★
Consistency	★ ★
Fees/Services	★ ★ ★ ★ ★
TWCUX	**10 Points**

With assets of more than $22 billion, the managers of the American Century–Twentieth Century Ultra Fund must take a very broad approach in selecting stocks for the portfolio. Fund managers James Stowers III and Bruce Wimberly focus on momentum in evaluating stocks, looking specifically for earnings and revenue growth acceleration. The fund has enjoyed an outstanding performance over the past decade, posting an average annual return of 22 percent. A $10,000 investment in the fund ten years ago would now be worth about $75,000.

The fund managers try to keep the fund on the upswing through close and continuous scrutiny of their holdings. They examine every stock in the portfolio each week to make sure the companies are still on an upward trend. They also keep their eye on their list of 20 to 30 prospective stocks that could find their way into the portfolio when some of the fund's holdings begin to weaken.

Generally speaking, the fund stays almost fully invested in stocks at all times. The portfolio managers maintain a fairly active trading policy. The fund has a 107 percent annual portfolio turnover ratio. The fund has about 200 stock holdings in all that are spread across a diverse range of industries. Leading industrial sectors include financial services, 12 percent of total assets; technology, 44 percent; health-related companies, 19 percent; and business and consumer services, 8 percent.

PERFORMANCE

The fund has enjoyed strong growth over the last five years. Including dividends and capital gains distributions, the Ultra Fund has provided a total return for the last five years (through mid-1998) of 163 percent. A $10,000 investment in 1993 would have grown to about $26,000 five years later. Average annual return: 21.2 percent.

CONSISTENCY

The fund has been somewhat inconsistent recently, trailing the Dow Jones Industrial Average in three of the last five years through 1997 (but it led the Dow through the first few months of 1998). Its biggest gain came in 1997, when it jumped 27.9 percent (compared with a 22.6 percent rise in the Dow).

FEES/SERVICES/MANAGEMENT

Like all American Century funds, the Ultra Fund is a true no-load—no fee to buy, no fee to sell. The fund's low total annual expense ratio of 1 percent (with no 12b-1 fee) compares favorably with other funds.

The fund offers all the standard services, such as retirement account availability, automatic withdrawal, and automatic checking account deduction. Its minimum initial investment of $2,500 and minimum subsequent investment of $50 is in line with most other funds.

The management team of James Stowers III and Bruce Wimberly has managed the fund since 1981. The American Century family of funds includes more than 20 funds, and allows shareholders to switch from fund to fund by telephone.

Top Ten Stock Holdings

1. General Electric	6. America Online
2. Pfizer	7. WorldCom
3. Warner-Lambert	8. Bristol-Myers Squibb
4. Eli Lilly	9. Microsoft
5. Cisco Systems	10. IBM

Asset mix: common stocks—99%; cash/equivalents—1%
Total net assets: $22.5 million
Dividend yield: 0.04%

Fees

Front-end load	*None*
Redemption fee	*None*
12b-1 fee	*None*
Management fee	1.00%
Other expenses	0.00
Total annual expense	1.00%
Minimum initial investment	$2,500
Minimum subsequent investment	$50

Services

Telephone exchanges	*Yes*
Automatic withdrawal	*Yes*
Automatic checking deduction	*Yes*
Retirement plan/IRA	*Yes*
Instant redemption	*Yes*
Financial statements	*Semiannual*
Income distributions	*Annual*
Capital gains distributions	*Annual*
Portfolio manager: years	17
Number of funds in family	22

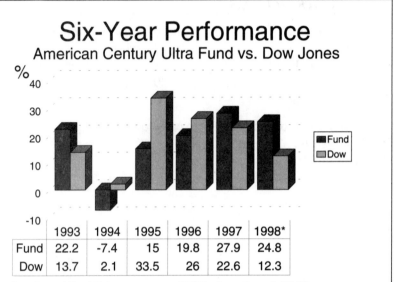

Six-Year Performance
American Century Ultra Fund vs. Dow Jones

	1993	1994	1995	1996	1997	1998*
Fund	22.2	-7.4	15	19.8	27.9	24.8
Dow	13.7	2.1	33.5	26	22.6	12.3

% Avg. Annual Total Return   *1998 returns through 8/1/98
Fund vs. Dow Jones Industrial Avg.   (5-year avg. annual return: 20.2%)

AGGRESSIVE

T. Rowe Price Small Cap Stock Fund

T. Rowe Price Funds
100 East Pratt Street
Baltimore, MD 21202

Fund manager: Gregory A. McCrickard   **Toll-free:** 800-225-5132
Fund objective: Aggressive growth   **In-state:** 410-547-2000
Web site: www.troweprice.com   **Fax:** 410-347-1572

Performance	★ ★
Consistency	★ ★ ★
Fees/Services	★ ★ ★ ★ ★
OTCFX	**10 Points**

Formerly the T. Rowe Price Over-the-Counter Securities Fund, the Small Cap Stock Fund focuses on fast-growth companies with market capitalizations of under $1 billion. "We seek soundly managed companies with strong, shareholder-oriented management and an equally strong business niche," says fund manager Gregory McCrickard. Over the past ten years, the fund has posted an average annual return of about 16 percent. A $10,000 investment in the fund ten years ago would now be worth about $43,000.

McCrickard looks for companies with veteran management, solid business franchises, sound financials, and proven ability to deliver increasing earnings. He invests in both "value" stocks—those trading at a discount to the market relative to their book value or earnings—and growth companies—those with strong growth momentum.

McCrickard takes a fairly conservative trading approach and the fund has an annual portfolio turnover ratio of 31 percent. The fund stays about 80 to 95 percent invested in the market all the time. It has about 120 stock holdings in all. Leading sectors include consumer nondurables, 13 percent of assets; financial services, 13 percent; business services and transportation, 23 percent; consumer services and cyclicals, 21 percent; and technology, 8 percent.

PERFORMANCE

The fund has enjoyed solid growth over the last five years. Including dividends and capital gains distributions, the T. Rowe Price Small Cap Stock Fund has provided a total return for the last five years (through mid-1998) of 154 percent. A $10,000 investment in 1993 would have grown to about $25,000 five years later. Average annual return: 20.5 percent.

CONSISTENCY

The fund has been fairly consistent recently, outperforming the Dow Jones Industrial Average in two of the last five years through 1997 (but it trailed the Dow through the first few months of 1998). Its biggest gain came in 1995, when it moved up 33.9 percent (compared with a 33.5 percent rise in the Dow).

FEES/SERVICES/MANAGEMENT

Like all T. Rowe Price funds, the Small Cap Fund is a true no-load—no fee to buy, no fee to sell. Its total annual expense ratio of 1.07 percent (with no 12b-1 fee) compares favorably with other funds.

The fund offers all the standard services, such as retirement account availability, automatic withdrawal, and automatic checking account deduction. Its minimum initial investment of $2,500 and minimum subsequent investment of $100 is a little high compared with other funds.

Gregory McCrickard has managed the fund since 1992. The T. Rowe Price family of funds includes 70 funds and allows shareholders to switch from fund to fund by telephone.

Top Ten Stock Holdings

1. U.S. Foodservice	6. Carson Pirie Scott
2. Aliant Communications	7. A.O. Smith
3. Analogic	8. Cionmach Laundry
4. PartnerRe	9. Harleysville Group
5. Summit Bancorp	10. Richfield Holdings

Asset mix: common stocks—90%; cash/equivalents—10%
Total net assets: $816 million
Dividend yield: 0.17%

Fees

Front-end load	*None*
Redemption fee	*None*
12b-1 fee	*None*
Management fee	0.78%
Other expenses	0.29
Total annual expense	1.07%
Minimum initial investment	$2,500
Minimum subsequent investment	$100

Services

Telephone exchanges	*Yes*
Automatic withdrawal	*Yes*
Automatic checking deduction	*Yes*
Retirement plan/IRA	*Yes*
Instant redemption	*Yes*
Financial statements	*Semiannual*
Income distributions	*Annual*
Capital gains distributions	*Annual*
Portfolio manager: years	6
Number of funds in family	70

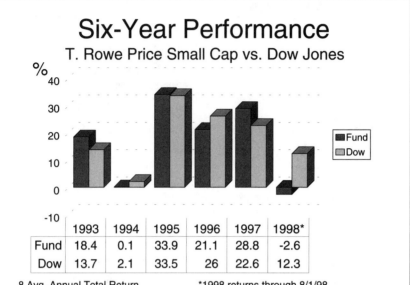

Six-Year Performance
T. Rowe Price Small Cap vs. Dow Jones

	1993	1994	1995	1996	1997	1998*
Fund	18.4	0.1	33.9	21.1	28.8	-2.6
Dow	13.7	2.1	33.5	26	22.6	12.3

8 Avg. Annual Total Return   *1998 returns through 8/1/98
Fund vs. Dow Jones Industrial Avg.   (5-year avg. annual return: 17.2%)

60
Strong Opportunity Fund

Strong Funds
P.O. Box 2936
Milwaukee, WI 53201-2936

Fund managers: Richard T. Weiss
   and Marina T. Carlson
Fund objective: Long-term growth
Web site: www.strong-funds.com

Toll-free: 800-368-1030
In-state: 414-359-3400
Fax: 414-359-3947

Performance	★ ★
Consistency	★ ★ ★
Fees/Services	★ ★ ★ ★ ★
SOPFX	**10 Points**

Strong Opportunity Fund managers Richard Weiss and Marina Carlson look for small and mid-size stocks that analysts on Wall Street have not yet discovered. "We evaluate a company as though we were considering buying the entire firm and compare the price we'd be willing to pay with the current stock price," explains Weiss. "If the cost of the stock doesn't reflect this private value—often because the stock is being ignored by analysts—we will consider adding it to the portfolio."

Most of the fund's holdings are little-known companies in a wide range of industries, such as Comcast Special, Tele-Communications Liberty Media, and NIPSCO Industries. But a few of the blue chips, such as General Motors, Kmart, and Office Depot, do show up in the portfolio.

Over the past ten years, the fund has had an average annual return of about 17 percent. A $10,000 investment in the fund ten years ago would now be worth about $45,000.

The fund has about 90 stock holdings in all. Leading industrial sectors include technology, 21 percent of assets; energy, 13 percent; financial services, 12 percent; consumer cyclicals, 11 percent; and retailing, 8 percent.

The fund generally stays 70 percent to 90 percent invested in stocks, the managers are fairly active in their trading approach, and the annual portfolio turnover ratio is 94 percent.

PERFORMANCE

The fund has enjoyed solid growth over the last five years. Including dividends and capital gains distributions, the Strong Opportunity Fund has provided a total return for the last five years (through mid-1998) of 152 percent. A $10,000 investment in 1993 would have grown to about $25,000 five years later. Average annual return: 20.3 percent.

CONSISTENCY

The fund has been fairly consistent recently, outperforming the Dow Jones Industrial Average in three of the last five years through 1997 (and it led the Dow through the first few months of 1998). Its biggest gain came in 1995, when it moved up 27.3 percent (compared with a 33.5 percent rise in the Dow).

FEES/SERVICES/MANAGEMENT

Like all Strong funds, the Opportunity Fund is a true no-load—no fee to buy, no fee to sell. Its total annual expense ratio of 1.27 percent (with no 12b-1 fee) compares favorably with other funds.

The fund offers all the standard services, such as retirement account availability, automatic withdrawal, and automatic checking account deduction. Its minimum initial investment of $1,000 and minimum subsequent investment of $50 compare favorably with other funds.

Richard Weiss and Marina Carlson have managed the fund since 1991. The Strong family of funds includes 21 funds and allows shareholders to switch from fund to fund by telephone.

Top Ten Stock Holdings

1. Tele-Communications
   Liberty Media
2. Cox Communications
3. Magna International
4. NIPSCO Industries
5. Comcast Special

6. Tele-Comm TCI Group
7. General Motors
8. Kmart
9. U.S. West Media Group
10. Office Depot

Asset mix: common stocks—90%; cash/equivalents—10%
Total net assets: $1.9 billion
Dividend yield: 0.21%

Fees

Front-end load	*None*
Redemption fee	*None*
12b-1 fee	*None*
Management fee	1.00%
Other expenses	0.27
Total annual expense	1.27%
Minimum initial investment	$1,000
Minimum subsequent investment	$50

Services

Telephone exchanges	*Yes*
Automatic withdrawal	*Yes*
Automatic checking deduction	*Yes*
Retirement plan/IRA	*Yes*
Instant redemption	*Yes*
Financial statements	*Semiannual*
Income distributions	*Annual*
Capital gains distributions	*Annual*
Portfolio manager: years	7
Number of funds in family	21

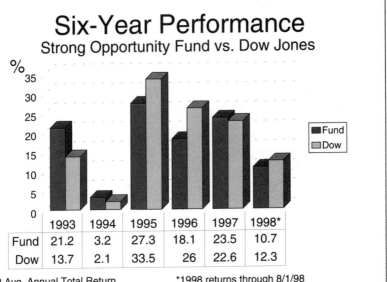

Six-Year Performance
Strong Opportunity Fund vs. Dow Jones

	1993	1994	1995	1996	1997	1998*
Fund	21.2	3.2	27.3	18.1	23.5	10.7
Dow	13.7	2.1	33.5	26	22.6	12.3

8 Avg. Annual Total Return   *1998 returns through 8/1/98
Fund vs. Dow Jones Industrial Avg.   (5-year avg. annual return: 18.3%)

61

Warburg Pincus Emerging Growth Fund

Warburg Pincus Funds
466 Lexington Avenue
New York, NY 10017-3147

Fund managers: Elizabeth B. Dater
and Stephen J. Lurit
Fund objective: Aggressive growth
Web site: www.warburg.com

Toll-free: 800-257-5614
In-state: 212-878-0600
Fax: 302-791-3067

Performance	★ ★
Consistency	★ ★ ★
Fees/Services	★ ★ ★ ★ ★
CUEGX	**10 Points**

The Warburg Pincus Emerging Growth Fund invests in companies that have progressed beyond the start-up phase but still have the potential for sustained growth. The fund, which opened in 1988, has posted an average annual return of about 18 percent since its inception. A $10,000 investment in the fund ten years ago would now be worth about $52,000.

The fund managers look for stocks that have "positive earnings momentum and have the potential to achieve significant capital gains within a relatively short period of time" through new products or services, technological improvements, or changes in management.

The fund has about 100 stock holdings in all. It stays almost fully invested in stocks most of the time. Its leading industrial sectors include computers, 8 percent of assets; electronics, 9 percent; business services, 10 percent; health care and pharmaceuticals, 7 percent; and financial services, 9 percent. The fund managers take a fairly active approach in their trading strategy. The annual portfolio turnover ratio is 87 percent.

PERFORMANCE

The fund has enjoyed solid growth over the last five years. Including dividends and capital gains distributions, the Warburg Pincus Emerging Growth Fund has provided a total return for the last five years (through mid-1998) of 151 percent. A $10,000 investment in 1993 would have grown to about $25,000 five years later. Average annual return: 20.2 percent.

CONSISTENCY

The fund has been fairly consistent recently, outperforming the Dow Jones Industrial Average in two of the last five years through 1997 and was nearly even with the Dow two other years. It was also about even with the Dow through the first few months of 1998. Its biggest gain came in 1995, when it moved up 46.2 percent (compared with a 33.5 percent rise in the Dow).

FEES/SERVICES/MANAGEMENT

Like all Warburg funds, the Emerging Growth Fund is a true no-load—no fee to buy, no fee to sell. Its total annual expense ratio of 1.22 percent (with no 12b-1 fee) compares favorably with other funds.

The fund offers all the standard services, such as retirement account availability, automatic withdrawal, and automatic checking account deduction. Its minimum initial investment of $2,500 and minimum subsequent investment of $100 are a little higher than many other funds.

Elizabeth Dater and Stephen Lurit have managed the fund since 1988. The Warburg Pincus family of funds includes 22 funds and allows shareholders to switch from fund to fund by telephone.

Top Ten Stock Holdings

1. PeopleSoft
2. Maxim Integrated Products
3. Robert Half International
4. Transaction Systems Architects
5. BMC Software
6. Outdoor Systems
7. Herman Miller
8. Border Group
9. Allmerica Financial
10. Nationwide Financial Services

Asset mix: common stocks—93%; cash/equivalents—7%
Total net assets: $1.6 billion
Dividend yield: none

Fees

Front-end load	*None*
Redemption fee	*None*
12b-1 fee	*None*
Management fee	0.90%
Other expenses	0.32
Total annual expense	1.22%
Minimum initial investment	$2,500
Minimum subsequent investment	$50

Services

Telephone exchanges	*Yes*
Automatic withdrawal	*Yes*
Automatic checking deduction	*Yes*
Retirement plan/IRA	*Yes*
Instant redemption	*Yes*
Financial statements	*Semiannual*
Income distributions	*Annual*
Capital gains distributions	*Annual*
Portfolio manager: years	10
Number of funds in family	22

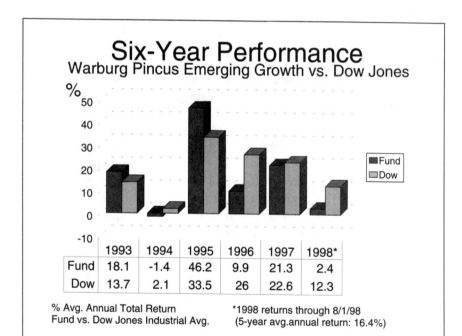

Six-Year Performance
Warburg Pincus Emerging Growth vs. Dow Jones

	1993	1994	1995	1996	1997	1998*
Fund	18.1	-1.4	46.2	9.9	21.3	2.4
Dow	13.7	2.1	33.5	26	22.6	12.3

% Avg. Annual Total Return
Fund vs. Dow Jones Industrial Avg.

*1998 returns through 8/1/98
(5-year avg.annual return: 16.4%)

62

Neuberger & Berman Focus Fund

LONG TERM

Neuberger Funds
605 Third Avenue
New York, NY 10158-0006

Fund managers: Kent Simons
   and Kevin Risen
Fund objective: Long-term growth
Web site: www.nbfunds.com

Toll-free: 800-877-9700
In-state: 212-476-8800
Fax: 212-476-8944

Performance	★ ★
Consistency	★ ★ ★
Fees/Services	★ ★ ★ ★ ★
NBSSX	**10 Points**

Opened in 1955, the Neuberger & Berman Focus Fund is one of the oldest mutual funds in America. Fund managers Kent Simons and Kevin Risen look for undervalued stocks with solid financial strength and proven management. In selecting their portfolio, the fund managers identify 6 economic sectors (out of a possible 13) that they believe to be the most undervalued. Then they try to invest in the well-managed, financially strong industry leaders in each of those sectors.

Over the past ten years, the fund has posted an annual average return of about 18 percent. A $10,000 investment in the fund ten years ago would now be worth about $50,000. The fund, which has about 40 stock holdings, invests in both major blue chip stocks, such as General Motors, Citicorp, and Banc One, and growing young companies, such as 3Com, Rational Software, and Applied Materials.

The six main industry sectors represented in the fund include financial services, 39 percent of assets; health care, 15 percent; heavy industry, 9 percent; technology, 19 percent; automotive, 9 percent; and retail, 8 percent. The fund managers take a fairly conservative trading approach, so the annual portfolio turnover ratio is 63 percent.

PERFORMANCE

The fund has enjoyed solid growth over the last five years. Including dividends and capital gains distributions, the Neuberger & Berman Focus Fund has provided a total return for the last five years (through mid-1998) of 155 percent. A $10,000 investment in 1993 would have grown to about $25,000 five years later. Average annual return: 20.5 percent.

CONSISTENCY

The fund has been fairly consistent recently, outperforming the Dow Jones Industrial Average in three of the last five years through 1997 (and it led the Dow through the first few months of 1998). Its biggest gain came in 1995, when it moved up 36.2 percent (compared with a 33.5 percent rise in the Dow).

FEES/SERVICES/MANAGEMENT

The Focus Fund is a true no-load—no fee to buy, no fee to sell. Its total annual expense ratio of 0.86 percent (with no 12b-1 fee) compares favorably with other funds.

The fund offers all the standard services, such as retirement account availability, automatic withdrawal, and automatic checking account deduction. Its minimum initial investment of $1,000 and minimum subsequent investment of $100 compare favorably with other funds.

Kent Simons has managed the fund since 1988; Kevin Risen recently joined as co-manager. The Neuberger & Berman family of funds includes seven funds and allows shareholders to switch from fund to fund by telephone.

Top Ten Stock Holdings

1. Chase Manhattan
2. Countrywide Credit Industry
3. Travelers Group
4. Citicorp
5. General Motors
6. Capital One Financial
7. Furniture Brands International
8. Wellpoint Health Networks
9. 3Com
10. Merrill Lynch

Asset mix: common stocks—99%; cash/equivalents—1%
Total net assets: $1.4 billion
Dividend yield: 0.14%

Fees

Front-end load	*None*
Redemption fee	*None*
12b-1 fee	*None*
Management fee	0.76%
Other expenses	0.10
Total annual expense	0.86%
Minimum initial investment	$1,000
Minimum subsequent investment	$100

Services

Telephone exchanges	*Yes*
Automatic withdrawal	*Yes*
Automatic checking deduction	*Yes*
Retirement plan/IRA	*Yes*
Instant redemption	*Yes*
Financial statements	*Semiannual*
Income distributions	*Annual*
Capital gains distributions	*Annual*
Portfolio manager: years	10
Number of funds in family	7

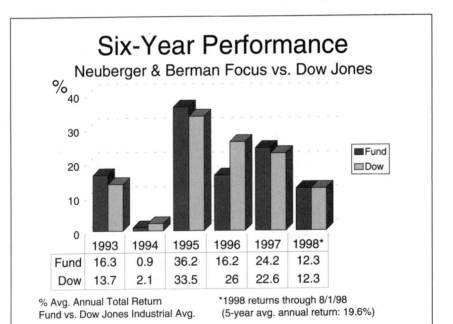

Six-Year Performance
Neuberger & Berman Focus vs. Dow Jones

	1993	1994	1995	1996	1997	1998*
Fund	16.3	0.9	36.2	16.2	24.2	12.3
Dow	13.7	2.1	33.5	26	22.6	12.3

% Avg. Annual Total Return
Fund vs. Dow Jones Industrial Avg.

*1998 returns through 8/1/98
(5-year avg. annual return: 19.6%)

63

Managers Special Equity Fund

Managers Funds
40 Richards Avenue
Norwalk, CT 06854

Fund managers: Tim Ebright,
  Andrew Knuth, Gary Pilgrim,
  and Robbert E. Kern
Fund objective: Aggressive growth

Toll-free: 800-835-3879
In-state: 203-857-5321
Fax: 203-857-5316

Performance	★ ★
Consistency	★ ★ ★
Fees/Services	★ ★ ★ ★ ★
MGSEX	**10 Points**

The Managers Special Equity Fund has a hired-gun approach to investment management. The company scours the investment industry for the top independent money managers and contracts with them to run its funds rather than hiring a specific manager for each fund. The Special Equity Fund, for instance, has four portfolio managers: Gary Pilgrim, the very successful manager of the PBHG Growth Fund; Timothy Ebright of Liberty Investment; Robert Kern of Kern Capital Management; and Andrew Knuth of Westport Asset Management. The four work together to select the portfolio and determine buy-and-sell strategy.

The managers invest in a diverse range of fast-growing small and midsize stocks. They are fairly conservative in their trading policy and have an annual portfolio turnover ratio of 56 percent. The fund stays almost fully invested in stocks most of the time.

Over the past ten years, the fund has grown at an average annual rate of about 19 percent. A $10,000 investment in the fund ten years ago would now be worth about $55,000. The fund has about 300 stock holdings. Its leading industrial sectors include financial services and insurance, 11 percent of assets; health care, 9 percent; technology, 8 percent; capital goods, 8 percent; entertainment and leisure, 7 percent; and computer software, 6 percent.

PERFORMANCE

The fund has enjoyed solid growth over the last five years. Including dividends and capital gains distributions, the Mangers Special Equity Fund has provided a total return for the last five years (through mid-1998) of 148 percent. A $10,000 investment in 1993 would have grown to about $25,000 five years later. Average annual return: 20 percent.

CONSISTENCY

The fund has been fairly consistent recently, outperforming the Dow Jones Industrial Average in two of the last five years through 1997 (and it led the Dow through the first few months of 1998). Its biggest gain came in 1995, when it moved up 33.9 percent (compared with a 33.5 percent rise in the Dow).

FEES/SERVICES/MANAGEMENT

Like all Managers funds, the Special Equity Fund is a true no-load—no fee to buy, no fee to sell. The fund's total annual expense ratio of 1.43 percent (with no 12b-1 fee) is in line with other funds.

The fund offers all the standard services, such as retirement account availability, automatic withdrawal, and automatic checking account deduction. Its minimum initial investment of $2,000 and minimum subsequent investment of $1 compare favorably with other funds.

The management team of Tim Ebright, Andy Knuth, Gary Pilgrim, and Bob Kern have managed the fund since 1988. The Managers family of funds includes 11 funds and allows shareholders to switch from fund to fund by telephone.

Top Ten Stock Holdings

1. XTRA
2. Airborne Freight
3. American Radio Systems
4. Emmis Broadcasting
5. Applied Capital International

6. Superior Services
7. Downey Financial
8. Pittston Brinks Group
9. American Disposal Services
10. Policy Management Systems

Asset mix: common stocks—91%; cash/equivalents—9%
Total net assets: $720 million
Dividend yield: 0.11%

Fees

Front-end load	*None*
Redemption fee	*None*
12b-1 fee	*None*
Management fee	0.90%
Other expenses	0.53
Total annual expense	1.43%
Minimum initial investment	$2,000
Minimum subsequent investment	$1

Services

Telephone exchanges	*Yes*
Automatic withdrawal	*Yes*
Automatic checking deduction	*Yes*
Retirement plan/IRA	*Yes*
Instant redemption	*Yes*
Financial statements	*Semiannual*
Income distributions	*Annual*
Capital gains distributions	*Annual*
Portfolio manager: years	13
Number of funds in family	11

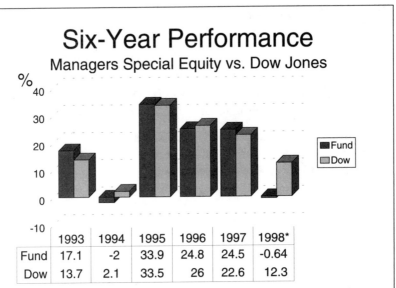

Six-Year Performance
Managers Special Equity vs. Dow Jones

	1993	1994	1995	1996	1997	1998*
Fund	17.1	-2	33.9	24.8	24.5	-0.64
Dow	13.7	2.1	33.5	26	22.6	12.3

8 Avg. Annual Total Return
Fund vs. Dow Jones Industrial Avg.

*1998 returns through 8/1/98
(5-year avg. annual return: 17.3%)

64

Fidelity Select Regional Banks Portfolio

Fidelity Investments
82 Devonshire Street
Boston, MA 02109

Fund manager: Christine Schaulat
Fund objective: Sector
Web site: www.fidelity.com

Toll-free: 800-544-8888
In-state: 801-534-1910
Fax: 617-476-9753

Performance	★ ★ ★ ★ ★
Consistency	★ ★ ★
Fees/Services	★ ★
FSRBX	**10 Points**

A strong economy and low interest rates have been good for business at banks throughout the United States. That's been good news for investors of the Fidelity Select Regional Banks Portfolio, which has been one of the nation's top-performing funds over the past decade. Several other factors have also contributed to the growth of the banking sector, including cost-cutting measures, new fee services, and major bank consolidations.

Over the past ten years, the Regional Banks Portfolio has posted a 26 percent average annual return. A $10,000 investment in the fund ten years ago would now be worth about $100,000.

The fund invests in large and midsize regional banks throughout the country, such as Banc One, First Chicago NBD, and Wells Fargo. It also invests in companies involved in discount brokerage, leasing, and insurance. In all, it has about 50 stock holdings. Its largest concentration of holdings is in the West (17 percent of assets), the Midwest (15 percent), and the Northeast (14 percent). Multiregional banks make up 12 percent of the portfolio, and money centers account for 11.5 percent. The fund has had a fairly modest trading record with a 43 percent annual portfolio ratio.

PERFORMANCE

The fund has enjoyed outstanding growth over the past five years. Including dividends and capital gains distributions, the Fidelity Select Regional Banks Portfolio has provided a total return for the past five years (through early 1998) of 220 percent. A $10,000 investment in 1993 would have grown to $32,200 five years later. Average annual return: 26.2 percent.

CONSISTENCY

The fund has been fairly consistent, outpacing the Dow Jones Industrial Average in three of the past five years (and it was even with the Dow through the first few months of 1998). Its biggest gains came in 1995 and 1997 when it climbed 46.8 percent and 45.6 percent, respectively.

FEES/SERVICES/MANAGEMENT

The fund has a low front-end load of 3 percent and a maximum redemption fee of 0.75 percent if it's sold out within 29 days. Its annual expense ratio of 1.46 percent (with no 12b-1 fee) is about average among all funds.

The fund offers many of the standard services, such as retirement account availability and automatic checking account deduction. Its minimum initial investment of $2,500 and minimum subsequent investment of $250 are a little high compared with other funds.

Christine Schaulat was appointed fund manager in 1998. The Fidelity family of funds includes more than 230 funds.

Top Ten Stock Holdings

1. BankAmerica
2. U.S. Bancorp
3. NationsBank
4. Bank of New York
5. Banc One
6. Wells Fargo
7. First Chicago NBD
8. Norwest
9. Comerica
10. American Express

Asset mix: common stocks—87%; cash/equivalents—13%
Total net assets: $1.35 billion
Dividend yield: 0.58%

Fees

Front-end load	3.00%
Redemption fee	0.75
12b-1 fee	*None*
Management fee	0.61
Other expenses	0.85
Total annual expense	1.46%
Minimum initial investment	$2,500
Minimum subsequent investment	$250

Services

Telephone exchanges	*Yes*
Automatic withdrawal	*Yes*
Automatic checking deduction	*Yes*
Retirement plan/IRA	*Yes*
Instant redemption	*Yes*
Financial statements	*Semiannual*
Income distributions	*Semiannual*
Capital gains distributions	*Semiannual*
Portfolio manager: years	0
Number of funds in family	235

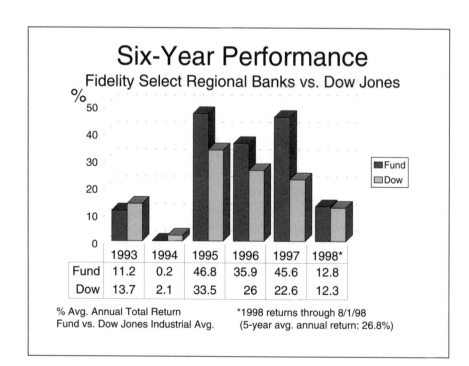

Six-Year Performance
Fidelity Select Regional Banks vs. Dow Jones

	1993	1994	1995	1996	1997	1998*
Fund	11.2	0.2	46.8	35.9	45.6	12.8
Dow	13.7	2.1	33.5	26	22.6	12.3

% Avg. Annual Total Return
Fund vs. Dow Jones Industrial Avg.

*1998 returns through 8/1/98
(5-year avg. annual return: 26.8%)

65

Fidelity Select Software and Computer Services Portfolio

SECTOR

Fidelity Investments
82 Devonshire Street
Boston, MA 02109

Fund manager: John Porter
Fund objective: Sector
Web site: www.fidelity.com

Toll-free: 800-544-8888
In-state: 801-534-1910
Fax: 617-476-9753

Performance	★ ★ ★ ★ ★
Consistency	★ ★
Fees/Services	★ ★ ★
FSCSX	**10 Points**

The computer revolution continues to drive the growth of the software and computer services sector. With software applications being developed for a broad range of personal, professional, industrial, and commercial uses, the software industry has been one of the fastest growing areas of the economy the past few years. The Fidelity Select Software and Computer Services Portfolio has ridden the crest of that growth by posting returns of about 23 percent per year over the past ten years. A $10,000 investment in the fund ten years ago would now be worth about $80,000.

The fund invests in a wide variety of computer and software stocks, such as Microsoft, Oracle, Cadence Design Systems, Intel, and Compaq as well as in some communications equipment manufacturers and some computer services companies, such as Electronic Data Systems, Accustaff, and Computer Horizons. About 60 percent of the fund's assets are invested in computer services and software stocks. Other leading sectors include computers and office equipment, 12 percent, and electronics companies, 9 percent.

Fund manager John Porter says the future should be promising for the software sector. "Software companies continue to roll out new products with high returns that are good investments for corporations as they reduce complexity and enhance productivity." He warns, however, that "intensive competition has tightened the profit margins of some companies, particularly those competing for large contracts. However, the fundamental outlook still is very strong for both software and computer services."

The fund manager maintains a very aggressive trading policy and so the annual turnover ratio is 279 percent.

PERFORMANCE

The fund has enjoyed outstanding growth over the past five years. Including dividends and capital gains distributions, the Fidelity Select Software and Computer Services Portfolio has provided a total return for the past five years (through early 1998) of 217 percent. A $10,000 investment in 1993 would have grown to $32,000 five years later. Average annual return: 26 percent.

CONSISTENCY

The fund has been somewhat inconsistent, trailing the Dow Jones Industrial Average in three of the past five years (but it outperformed the market through the first few months of 1998). Its biggest gain came in 1995, when it jumped 46.3 percent (compared with a 33.5 percent rise in the Dow).

FEES/SERVICES/MANAGEMENT

The fund has a low front-end load of 3 percent and a maximum redemption fee of 0.75 percent if sold out within 29 days. Its annual expense ratio of 1.54 percent (with no 12b-1 fee) is about average among all funds.

The fund offers many of the standard services, such as retirement account availability and automatic checking account deduction. Its minimum initial investment of $2,500 and minimum subsequent investment of $250 are a little high compared with other funds.

John Porter has been with Fidelity since 1995 and has managed the fund only since 1997. The Fidelity family of funds includes more than 230 funds.

Top Ten Stock Holdings

1. Microsoft
2. PeopleSoft
3. BMC Software
4. Oracle
5. Compuware

6. Computer Associates
7. Siebel Systems
8. Electronic Data Systems
9. HBO
10. Automatic Data Processing

Asset mix: common stocks—93%; cash/equivalents—7%
Total net assets: $426 million
Dividend yield: none

Fees

Front-end load	3.00%
Redemption fee	0.75
12b-1 fee	*None*
Management fee	0.60
Other expenses	0.94
Total annual expense	1.54%
Minimum initial investment	$2,500
Minimum subsequent investment	$250

Services

Telephone exchanges	*Yes*
Automatic withdrawal	*Yes*
Automatic checking deduction	*Yes*
Retirement plan/IRA	*Yes*
Instant redemption	*Yes*
Financial statements	*Semiannual*
Income distributions	*Semiannual*
Capital gains distributions	*Semiannual*
Portfolio manager: years	1
Number of funds in family	235

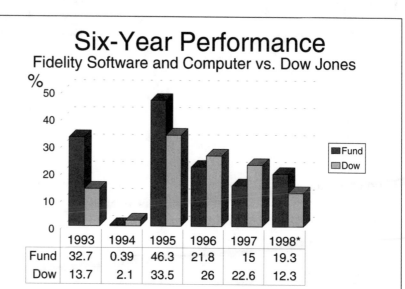

Six-Year Performance
Fidelity Software and Computer vs. Dow Jones

	1993	1994	1995	1996	1997	1998*
Fund	32.7	0.39	46.3	21.8	15	19.3
Dow	13.7	2.1	33.5	26	22.6	12.3

% Avg. Annual Total Return
Fund vs. Dow Jones Industrial Avg.

*1998 returns through 8/1/98
(5-year avg. annual return: 22.2%)

66
Fidelity Select Technology Portfolio

SECTOR

Fidelity Investments
82 Devonshire Street
Boston, MA 02109

Fund manager: Adam Hetnarski
Fund objective: Sector
Web site: www.fidelity.com

Toll-free: 800-544-8888
In-state: 801-534-1910
Fax: 617-476-9753

Performance	★ ★ ★ ★
Consistency	★ ★ ★
Fees/Services	★ ★ ★
FSPTX	**10 Points**

The Fidelity Select Technology Portfolio is a fund that's been in the right place at the right time. As the high-tech market has boomed, so has the fund's performance. The fund, which invests in a broad range of technology issues, includes a combination of large companies such as Compaq, IBM, and Digital Equipment, and emerging growth stocks, such as Cisco Systems, PeopleSoft, Electronic Arts, and Linear Technology. The fund's strategy with the larger stocks has been to buy when the gross profit margin is high and the stock price is low based on the PE ratio and other valuation measures. The fund takes a different approach with the small stocks, seeking companies with soaring earnings growth.

Over the past ten years the fund has grown at about 21 percent per year. A $10,000 investment in the fund ten years ago would now be worth about $65,000. Fund manager Adam Hetnarski takes a very aggressive portfolio trading approach that results in an annual portfolio turnover ratio of 549 percent.

In all, the fund has about 100 stock holdings. Its leading sectors include computers and office equipment, 18 percent of total assets; electronic instruments, 29 percent; electronics, 15 percent; and computer services and software, 5 percent.

Hetnarski has high expectations for the future of the technology sector. "Technology companies have better operating margins, return on equity, and return on assets than most other segments. They are the beneficiaries of government, corporate, and consumer spending as technological change becomes more of a driving force behind the growing global economy."

PERFORMANCE

The fund has enjoyed excellent growth over the past five years. Including dividends and capital gains distributions, the Fidelity Select Technology Portfolio has provided a total return for the past five years (through early 1998) of 198 percent. A $10,000 investment in 1993 would have grown to about $30,000 five years later. Average annual return: 24.4 percent.

CONSISTENCY

The fund has been fairly consistent, outpacing the Dow Jones Industrial Average in three of the past five years (and again through the first few months of 1998). Its biggest gain came in 1995, when it jumped 43.8 percent (compared with a 33.5 percent rise in the Dow).

FEES/SERVICES/MANAGEMENT

The fund has a low front-end load of 3 percent and a maximum redemption fee of 0.75 percent if it's sold out within 29 days. Its annual expense ratio of 1.49 percent (with no 12b-1 fee) is about average among all funds.

The fund offers many of the standard services, such as retirement account availability and automatic checking account deduction. Its minimum initial investment of $2,500 and minimum subsequent investment of $250 are a little high compared with other funds.

Adam Hetnarski has been with Fidelity since 1991 but has managed the fund only since 1996. The Fidelity family of funds includes more than 230 funds.

Top Ten Stock Holdings

1. Compaq Computer
2. Applied Materials
3. Teradyne
4. Advantest
5. KLA-Tencor

6. Lucent Technologies
7. Lam Research
8. Read-Rite
9. Western Digital
10. Silicon Graphics

Asset mix: common stocks—92%; cash/equivalents—8%
Total net assets: $526.5 million
Dividend yield: none

Fees

Front-end load	3.00%
Redemption fee	0.75
12b-1 fee	*None*
Management fee	0.60
Other expenses	0.89
Total annual expense	1.49%
Minimum initial investment	$2,500
Minimum subsequent investment	$250

Services

Telephone exchanges	*Yes*
Automatic withdrawal	*Yes*
Automatic checking deduction	*Yes*
Retirement plan/IRA	*Yes*
Instant redemption	*Yes*
Financial statements	*Semiannual*
Income distributions	*Semiannual*
Capital gains distributions	*Semiannual*
Portfolio manager: years	2
Number of funds in family	235

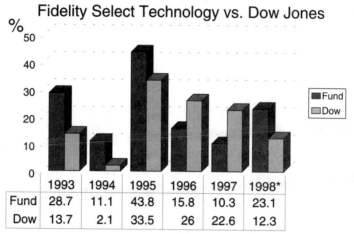

Six-Year Performance
Fidelity Select Technology vs. Dow Jones

	1993	1994	1995	1996	1997	1998*
Fund	28.7	11.1	43.8	15.8	10.3	23.1
Dow	13.7	2.1	33.5	26	22.6	12.3

% Avg. Annual Total Return
Fund vs. Dow Jones Industrial Avg.

*1998 returns through 8/1/98
(5-year return avg. annual: 22.6%)

67
PaineWebber Financial Services Growth Fund

SECTOR

PaineWebber Funds
1285 Avenue of the Americas, 14th Floor
New York, NY 10019

Fund manager: Karen Levy Finkel
Fund objective: Sector

Toll-free: 800-647-1568
In-state: 201-902-7341
Fax: 201-713-4715

Performance	★ ★ ★ ★
Consistency	★ ★ ★
Fees/Services	★ ★ ★
PREAX	**10 Points**

The financial services sector has been one of the top-performing industries of this decade, which has helped the PaineWebber Financial Services Growth Fund achieve outstanding success. Founded in 1986, the fund invests in a variety of regional banks, insurance companies, money centers, and other financial institutions. Over the past ten years, the fund has posted an average annual return of about 24 percent. A $10,000 investment in the fund ten years ago would now be worth about $83,000.

Fund manager Karen Levy Finkel, who has been with the fund since it opened, has sifted out many of the most successful banks from each region of the country. Among the fund's holdings are FINOVA Group, First Empire State, and ReliaStar Financial. Finkel takes a very conservative trading approach. The annual portfolio turnover ratio is 40 percent.

The fund focuses on stocks of banks that are located in geographic regions experiencing strong growth, are well managed and currently providing above-average returns on assets and shareholder equity, and are expanding into new services or geographic areas. Among the leading sectors in the portfolio are regional banks, 38 percent of assets; financial services, 10 percent; insurance, 20 percent; thrifts, 8 percent; and real estate, 4 percent.

PERFORMANCE

The fund has enjoyed excellent growth over the last five years. Including dividends and capital gains distributions, the PaineWebber Financial Services Growth Fund has provided a total return for the last five years (through mid-1998) of 189 percent. A $10,000 investment in 1993 would have grown to about $29,000 five years later. Average annual return: 23.7 percent.

CONSISTENCY

The fund has been fairly consistent recently, outperforming the Dow Jones Industrial Average in three of the last five years through 1997 (but it trailed the Dow through the first few months of 1998). Its biggest gain came in 1995, when it moved up 47.7 percent (compared with a 33.5 percent rise in the Dow).

FEES/SERVICES/MANAGEMENT

The fund has a front-end load of 4.50 percent. Its total annual expense ratio of 1.52 percent (including a 0.25 percent 12b-1 fee) compares favorably with other funds.

The fund offers some of the standard services such as automatic withdrawal and automatic checking account deduction. Its minimum initial investment of $1,000 and minimum subsequent investment of $100 compare favorably with other funds.

Karen Levy Finkel has managed the fund since 1986. The PaineWebber family of funds includes 21 funds.

Top Ten Stock Holdings

1. FINOVA Group
2. Ambac Financial Group
3. Enhance Financial Services Group
4. Life Re
5. First Empire State
6. ReliaStar Financial
7. Westamerica Bancorporation
8. Comerica
9. Countrywide Credit Industry
10. CB Commercial Real Estate Services

Asset mix: common stocks—87%; cash/equivalents—13%
Total net assets: $167 million
Dividend yield: 0.56%

Fees

Front-end load	4.50%
Redemption fee	*None*
12b-1 fee	0.25
Management fee	0.70
Other expenses	0.57
Total annual expense	1.52%
Minimum initial investment	$1,000
Minimum subsequent investment	$100

Services

Telephone exchanges	*No*
Automatic withdrawal	*Yes*
Automatic checking deduction	*Yes*
Retirement plan/IRA	*No*
Instant redemption	*Yes*
Financial statements	*Semiannual*
Income distributions	*Annual*
Capital gains distributions	*Annual*
Portfolio manager: years	13
Number of funds in family	21

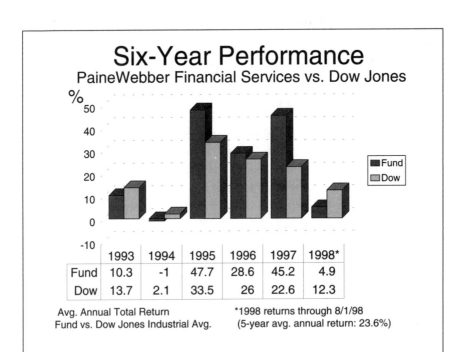

Six-Year Performance
PaineWebber Financial Services vs. Dow Jones

	1993	1994	1995	1996	1997	1998*
Fund	10.3	-1	47.7	28.6	45.2	4.9
Dow	13.7	2.1	33.5	26	22.6	12.3

Avg. Annual Total Return
Fund vs. Dow Jones Industrial Avg.

*1998 returns through 8/1/98
(5-year avg. annual return: 23.6%)

68
John Hancock Global Technology Fund

John Hancock Funds
101 Huntington Avenue
Boston, MA 02199-7603

Fund managers: Barry J. Gordon
and Marc Klee
Fund objective: Sector
Web site: www.jhancock.com/funds

Toll-free: 800-225-5291
In-state: 617-375-1500
Fax: 617-375-1819

Performance	★ ★ ★ ★
Consistency	★ ★ ★
Fees/Services	★ ★ ★
NTTFX	**10 Points**

The John Hancock Global Technology Fund has been an outstanding fund for investors, but the name is very misleading. Technology, yes; global, no way! Not one stock in its top 10 holdings comes from outside the U.S., and well under 10 percent of its total assets are invested in foreign stocks.

Fund managers Barry Gordon and Marc Klee take a top-down stock selection approach, first identifying the fastest growing sectors of the technology area, then ferreting out the most promising stocks within the sector. Gordon and Klee take a fairly conservative trading approach. The annual portfolio turnover ratio is 64 percent. Over the past ten years, the fund has posted an average annual return of 16 percent. A $10,000 investment in the fund ten years ago would now be worth about $44,000.

The fund has about 70 stock holdings in all, heavily weighted in the computer area. Leading sectors include computer software, 23 percent of total assets; computer services, 8 percent; semiconductors, 19 percent; other computer equipment, 21 percent; telecommunications, 10 percent; and transport companies, 6 percent.

PERFORMANCE

The fund has enjoyed strong growth over the last five years. Including dividends and capital gains distributions, the Global Technology Fund has provided a total return for the last five years (through mid-1998) of 184 percent. A $10,000 investment in 1993 would have grown to about $28,000 five years later. Average annual return: 23.3 percent.

CONSISTENCY

The fund has been fairly consistent recently, outperforming the Dow Jones Industrial Average in three of the last five years through 1997 (and it led the Dow through the first few months of 1998). Its biggest gain came in 1995, when it moved up 46.5 percent (compared with a 33.5 percent rise in the Dow).

FEES/SERVICES/MANAGEMENT

The fund has a front-end load of 5 percent. Its total annual expense ratio of 1.51 percent (including a 0.30 percent 12b-1 fee) is in line with other funds.

The fund offers all the standard services, such as retirement account availability, automatic withdrawal, and automatic checking account deduction. Its minimum initial investment of $1,000 and minimum subsequent investment of $25 compare favorably with other funds.

The management team of Barry Gordon and Marc Klee has managed the fund since 1983. The John Hancock family of funds includes 31 funds and allows shareholders to switch from fund to fund by telephone.

Top Ten Stock Holdings

1. Computer Associates
2. Microsoft
3. Cisco Systems
4. UAL
5. Intel
6. America Online
7. AMR
8. Network Associates
9. EMC
10. Cadence Design Systems

Asset mix: common stocks—91%; cash/equivalents—9%
Total net assets: $170 million
Dividend yield: none

Fees

Front-end load	5.00%
Redemption fee	*None*
12b-1 fee	0.30
Management fee	0.79
Other expenses	0.42
Total annual expense	1.51%
Minimum initial investment	$1,000
Minimum subsequent investment	$25

Services

Telephone exchanges	*Yes*
Automatic withdrawal	*Yes*
Automatic checking deduction	*Yes*
Retirement plan/IRA	*Yes*
Instant redemption	*Yes*
Financial statements	*Quarterly*
Income distributions	*Annual*
Capital gains distributions	*Annual*
Portfolio manager: years	15
Number of funds in family	31

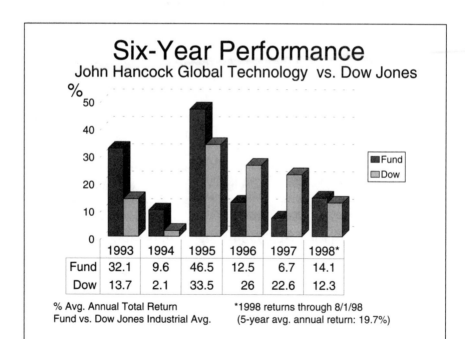

Six-Year Performance
John Hancock Global Technology vs. Dow Jones

	1993	1994	1995	1996	1997	1998*
Fund	32.1	9.6	46.5	12.5	6.7	14.1
Dow	13.7	2.1	33.5	26	22.6	12.3

% Avg. Annual Total Return
Fund vs. Dow Jones Industrial Avg.

*1998 returns through 8/1/98
(5-year avg. annual return: 19.7%)

69

GAM International Fund

Global Asset Management Funds
135 East 57th Street, 25th Floor
New York, NY 10022

INTERNATIONAL

Fund manager: John R. Horseman
Fund objective: International equity
Web site: www.usinfo.gam.com

Toll-free: 800-426-4685
In-state: 212-407-4700
Fax: 212-407-4684

Performance	★ ★ ★ ★
Consistency	★ ★
Fees/Services	★ ★ ★
GAMNX	**9 Points**

The GAM International Fund spreads its assets around the globe, investing in some of the world's top blue chip stocks. Among its holdings are Hong Kong and China Gas, L'Oreal of France, Canon and Sony of Japan, Nestlé of Switzerland, and the Bank of Scotland. In all, the fund has stock holdings in about 12 countries. While the asset mix is subject to wide swings, the fund recently had about 85 percent of its assets in stocks.

Over the past ten years, the fund has posted an average annual return of about 18 percent. A $10,000 investment in the fund ten years ago would now be worth about $53,000.

The fund has about 50 stock holdings in all. Leading industrial sectors include banking, 20 percent of assets; health and personal care, 14 percent; insurance, 9 percent; transportation, 6 percent; and business and public services, 7 percent. Geographically, 35 percent of the fund's assets are in British stocks, 17 percent in Japanese stocks, 12 percent in French stocks, and 10 percent in Swiss stocks.

Fund manager John Horseman takes a fairly conservative trading approach. The annual portfolio turnover ratio is 82 percent.

PERFORMANCE

The fund has enjoyed outstanding growth over the last five years. Including dividends and capital gains distributions, the GAM International Fund has provided a total return for the last five years (through mid-1998) of 203 percent. A $10,000 investment in 1993 would have grown to about $30,000 five years later. Average annual return: 24.8 percent.

CONSISTENCY

Understandably, the fund does not move in step with the U.S. market. It has outperformed the Dow Jones Industrial Average in only two of the last five years through 1997 (but it led the Dow through the first few months of 1998). Its biggest gain came in 1993, when it moved up 80 percent.

FEES/SERVICES/MANAGEMENT

The GAM International Fund has a front-end load of 5 percent. The fund's total annual expense ratio of 1.68 percent (including a 0.30 percent 12b-1 fee) is in line with other funds.

The fund offers all the standard services, such as retirement account availability, automatic withdrawal, and automatic checking account deduction. Its minimum initial investment of $5,000 and minimum subsequent investment of $500 are high compared with other funds.

John Horseman has managed the fund since 1990. The GAM family of funds includes eight funds and allows shareholders to switch from fund to fund by telephone.

Top Ten Stock Holdings

1. Bank of Scotland	6. Fortis AMEV
2. Barclays	7. National Express Group
3. Novartis	8. Prudential UK
4. Roche Holding Genusscheine	9. Severn Trent UK
5. Credit Lyonnais	10. Canon

Asset mix: common stocks—86%; adjustable rate index notes—5%; bond/currency warrants—3%; cash/equivalents—6%
Total net assets: $1.8 billion
Dividend yield: 0.54%

Fees

Front-end load	5.00%
Redemption fee	*None*
12b-1 fee	0.30
Management fee	1.00
Other expenses	0.38
Total annual expense	1.68%
Minimum initial investment	$5,000
Minimum subsequent investment	$500

Services

Telephone exchanges	*Yes*
Automatic withdrawal	*Yes*
Automatic checking deduction	*Yes*
Retirement plan/IRA	*Yes*
Instant redemption	*Yes*
Financial statements	*Semiannual*
Income distributions	*Annual*
Capital gains distributions	*Annual*
Portfolio manager: years	8
Number of funds in family	8

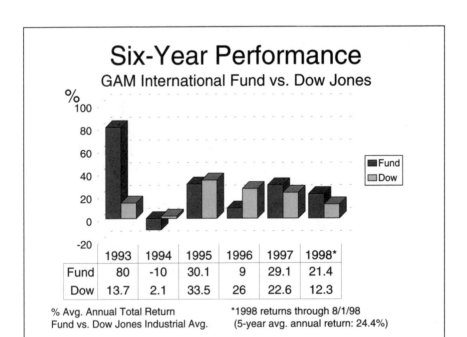

Six-Year Performance
GAM International Fund vs. Dow Jones

	1993	1994	1995	1996	1997	1998*
Fund	80	-10	30.1	9	29.1	21.4
Dow	13.7	2.1	33.5	26	22.6	12.3

% Avg. Annual Total Return
Fund vs. Dow Jones Industrial Avg.

*1998 returns through 8/1/98
(5-year avg. annual return: 24.4%)

LONG TERM

Alliance Premier Growth Fund "A"

Alliance Funds Group
1345 Avenue of the Americas
New York, NY 10105

Fund manager: Alfred Harrison
Fund objective: Long-term growth
Web site: www.alliancecapital.com

Toll-free: 800-221-5672
In-state: 201-319-4000
Fax: 201-319-4139

Performance	★ ★ ★ ★
Consistency	★ ★
Fees/Services	★ ★ ★
APGAX	**9 Points**

The Alliance Premier Growth Fund invests in an all-star cast of well-established blue chip growth companies, such as Wal-Mart, Coca-Cola, Johnson & Johnson, and General Electric. Fund manager Alfred Harrison tries to balance the fund's exposure to high-technology stocks with an equal exposure to lower-valued stocks in the financial area. A core portfolio of 25 premier stocks constitutes about 70 percent of the portfolio. The fund has provided outstanding returns the past few years, climbing nearly 24 percent per year over the past five years.

The fund maintains a fairly conservative trading policy and has a 76 percent annual portfolio turnover ratio. It has about 50 stock holdings in all. Leading industrial sectors include technology, 30 percent; financial services, 20 percent; and consumer products and services, 43 percent. The fund includes a handful of foreign stocks.

PERFORMANCE

The fund has enjoyed excellent growth over the last five years. Including dividends and capital gains distributions, the Alliance Premier Growth Fund has provided a total return for the last five years (through mid-1998) of 193 percent. A $10,000 investment in 1993 would have grown to about $29,000 five years later. Average annual return: 24 percent.

CONSISTENCY

The fund tends to be somewhat inconsistent. It trailed the Dow Jones Industrial Average in three of the last five years through 1997 (but it led the Dow through the first few months of 1998). Its biggest gain came in 1995, when it jumped 46.9 percent (compared with a 33.5 percent rise in the Dow).

FEES/SERVICES/MANAGEMENT

The Alliance Premier Growth Fund has a front-end load of 4.25 percent. Its annual expense ratio of 1.57 percent (including a 0.33 percent 12b-1 fee) is in line with other funds.

The fund offers all the standard services, such as retirement account availability, automatic withdrawal, and automatic checking account deduction. Its minimum initial investment of $250 and minimum subsequent investment of $50 compare very favorably with other funds.

Alfred Harrison has managed the fund since 1992. The Alliance family of funds includes more than 50 funds and allows shareholders to switch from fund to fund by telephone.

Top Ten Stock Holdings

1. Philip Morris
2. Nokia
3. Cisco Systems
4. MBNA
5. Compaq Computer
6. Dell Computer
7. Home Depot
8. Pfizer
9. Tyco International
10. UAL

Asset mix: common stocks—93%; cash/equivalents—7%
Total net assets: $407 million
Dividend yield: none

Fees

Front-end load	4.25%
Redemption fee	*None*
12b-1 fee	0.33
Management fee	1.00
Other expenses	0.24
Total annual expense	1.57%
Minimum initial investment	$250
Minimum subsequent investment	$50

Services

Telephone exchanges	*Yes*
Automatic withdrawal	*Yes*
Automatic checking deduction	*Yes*
Retirement plan/IRA	*Yes*
Instant redemption	*Yes*
Financial statements	*Semiannual*
Income distributions	*Annual*
Capital gains distributions	*Annual*
Portfolio manager: years	6
Number of funds in family	53

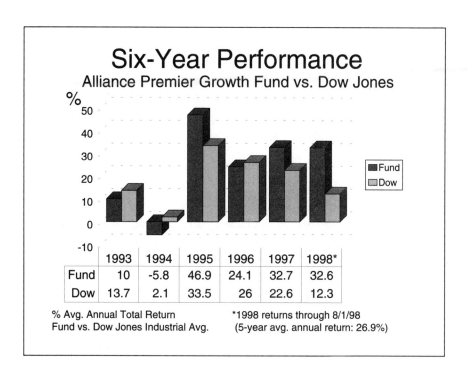

Six-Year Performance
Alliance Premier Growth Fund vs. Dow Jones

	1993	1994	1995	1996	1997	1998*
Fund	10	-5.8	46.9	24.1	32.7	32.6
Dow	13.7	2.1	33.5	26	22.6	12.3

% Avg. Annual Total Return
Fund vs. Dow Jones Industrial Avg.

*1998 returns through 8/1/98
(5-year avg. annual return: 26.9%)

71

Fidelity Destiny I Portfolio

LONG TERM

Fidelity Investments
82 Devonshire Street
Boston, MA 02109

Fund manager: George Vanderheiden
Fund objective: Long-term growth
Web site: www.fidelity.com

Toll-free: 800-544-6666
In-state: 801-534-1910
Fax: 617-476-9743

Performance	★ ★ ★
Consistency	★ ★ ★ ★
Fees/Services	★ ★
FDESX	**9 Points**

Fidelity Destiny I Portfolio manager George Vanderheiden looks for the stocks that most of his colleagues on Wall Street have overlooked or forgotten. "It can be lonely to buy when you don't have much company, but that's when you get the best values. I like to buy stocks when most of the risk has already been squeezed out." Vanderheiden has been with Fidelity since 1971 and has managed the Destiny I fund since 1980. The Destiny I Portfolio (as well as its clone, Destiny II) invests in major blue chip companies with strong earnings growth that are selling at an attractive price. The fund tends to be a little more conservative than other stock funds, which helps its performance in down markets but can dampen its returns in bull markets. Its leading holding recently was U.S. Treasury bonds paying 8.125 percent. The rest of its top ten list, however, was packed with such blue chip stocks such as IBM, Philip Morris, and General Motors.

Over the past ten years, the fund has grown at about 21 percent per year. A $10,000 investment in the fund ten years ago would now be worth about $56,000. With Vanderheiden, the fund has one of the nation's most respected and successful money managers. But with the Destiny I fund, Fidelity makes its investors jump through some very expensive and annoying hoops. Shares may only be purchased through a dollar-cost-averaging plan over a period of at least ten years. And the fees can be staggering. On a $50-a-month plan, investors are assessed a fee of 8.24 percent. The more you pay, the lower the fee. If you plan to invest $10,000 a month in the fund, you'd pay just 0.64 percent.

Vanderheiden takes a fairly conservative approach in managing the fund resulting in a 32 percent annual turnover ratio. But he will sell quickly if a stock appears to be in trouble. "As soon as I see the first crack, I get out. I want to sell my mistakes quickly. For instance, if I buy a stock thinking the company's new concept will do well, and it doesn't work out, I'll sell. Usually the first piece of bad news is not the last piece of bad news."

Vanderheiden is well aware that not all of his picks are going to go up, so he tries to build the largest positions in the stocks he believes have the best long-term promise. "You want to make sure you've put a lot of assets in your 'home run' stocks. I could have a 30–70 win-loss record with my stock picks and still do fabulously if I have the mass of my assets in the good stocks."

In selecting stocks, Vanderheiden tries to look beyond the sizzle. "Wall Street lives on perception," he says. Sometimes those perceptions are responsible for pushing the price of stocks of certain industries beyond reasonable levels. "I try to avoid fads. When the cellular industry got hot a few years ago, I didn't know how to value those stocks. They had no earnings."

Vanderheiden has put together the following top ten list of investment tips (reprinted with permission).

Ten Commandments for Reaching Financial Heaven

1. *Thou shalt avoid the BIG loss.* When you buy a stock, don't be blinded by the upside potential and ignore the downside risk. Moderate gains every year are better than big gains and big losses. Remember, if you start with $100 and you're up 50 percent one year and down 50 percent the next, you're left with only $75. (Corollary: There is no limit to how bad things can get.)
2. *Thou shalt develop conviction in your ideas.* Write down your reasons for buying a stock and if a stock goes down for a temporary or unrelated reason, you won't be panicked out of it. (Corollary: Where all think alike, no one thinks very much.)
3. *Thou shalt invest with the person.* The business world is full of successful managers and proven moneymakers, and you can

become their partners for the mere price of a stock. Stan Gault is a talented, GE-trained manager who helped turn Rubbermaid into a premier growth company. The day he announced he was joining Goodyear, its stock went from $25 to $29. It never saw $29 again and went straight to $75 over the next nine months. (Corollary: Trust everyone, but cut the cards.)

4. *Thou shalt honor pricing power.* Pricing power is the ability of companies to raise their prices well in excess of their costs or inflation. Companies with improving pricing power are ones to own, and companies with deteriorating pricing power are ones to sell. (Corollary: The price of a dinner varies inversely with the amount of light.)

5. *Thou shalt respect the force of government action.* As a government directs the full force of its resources at an objective, invest with the objective and not counter to it. When the U.S. government entered the space race in 1957, it launched a great technology bull market that lasted for over a decade. The advent of Medicare in 1964 launched a multiyear bull market in health care stocks. (Corollary: Government expands to absorb revenue and then some.)

6. *Thou shalt recognize fear and greed in yourselves and in others and act accordingly.* Someone once said, "The stock market is only distantly related to economics; it is a function of fear, apprehension, and greed, all superimposed on a business cycle." The more gut-wrenching a decision, the bigger the potential for capital gains. (Corollary: The chief cause of problems is solutions.)

7. *Thou shalt learn how to live with uncertainty and failure.* The only certainty about the stock market is that there is none. Every successful investor constantly makes mistakes. Don't be afraid of failure. While Babe Ruth had 714 homers, he also had 1,330 strikeouts. (Corollary: The person who can smile when things fail has thought of someone else to blame.)

8. *Thou shalt avoid investment bias.* A good stock can be found anywhere, whether it is a cyclical stock, a growth stock, a value stock, or a high yielder. (Corollary: A bird in the hand is safer than overhead.)

9. *Thou shalt not be frozen by inertia when events change.* Most investors don't recognize turning points and wrongly stay on their existing course after the dynamics have clearly changed. After the Allies attacked Iraq on January 16, 1991, the market surged 115

points instead of going down as everyone expected. Something changed, and the market moved up more than 700 points over the next two years. (Corollary: When in charge, ponder. When in trouble, delegate. When in doubt, mumble.)

10. *Thou shalt have patience.* Start with modest expectations about your stocks and be prepared to be patient. In 1919, Coca-Cola went public and gave 5,000 shares of its stock (worth $110,000) as part of the underwriting fee to the two underwriters, J.P. Morgan Bank and the Trust Company of Georgia (now SunTrust Banks). J. P. Morgan sold its stock, but SunTrust kept its original shares. After years of growth and stock splits, the stock now amounts to 24 million shares worth $900 million. (Corollary: Friends may come and go, but enemies accumulate.)

Final rule: As George Bernard Shaw wrote, "There are no golden rules." In other words, once you think you've found the key to the market, someone always comes along and changes the lock. Successful investing requires imagination, independent thinking, patience, and a touch of contrariness rather than a mechanistic following of rules.

PERFORMANCE

The fund has enjoyed outstanding growth over the past five years. Including dividends and capital gains distributions, the Fidelity Destiny 1 Portfolio has provided a total return for the past five years (through early 1998) of 185 percent. A $10,000 investment in 1993 would have grown to $28,500 five years later. Average annual return: 23.3 percent.

CONSISTENCY

The fund has been consistent recently, outperforming the Dow Jones Industrial Average in four of the past five years through 1997 (and it was about even with the Dow through the first few months of 1998). Its biggest gain came in 1995, when it jumped 37 percent (compared with a 33.5 percent rise in the Dow).

FEES/SERVICES/MANAGEMENT   ★ ★

As noted above, the fund has a maximum front-end load of 8.24 percent. It has a very low annual expense ratio of about 0.40 percent (with no 12b-1 fee).

The fund offers many of the standard services, such as retirement account availability and automatic checking account deduction. It has a minimum initial investment requirement of just $50—but only if you are willing to sign up for at least ten years of monthly contributions.

The Fidelity family of funds includes more than 230 funds.

Top Ten Stock Holdings

1. U.S. Treasury bonds
2. Fannie Mae
3. Philip Morris
4. Fleet Financial Group
5. General Motors
6. FHLMC
7. Columbia/HCA Healthcare
8. IBM
9. Wal-Mart
10. Vodafone Group (ADR)

Asset mix: common stocks—84%; corporate bonds—11%; cash/equivalents—5%
Total net assets: $6.14 billion
Dividend yield: 1.67%

Fees

Front-end load (max)	8.24%
Redemption fee	*None*
12b-1 fee	*None*
Management fee	0.39
Other expenses	0.00
Total annual expense	0.39%
Minimum initial investment	$50/month
Minimum subsequent investment	$50/month

Services

Telephone exchanges	*Yes*
Automatic withdrawal	*Yes*
Automatic checking deduction	*Yes*
Retirement plan/IRA	*Yes*
Instant redemption	*Yes*
Financial statements	*Semiannual*
Income distributions	*Annual*
Capital gains distributions	*Annual*
Portfolio manager: years	18
Number of funds in family	235

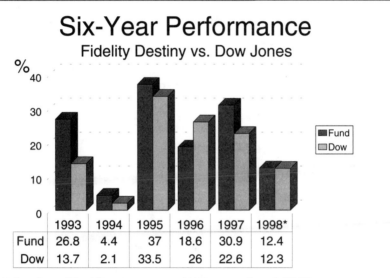

Six-Year Performance
Fidelity Destiny vs. Dow Jones

	1993	1994	1995	1996	1997	1998*
Fund	26.8	4.4	37	18.6	30.9	12.4
Dow	13.7	2.1	33.5	26	22.6	12.3

% Avg. Annual Total Return
Fund vs. Dow Jones Industrial Avg.

*1998 returns through 8/1/98
(5-year avg. annual return: 22.4%)

72
Fidelity Blue Chip Growth Fund

LONG TERM

Fidelity Investments
82 Devonshire Street
Boston, MA 02109

Fund manager: John McDowell
Fund objective: Long-term growth
Web site: www.fidelity.com

Toll-free: 800-544-6666
In-state: 801-534-1910
Fax: 617-476-9743

Performance	★ ★ ★
Consistency	★ ★ ★
Fees/Services	★ ★ ★
FBGRX	**9 Points**

The Fidelity Blue Chip Growth Fund invests in some of the largest, most well-known names in corporate America. Its largest holdings include such corporate giants as Microsoft, General Electric, Merck, Bristol-Myers, and Procter & Gamble. Since its inception in 1988, the fund has grown at an average annual rate of nearly 22 percent. A $10,000 investment in the fund when it opened would have grown to about $61,000 over the next nine years.

The fund's strategy is a diversified portfolio of established companies that maintains at least 65 percent of assets in blue chip stocks. Most of its stock holdings are included in the Standard and Poor's 500, although the fund may also invest in some smaller, emerging companies. Fund manager John McDowell, who has been with the fund since 1996, maintains a fairly modest trading policy. The annual portfolio turnover ratio is about 51 percent.

In all, the fund has more than 250 stock holdings. It is well diversified across a range of industries, although its heaviest weighting is in the high-tech area. Health-related stocks account for about 18 percent of its holdings, while other technology issues make up about 20 percent of the portfolio. The other leading segment, which accounts for about 12 percent of the portfolio, is financial services.

Because of its long run of success, the fund has become very popular with investors, and its assets have grown to more than $13 billion.

PERFORMANCE

The fund has enjoyed outstanding growth over the past five years. Including dividends and capital gains distributions, the Fidelity Blue Chip Growth Fund has provided a total return for the past five years (through early 1998) of 181 percent. A $10,000 investment in 1993 would have grown to $28,100 five years later. Average annual return: 23 percent.

CONSISTENCY

The fund has been fairly consistent recently, outperforming the Dow Jones Industrial Average in three of the past five years through 1997 (and it led the Dow through the first few months of 1998). Its biggest gain came in 1995, when it jumped 28.4 percent (compared with a 33.5 percent rise in the Dow).

FEES/SERVICES/MANAGEMENT

The fund has a low front-end load of 3 percent. Its low annual expense ratio of just 0.80 percent (with no 12b-1 fee) compares very favorably with other funds.

The fund offers many of the standard services, such as retirement account availability and automatic checking account deduction, but it does not offer an automatic withdrawal plan. Its minimum initial investment of $2,500 and minimum subsequent investment of $250 are a little high compared with other funds.

John McDowell has managed the fund only since 1996. The Fidelity family of funds includes more than 230 funds.

Top Ten Stock Holdings

1. General Electric	6. American Home Products
2. Merck	7. Johnson & Johnson
3. Microsoft	8. Wal-Mart
4. Philip Morris	9. Procter & Gamble
5. Bristol-Myers Squibb	10. Schering-Plough

Asset mix: common stocks—96%; cash/equivalents—4%
Total net assets: $13.43 billion
Dividend yield: 0.54%

Fees

Front-end load	3.00%
Redemption fee	*None*
12b-1 fee	*None*
Management fee	0.51
Other expenses	0.29
Total annual expense	0.80%
Minimum initial investment	$2,500
Minimum subsequent investment	$250

Services

Telephone exchanges	*Yes*
Automatic withdrawal	*No*
Automatic checking deduction	*Yes*
Retirement plan/IRA	*Yes*
Instant redemption	*Yes*
Financial statements	*Semiannual*
Income distributions	*Annual*
Capital gains distributions	*Annual*
Portfolio manager: years	2
Number of funds in family	235

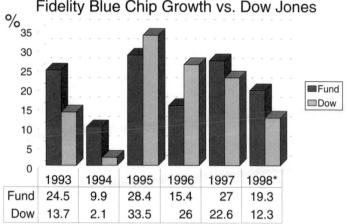

Six-Year Performance
Fidelity Blue Chip Growth vs. Dow Jones

	1993	1994	1995	1996	1997	1998*
Fund	24.5	9.9	28.4	15.4	27	19.3
Dow	13.7	2.1	33.5	26	22.6	12.3

% Avg. Annual Total Return   *1998 returns through 8/1/98
Fund vs. Dow Jones Industrial Avg.   (5-year avg. annual return: 22.2%)

73
MFS Research Fund

LONG TERM

MFS Funds Distributors, Inc.
500 Boylston Street
Boston, MA 02116

Fund manager: Kevin R. Parke
Fund objective: Long-term growth
Web site: www.mfs.com

Toll-free: 800-225-2606
In-state: 617-954-5000
Fax: 617-954-6617

Performance	★ ★ ★ ★
Consistency	★ ★ ★
Fees/Services	★ ★
MFRFX	**9 Points**

At the MFS Research Fund, majority rules. The stocks in the fund—primarily major blue chip growth companies—are selected by a committee of about 25 analysts. The committee meets regularly, with Kevin Parke as monitor, and votes on how to spend its investment dollars. It decides which industries should carry the heaviest weighting in the portfolio and then suggests the best stocks for its assets.

The committee approach has proven to be very successful. Over the past ten years, the fund has provided an annual average return of about 18 percent. A $10,000 investment in the fund ten years ago would now be worth about $53,000. The fund manager takes a fairly conservative trading approach, so the annual portfolio turnover ratio is 79 percent.

The fund invests worldwide across a variety of industrial sectors. It looks for solid companies with outstanding long-term earnings growth, such as Coca-Cola, Gillette, and Microsoft. Its leading industrial sectors (as selected by the committee of 25) include financial services, 20 percent of assets; technology, 20 percent; consumer staples, 14 percent; health care, 10 percent; and retailing, 8 percent.

PERFORMANCE

The fund has enjoyed outstanding growth over the last five years. Including dividends and capital gains distributions, the MFS Research Fund has provided a total return for the last five years (through mid-1998) of 182 percent. A $10,000 investment in 1993 would have grown to about $28,000 five years later. Average annual return: 23.1 percent.

CONSISTENCY

The fund has been fairly consistent recently, outperforming the Dow Jones Industrial Average in two of the last five years (and it was nearly even with the Dow two other years) through 1997 (and it led the Dow through the first few months of 1998). Its biggest gain came in 1995, when it moved up 38.6 percent (compared with a 33.5 percent rise in the Dow).

FEES/SERVICES/MANAGEMENT

The MFS Research Fund has a front-end load of 5.75 percent. Its total annual expense ratio of 0.96 percent (including a 0.34 percent 12b-1 fee) compares very favorably with other funds.

The fund offers all the standard services, such as retirement account availability, automatic withdrawal, and automatic checking account deduction. Its minimum initial investment of $1,000 and minimum subsequent investment of $50 compare favorably with other funds.

The fund management committee has been led by Kevin Parke since 1995. The MFS family of funds includes 50 funds and allows shareholders to switch from fund to fund by telephone.

Top Ten Stock Holdings

1. Microsoft
2. Bristol-Myers Squibb
3. Tyco International
4. Cendant
5. United Technology
6. Novartis
7. Philip Morris
8. United Healthcare
9. Intel
10. Coca-Cola

Asset mix: common stocks—97%; cash/equivalents—3%
Total net assets: $2.4 billion
Dividend yield: none

Fees

Front-end load	5.75%
Redemption fee	*None*
12b-1 fee	0.34
Management fee	0.40
Other expenses	0.22
Total annual expense	0.96%
Minimum initial investment	$1,000
Minimum subsequent investment	$50

Services

Telephone exchanges	*Yes*
Automatic withdrawal	*Yes*
Automatic checking deduction	*Yes*
Retirement plan/IRA	*Yes*
Instant redemption	*Yes*
Financial statements	*Semiannual*
Income distributions	*Annual*
Capital gains distributions	*Annual*
Portfolio manager: years	3
Number of funds in family	50

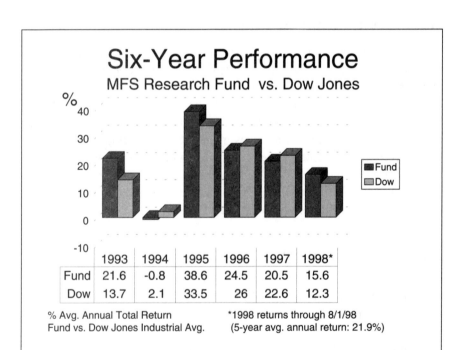

Six-Year Performance
MFS Research Fund vs. Dow Jones

	1993	1994	1995	1996	1997	1998*
Fund	21.6	-0.8	38.6	24.5	20.5	15.6
Dow	13.7	2.1	33.5	26	22.6	12.3

% Avg. Annual Total Return
Fund vs. Dow Jones Industrial Avg.

*1998 returns through 8/1/98
(5-year avg. annual return: 21.9%)

GROWTH

Kemper-Dreman High Return Equity Fund

Kemper Funds
222 South Riverside Plaza
Chicago, IL 60606-5808

Fund manager: David N. Dreman
Fund objective: Growth and income
Web site: www.kemper.com

Toll-free: 800-621-1048
In-state: 312-781-1121
Fax: 312-537-1644

Performance	★ ★ ★
Consistency	★ ★ ★
Fees/Services	★ ★ ★
KDHAX	**9 Points**

Kemper-Dreman High Return Equity Fund manager David Dreman, who has run the fund since its inception in 1988, looks for solid companies—most of which pay dividends—that appear to be undervalued.

Dreman looks for stocks with low PE ratios, a record of solid earnings and dividend growth, reasonable returns on equity and sound finances. As part of this strategy, the fund sells call options on stocks it holds and put options on stocks it may wish to acquire. It also buys and sells securities index futures and options, although most of its assets are in common stocks.

Dreman takes a very conservative buy-and-hold approach resulting in an annual portfolio turnover ratio of just 10 percent. The fund has provided outstanding returns over the past decade, posting an average annual return of about 20 percent the past ten years. A $10,000 investment in the fund ten years ago would now be worth about $65,000.

The fund's 50 stock holdings have a decidedly nontech flavor, primarily because high-tech stocks don't pay dividends. The High Return Equity Fund is one of the few top-performing funds without a single computer stock in its portfolio. It is heavily concentrated in banks and financial stocks, which make up 20 percent of total assets. Other leading segments include consumer products, 17 percent; energy, 14 percent; and health care, 4 percent. Nearly 40 percent of the fund's assets are in money market instruments.

PERFORMANCE

The fund has enjoyed strong growth over the last five years. Including dividends and capital gains distributions, the Kemper-Dreman High Return Equity Fund has provided a total return for the last five years (through mid-1998) of 180 percent. A $10,000 investment in 1993 would have grown to about $28,000 five years later. Average annual return: 22.9 percent.

CONSISTENCY

The fund has been fairly consistent recently, outperforming the Dow Jones Industrial Average in three of the last five years through 1997 (but it trailed the Dow through the first few months of 1998). Its biggest gain came in 1995, when it moved up 46.9 percent (compared with a 33.5 percent rise in the Dow).

FEES/SERVICES/MANAGEMENT

The fund has a front-end load of 5.75 percent. Its total annual expense ratio of 1.21 percent (with no 12b-1 fee) compares favorably with other funds.

The fund offers all the standard services, such as retirement account availability, automatic withdrawal, and automatic checking account deduction. Its minimum initial investment of $1,000 and minimum subsequent investment of $100 are in line with other funds.

David Dreman has managed the fund since 1988. The Kemper fund family includes 37 funds and allows shareholders to switch from fund to fund by telephone.

Top Ten Stock Holdings

1. Philip Morris
2. UST
3. Atlantic Richfield
4. Amoco
5. RJR Nabisco

6. Texaco
7. Fannie Mae
8. FHLMC
9. AT&T
10. Columbia/HCA Healthcare

Asset mix: common stocks—94%; cash/equivalents—6%
Total net assets: $3.2 billion
Dividend yield: 1.75%

Fees

Front-end load	5.75%
Redemption fee	*None*
12b-1 fee	*None*
Management fee	0.74
Other expenses	0.47
Total annual expense	1.21%
Minimum initial investment	$1,000
Minimum subsequent investment	$100

Services

Telephone exchanges	*Yes*
Automatic withdrawal	*Yes*
Automatic checking deduction	*Yes*
Retirement plan/IRA	*Yes*
Instant redemption	*Yes*
Financial statements	*Semiannual*
Income distributions	*Quarterly*
Capital gains distributions	*Annual*
Portfolio manager: years	10
Number of funds in family	37

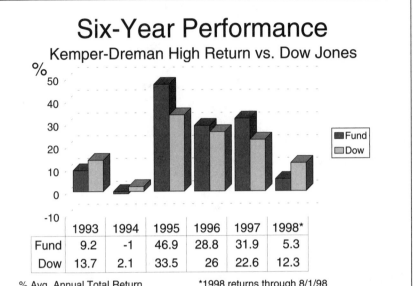

Six-Year Performance
Kemper-Dreman High Return vs. Dow Jones

	1993	1994	1995	1996	1997	1998*
Fund	9.2	-1	46.9	28.8	31.9	5.3
Dow	13.7	2.1	33.5	26	22.6	12.3

% Avg. Annual Total Return   *1998 returns through 8/1/98
Fund vs. Dow Jones Industrial Avg.   (5-year avg. annual return: 22.7%)

AGGRESSIVE

Alliance Quasar Fund

Alliance Funds Group
1345 Avenue of the Americas
New York, NY 10105

Fund managers: Alden Stewart
and Randall Hasse
Fund objective: Aggressive growth
Web site: www.alliancecapital.com

Toll-free: 800-221-5672
In-state: 201-319-4000
Fax: 201-319-4139

Performance	★ ★ ★
Consistency	★ ★ ★
Fees/Services	★ ★ ★
QUASX	**9 Points**

The Alliance Quasar Fund is an aggressive growth fund that has managed to post outstanding long-term returns without becoming overloaded in the high-technology sector. While the fund keeps about 25 percent of its assets in high-tech-related industries, it also has a wide range of holdings in other areas, such as retailing, transportation, apparel, and manufacturing.

"Our strategy is to invest in quality companies selling at undervalued market prices relative to expected earnings, fundamentals, and future prospects," says fund comanager Randall Haase. "We buy stocks of companies that have strong, experienced management teams, quality products selling at reasonable prices and dominant market share with the potential for faster-than-average growth. Currently, we continue to focus on companies with strong earnings growth in both growth and cyclical industries."

Over the past ten years, the fund has grown at an average annual rate of about 15.6 percent. A $10,000 investment in the fund ten years ago would now be worth about $43,000. The fund managers maintain a fairly active trading approach. The annual portfolio turnover ratio is 135 percent.

The fund has about 90 stock holdings in all. Health care stocks account for about 10 percent of the portfolio; technology, 14 percent; consumer products and services, 30 percent; basic industries, 20 percent; and energy stocks, about 6 percent.

PERFORMANCE

The fund has enjoyed strong growth over the last five years. Including dividends and capital gains distributions, the Alliance Quasar Fund has provided a total return for the last five years (through mid-1998) of 179 percent. A $10,000 investment in 1993 would have grown to about $28,000 five years later. Average annual return: 22.8 percent.

CONSISTENCY

The fund has been fairly consistent recently, outperforming the Dow Jones Industrial Average in three of the last five years through 1997 (and it led the Dow through the first few months of 1998). Its biggest gain came in 1995, when it jumped 47.6 percent (compared with a 33.5 percent rise in the Dow).

FEES/SERVICES/MANAGEMENT

The Alliance Quasar Fund has a front-end load of 4.25 percent. Its annual expense ratio of 1.67 percent (including a 0.22 percent 12b-1 fee) compares favorably with other funds.

The fund offers all the standard services, such as retirement account availability, automatic withdrawal, and automatic checking account deduction. Its minimum initial investment of $250 and minimum subsequent investment of $50 compare very favorably with other funds.

Alden Stewart and Randall Haase have managed the fund since 1994. The Alliance family of funds includes more than 50 funds and allows shareholders to switch from fund to fund by telephone.

Top Ten Stock Holdings

1. Parker Drilling	6. Continental Airlines
2. OMI	7. GelTex Pharmaceuticals
3. Mohawk Industries	8. Miller Industries
4. Consolidated Freightways	9. Security Capital Group
5. Budget Group	10. Telephone and Data Systems

Asset mix: common stocks—93%; cash/equivalents—7%
Total net assets: $414 million
Dividend yield: none

Fees

Front-end load	4.25%
Redemption fee	*None*
12b-1 fee	0.22
Management fee	1.16
Other expenses	0.29
Total annual expense	1.67%
Minimum initial investment	$250
Minimum subsequent investment	$50

Services

Telephone exchanges	*Yes*
Automatic withdrawal	*Yes*
Automatic checking deduction	*Yes*
Retirement plan/IRA	*Yes*
Instant redemption	*Yes*
Financial statements	*Semiannual*
Income distributions	*Annual*
Capital gains distributions	*Annual*
Portfolio manager: years	4
Number of funds in family	53

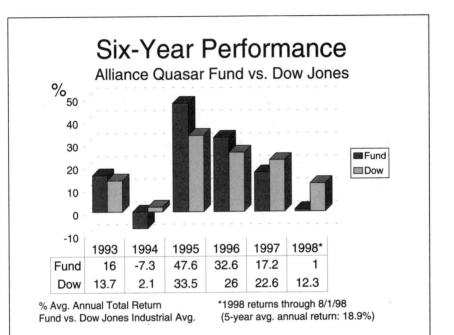

Six-Year Performance
Alliance Quasar Fund vs. Dow Jones

	1993	1994	1995	1996	1997	1998*
Fund	16	-7.3	47.6	32.6	17.2	1
Dow	13.7	2.1	33.5	26	22.6	12.3

% Avg. Annual Total Return   *1998 returns through 8/1/98
Fund vs. Dow Jones Industrial Avg.   (5-year avg. annual return: 18.9%)

GROWTH

Victory Diversified Stock Fund

Victory Funds
127 Public Square, 19th Floor
Cleveland, OH 44114

Fund manager: Lawrence G. Babin
Fund objective: Growth and income

Toll-free: 800-423-0898
In-state: 216-813-4367
Fax: 216-813-4389

Performance	★ ★ ★
Consistency	★ ★ ★
Fees/Services	★ ★ ★
SRVEX	**9 Points**

The Victory Diversified Stock Fund invests primarily in large, well-established companies such as IBM, Pfizer, and American Home Products. And, as its name implies, it is well diversified across a wide range of industrial sectors. Fund manager Lawrence Babin selects stocks based on an analysis of a company's cash flow, book value, quality of management, revenue, and prospects for future earnings and dividend growth.

Babin uses a combination of value and growth-oriented investment strategies to time his buy-and-sell decisions. He takes a fairly conservative trading approach, so the annual portfolio turnover ratio is 63 percent. He stays almost 100 percent invested in stocks under normal circumstances.

Leading industrial sectors include consumer staples, 18 percent of assets; technology, 18 percent; financial services, 15 percent; consumer cyclicals, 14 percent; utilities, 11 percent; energy, 8 percent; and basic materials, 8 percent.

PERFORMANCE

The fund has enjoyed strong growth over the last five years. Including dividends and capital gains distributions, the Victory Diversified Stock Fund has provided a total return for the last five years (through mid-1998) of 175 percent. A $10,000 investment in 1993 would have grown to about $27,500 five years later. Average annual return: 22.4 percent.

CONSISTENCY

The fund has been fairly consistent recently, outperforming the Dow Jones Industrial Average in three of the last five years through 1997 (and it led the Dow through the first few months of 1998). Its biggest gain came in 1995, when it moved up 35.4 percent (compared with a 33.5 percent rise in the Dow).

FEES/SERVICES/MANAGEMENT

The Victory Diversified Stock Fund has a front-end load of 5.75 percent. Its total annual expense ratio of 1.05 percent (with no 12b-1 fee) compares favorably with other funds.

The fund offers all of the standard services, such as retirement account availability, automatic withdrawal, and automatic checking account deduction. Its minimum initial investment of $500 and minimum subsequent investment of $25 compare very favorably with other funds.

Lawrence Babin has managed the fund since 1989. The Victory family of funds includes 18 funds and allows shareholders to switch from fund to fund by telephone.

Top Ten Stock Holdings

1. IBM
2. Pfizer
3. GTE
4. American Home Products
5. Intel
6. Enron
7. MCI Communications
8. Tele-Communications TCI
9. Unocal
10. Avon Products

Asset mix: common stocks—97%; cash/equivalents—4%
Total net assets: $796 million
Dividend yield: none

Fees

Front-end load	5.75%
Redemption fee	*None*
12b-1 fee	*None*
Management fee	0.54
Other expenses	0.51
Total annual expense	1.05%
Minimum initial investment	$500
Minimum subsequent investment	$25

Services

Telephone exchanges	*Yes*
Automatic withdrawal	*Yes*
Automatic checking deduction	*Yes*
Retirement plan/IRA	*Yes*
Instant redemption	*Yes*
Financial statements	*Semiannual*
Income distributions	*Annual*
Capital gains distributions	*Annual*
Portfolio manager: years	9
Number of funds in family	18

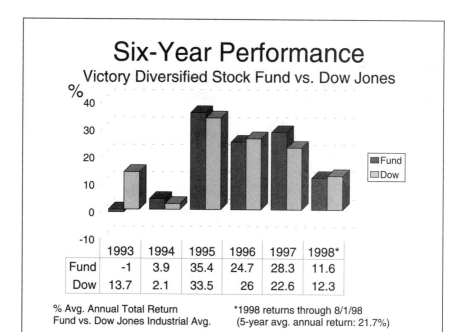

Six-Year Performance
Victory Diversified Stock Fund vs. Dow Jones

	1993	1994	1995	1996	1997	1998*
Fund	-1	3.9	35.4	24.7	28.3	11.6
Dow	13.7	2.1	33.5	26	22.6	12.3

% Avg. Annual Total Return
Fund vs. Dow Jones Industrial Avg.

*1998 returns through 8/1/98
(5-year avg. annual return: 21.7%)

77

MFS Massachusetts Investors Trust

GROWTH

MFS Funds Distributors, Inc.
500 Boylston Street
Boston, MA 02116

Fund managers: Mitchell Dynan,
  Kevin Parke, and John Laupheimer
Fund objective: Growth and income
Web site: www.mfs.com

Toll-free: 800-225-2606
In-state: 617-954-5000
Fax: 617-954-6617

Performance	★ ★ ★
Consistency	★ ★ ★
Fees/Services	★ ★ ★
MITTX	**9 Points**

The MFS Massachusetts Investors Trust has been around since 1924, making it one of the oldest investment vehicles in existence. The trust invests in a diverse cross section of blue chip growth companies such as Bristol-Myers, Gillette, and Lockheed Martin. Over the past ten years, the fund has posted average annual returns of about 19 percent. A $10,000 investment in the fund ten years ago would now be worth about $57,000.

The fund managers take a fairly conservative trading approach, so the fund has a 47 percent annual portfolio turnover ratio. The fund stays nearly 100 percent invested in stocks most of the time. Fund managers Mitchell Dynan, Kevin Parke, and John Laupheimer say they look for high-quality blue chip companies with above-average growth rates that they can buy at a fair price.

The fund maintains a portfolio of about 150 stocks. Foreign stocks account for about 7 percent of the portfolio. Leading industrial sectors include financial services, 26 percent of assets; health care, 12 percent; consumer staples, 11 percent; industrial goods and services, 10 percent; and utilities and communications, 8 percent.

PERFORMANCE

The fund has enjoyed strong growth over the last five years. Including dividends and capital gains distributions, the Investors Trust has provided a total return for the last five years (through mid-1998) of 173 percent. A $10,000 investment in 1993 would have grown to about $27,000 five years later. Average annual return: 22.2 percent.

CONSISTENCY

The fund has been fairly consistent recently, outperforming the Dow Jones Industrial Average in two of the last five years through 1997, and it was nearly even with the Dow the other three years. (It was leading the Dow through the first few months of 1998). Its biggest gain came in 1995, when it moved up 39.3 percent (compared with a 33.5 percent rise in the Dow).

FEES/SERVICES/MANAGEMENT

The Investors Trust has a front-end load of 5.75 percent. Its total annual expense ratio of 0.79 percent (including a 0.33 percent 12b-1 fee) compares very favorably with other funds.

The fund offers all the standard services, such as retirement account availability, automatic withdrawal, and automatic checking account deduction. Its minimum initial investment of $1,000 and minimum subsequent investment of $50 compare favorably with other funds.

All of the fund managers have many years of experience. Dynan has been with MFS since 1986 and joined the management team in 1995; Laupheimer joined MFS in 1981 and has been with the fund since 1992; and Parke has been with MFS since 1985 and with the fund since 1992. The MFS family of funds includes 50 funds and allows shareholders to switch from fund to fund by telephone.

Top Ten Stock Holdings

1. Bristol-Myers Squibb	6. Air Products and Chemicals
2. Norwest	7. Gillette
3. U.S. Bancorp	8. Hartford Financial Services
4. Philip Morris	9. United Technologies
5. British Petroleum	10. Lockheed Martin

Asset mix: common stocks—97%; cash/equivalents—3%
Total net assets: $4.3 billion
Dividend yield: 0.81%

Fees

Front-end load	5.75%
Redemption fee	*None*
12b-1 fee	0.33
Management fee	0.23
Other expenses	0.23
Total annual expense	0.79%
Minimum initial investment	$1,000
Minimum subsequent investment	$50

Services

Telephone exchanges	*Yes*
Automatic withdrawal	*Yes*
Automatic checking deduction	*Yes*
Retirement plan/IRA	*Yes*
Instant redemption	*Yes*
Financial statements	*Semiannual*
Income distributions	*Quarterly*
Capital gains distributions	*Quarterly*
Portfolio manager: years	6
Number of funds in family	50

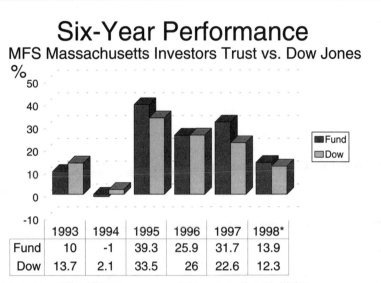

Six-Year Performance
MFS Massachusetts Investors Trust vs. Dow Jones

	1993	1994	1995	1996	1997	1998*
Fund	10	-1	39.3	25.9	31.7	13.9
Dow	13.7	2.1	33.5	26	22.6	12.3

% Avg. Annual Total Return   *1998 returns through 8/1/98
Fund vs. Dow Jones Industrial Avg.   (5-year avg. annual return: 22.4%)

78
IDS Growth Fund

IDS Funds
IDS Tower 10
Minneapolis, MN 55440

LONG TERM

Fund manager: Mitzi Malevich
Fund objective: Long-term growth

Toll-free: 800-328-8300
In-state: 612-671-3733
Fax: 612-671-5113

Performance	★ ★ ★
Consistency	★ ★ ★
Fees/Services	★ ★ ★
INIDX	**9 Points**

IDS Growth Fund manager Mitzi Malevich scans the market for the fastest-growing companies. The result is a portfolio heavily stocked with technology and medical companies. The fund, with assets of just over $3 billion, stays 90 to 100 percent invested in stocks at almost all times. Over the past ten years, the fund has posted an average annual return of about 19 percent. A $10,000 investment in the fund ten years ago would now be worth nearly $60,000.

Although the fund does have stock holdings in a diverse array of industries, technology-related stocks, such as Cisco Systems, Oracle, and Intel, dominate the portfolio. The fund has about 60 stock holdings in all. Leading sectors include computers and office equipment, 18 percent of assets; electronics, 8 percent; communications equipment, 6 percent; health care products and services, 16 percent; and banks and financial services, 12 percent. Foreign stocks make up about 7 percent of the portfolio.

Malevich maintains a conservative buy-and-hold approach that results in an annual portfolio turnover ratio of 24 percent.

PERFORMANCE

The fund has enjoyed strong growth over the last five years. Including dividends and capital gains distributions, the IDS Growth Fund has provided a total return for the last five years (through mid-1998) of 165 percent. A $10,000 investment in 1993 would have grown to about $27,000 five years later. Average annual return: 21.5 percent.

CONSISTENCY

The fund has been fairly consistent recently, outperforming the Dow Jones Industrial Average in two of the last five years through 1997 and nearly matching the market two other years. (It also led the Dow through the first few months of 1998). Its biggest gain came in 1995, when it moved up 41.2 percent (compared with a 33.5 percent rise in the Dow).

FEES/SERVICES/MANAGEMENT

The IDS Growth Fund has a front-end load of 5 percent. Its annual expense ratio of 0.97 percent (with no 12b-1 fee) compares very favorably with other funds.

The fund offers all the standard services, such as retirement account availability, automatic withdrawal, and automatic checking account deduction. Its minimum initial investment of $2,000 and minimum subsequent investment of $100 is in line with other funds.

Mitzi Malevich has managed the fund since 1992. The IDS family of funds includes 37 funds and allows shareholders to switch from fund to fund by telephone.

Top Ten Stock Holdings

1. Travelers Group	6. HEALTHSOUTH
2. Washington Mutual	7. Tellabs
3. Merrill Lynch	8. Pfizer
4. Schlumberger	9. Hewlett-Packard
5. Coca-Cola	10. Intel

Asset mix: common stocks—98%; cash/equivalents—2%
Total net assets: $3.1 billion
Dividend yield: 0.11%

Fees

Front-end load	5.00%
Redemption fee	*None*
12b-1 fee	*None*
Management fee	0.61
Other expenses	0.36
Total annual expense	0.97%
Minimum initial investment	$2,000
Minimum subsequent investment	$100

Services

Telephone exchanges	*Yes*
Automatic withdrawal	*Yes*
Automatic checking deduction	*Yes*
Retirement plan/IRA	*Yes*
Instant redemption	*Yes*
Financial statements	*Quarterly*
Income distributions	*Annual*
Capital gains distributions	*Annual*
Portfolio manager: years	6
Number of funds in family	37

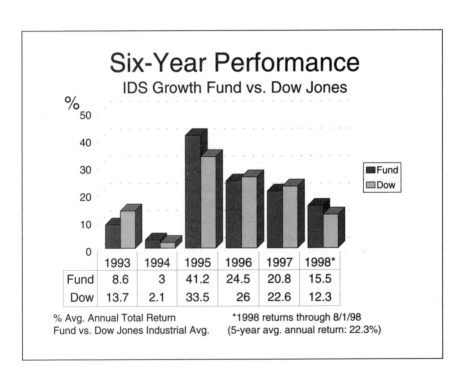

Six-Year Performance
IDS Growth Fund vs. Dow Jones

	1993	1994	1995	1996	1997	1998*
Fund	8.6	3	41.2	24.5	20.8	15.5
Dow	13.7	2.1	33.5	26	22.6	12.3

% Avg. Annual Total Return
Fund vs. Dow Jones Industrial Avg.

*1998 returns through 8/1/98
(5-year avg. annual return: 22.3%)

79
William Blair Growth Fund

LONG TERM

William Blair Funds
222 W. Adams Street
Chicago, IL 60606

Fund managers: Rocky Barber
and Mark Fuller III
Fund objective: Long-term growth

Toll-free: 800-742-7272
In-state: 312-364-8000
Fax: 312-236-1497

Performance	★ ★
Consistency	★ ★
Fees/Services	★ ★ ★ ★ ★
WBGSX	**9 Points**

Established in 1946, the William Blair Growth Fund invests in a broad range of emerging growth stocks, including Amgen, Electronic Arts, and AirTouch Communications. "We believe that smaller and midsize companies with a domestic focus offer greater protection from outside forces and more attractive value in the market," says fund manager Rocky Barber. The fund also has a few blue chip holdings, such as Microsoft, Intel, and Walgreen.

Over the past ten years, the fund has produced an average annual return of about 17 percent. A $10,000 investment in the fund ten years ago would now be worth about $50,000. Barber and comanager Mark Fuller like stocks that have averaged 15 to 20 percent in annual earnings growth over the past five to ten years. The fund maintains a modest portfolio turnover ratio of 43 percent.

The fund stays fully invested in the market most of the time. It has about 70 stock holdings, concentrated in fast-growing industries. Leading sectors include applied technology, 21 percent of assets; financial services, 11 percent; medical-related businesses, 18 percent; technology, 13 percent; distribution, 6 percent; retailing, 11 percent; business services, 8 percent; and industrial products, 5 percent.

PERFORMANCE

The fund has enjoyed solid growth over the last five years. Including dividends and capital gains distributions, the William Blair Growth Fund has provided a total return for the last five years (through mid-1998) of 153 percent. A $10,000 investment in 1993 would have grown to about $25,000 five years later. Average annual return: 20.4 percent.

CONSISTENCY

The fund has been fairly inconsistent recently, outperforming the Dow Jones Industrial Average in only two of the last five years through 1997 (and it led the Dow through the first few months of 1998). Its biggest gain came in 1995, when it moved up 29.1 percent (compared with a 33.5 percent rise in the Dow).

FEES/SERVICES/MANAGEMENT

Like all William Blair funds, the Growth Fund is a true no-load—no fee to buy, no fee to sell. Its total annual expense ratio of 0.79 percent (with no 12b-1 fee) compares very favorably with other funds.

The fund offers all the standard services, such as retirement account availability, automatic withdrawal, and automatic checking account deduction. Its minimum initial investment of $5,000 and minimum subsequent investment of $1,000 are higher than most other funds.

Rocky Barber and Mark Fuller III have managed the fund since 1993. The William Blair family of funds includes four funds and allows shareholders to switch from fund to fund by telephone.

Top Ten Stock Holdings

1. Automatic Data Processing
2. Microsoft
3. Amgen
4. Elan
5. Omnicare
6. Electronic Arts
7. AirTouch Communications
8. Boston Scientific
9. Concord EFS
10. Viking Office Products

Asset mix: common stocks—94%; cash/equivalents—6%
Total net assets: $591 million
Dividend yield: none

Fees

Front-end load	*None*
Redemption fee	*None*
12b-1 fee	*None*
Management fee	0.68%
Other expenses	0.11
Total annual expense	0.79%
Minimum initial investment	$5,000
Minimum subsequent investment	$1,000

Services

Telephone exchanges	*Yes*
Automatic withdrawal	*Yes*
Automatic checking deduction	*Yes*
Retirement plan/IRA	*Yes*
Instant redemption	*Yes*
Financial statements	*Semiannual*
Income distributions	*Annual*
Capital gains distributions	*Annual*
Portfolio manager: years	5
Number of funds in family	4

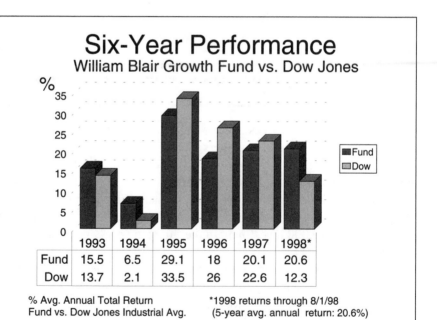

Six-Year Performance
William Blair Growth Fund vs. Dow Jones

	1993	1994	1995	1996	1997	1998*
Fund	15.5	6.5	29.1	18	20.1	20.6
Dow	13.7	2.1	33.5	26	22.6	12.3

% Avg. Annual Total Return
Fund vs. Dow Jones Industrial Avg.

*1998 returns through 8/1/98
(5-year avg. annual return: 20.6%)

80

AIM Value Fund

LONG TERM

AIM Funds Group
11 Greenway Plaza, Suite 100
Houston, TX 77046-1173

Fund managers: Joel Dobberpuhl
   and Robert Shelton
Fund objective: Long-term growth
Web site: www.aimfunds.com

Toll-free: 800-347-4246
In-state: 713-626-1919
Fax: 713-993-9890

Performance	★ ★
Consistency	★ ★ ★ ★
Fees/Services	★ ★ ★
AVLFX	**9 Points**

The AIM Value Fund invests in undervalued stocks with strong turn-around potential. The fund managers track a list of stocks they consider to be undervalued, and when they detect signs of a potential resurgence in a company, they add its stock to the portfolio.

The AIM Value Fund has enjoyed excellent long-term success. Over the past ten years, the fund has posted an average annual return of nearly 21 percent. A $10,000 investment in the fund ten years ago would now be worth about $65,000.

The fund portfolio consists of about 50 percent medium-sized companies and 50 percent large-capitalization companies. In all, the fund portfolio includes about 150 stocks, with about 11 percent of its holdings in foreign issues.

The fund managers are fairly active in their trading approach, so the annual portfolio turnover ratio is 126 percent. The fund invests heavily in high-tech and financial stocks. Computer stocks make up about 7 percent of total assets; telecommunications, 6 percent; and health care–related stocks about 7 percent. Banking and financial stocks make up about 13 percent of the portfolio and insurance companies 12 percent.

PERFORMANCE

The fund has enjoyed solid growth over the last five years. Including dividends and capital gains distributions, the AIM Value Fund portfolio has provided a total return for the last five years (through mid-1998) of 150 percent. A $10,000 investment in 1993 would have grown to about $25,000 five years later. Average annual return: 20 percent.

CONSISTENCY

The fund has been very consistent recently, outperforming the Dow Jones Industrial Average in four of the last five years through 1997 (and again through the first few months of 1998). Its biggest gain came in 1995, when it jumped 34.9 percent (compared with a 33.5 percent rise in the Dow).

FEES/SERVICES/MANAGEMENT

The fund charges a 5.50 percent front-end load. The fund's total annual expense ratio of 1.11 percent (with a 0.25 percent 12b-1 fee) compares favorably with other funds.

The fund offers all the standard services, such as retirement account availability, automatic withdrawal, and automatic checking account deduction. Its minimum initial investment of $500 and minimum subsequent investment of $50 compare favorably with other funds.

Joel Dobberpuhl has managed the fund since 1992, and Robert Shelton recently joined the management team. The AIM family of funds includes 30 funds and allows shareholders to switch from fund to fund by telephone.

Top Ten Stock Holdings

1. Royal Bank of Canada
2. Allstate
3. WorldCom
4. American International Group
5. MCI Communications
6. BankAmerica
7. Citicorp
8. SmithKline Beecham
9. Computer Associates
10. Philip Morris

Asset mix: common stocks—80%; repurchase agreements—20%
Total net assets: $14 billion
Dividend yield: 0.09%

Fees

Front-end load	5.50%
Redemption fee	*None*
12b-1 fee	0.25
Management fee	0.61
Other expenses	0.25
Total annual expense	1.11%
Minimum initial investment	$500
Minimum subsequent investment	$50

Services

Telephone exchanges	*Yes*
Automatic withdrawal	*Yes*
Automatic checking deduction	*Yes*
Retirement plan/IRA	*Yes*
Instant redemption	*Yes*
Financial statements	*Semiannual*
Income distributions	*Annual*
Capital gains distributions	*Annual*
Portfolio manager: years	6
Number of funds in family	30

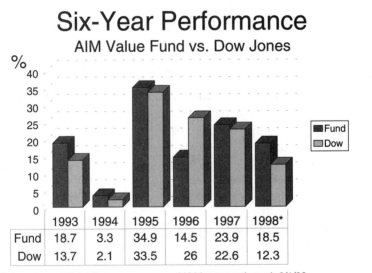

Six-Year Performance
AIM Value Fund vs. Dow Jones

	1993	1994	1995	1996	1997	1998*
Fund	18.7	3.3	34.9	14.5	23.9	18.5
Dow	13.7	2.1	33.5	26	22.6	12.3

% Avg. Annual Total Return
Fund vs. Dow Jones Industrial Avg.

*1998 returns through 8/1/98
(5-year avg. annual return: 20.4%)

LONG TERM

Fidelity Value Fund

Fidelity Investments
82 Devonshire Street
Boston, MA 02109

Fund manager: Richard Fentin
Fund objective: Long-term growth
Web site: www.fidelity.com

Toll-free: 800-544-6666
In-state: 801-534-1910
Fax: 617-476-9743

Performance	★ ★
Consistency	★ ★
Fees/Services	★ ★ ★ ★ ★
FDVLX	**9 Points**

The Fidelity Value Fund focuses on undervalued stocks that appear to be primed for a turn-around. Fund manager Richard Fentin likes well-known blue chip stocks but, generally speaking, only if they have survived some slow financial times and seem to be ready for a rebound. Several of the fund's leading holdings have trailed the overall market during the bull run of the 1990s, such as Rubbermaid, R. R. Donnelley, Browning-Ferris, and Wal-Mart.

The fund has enjoyed pretty good growth in recent years, although it has trailed the overall market. Value portfolios typically trail the averages during strong bull markets but tend to do better relative to the overall market during slower periods. That's why value funds can be a key component of a diversified portfolio.

Over the past ten years, the fund has climbed about 17.4 percent per year. A $10,000 investment in the fund ten years ago would now be worth about $50,000.

"My primary emphasis is on finding cheap stocks that I feel have the potential to appreciate over a period of time," says Fentin. "This discipline, I think, leads me to a wider cross section of stocks than many of the fund's competitors." The objective of the fund is to invest in companies with valuable fixed assets or stocks that appear to be undervalued based on the company's assets, earnings, or growth potential. Fentin also looks for companies that have recently changed management and seem to be on the verge of a rebound in earnings.

The Fidelity Value Fund, which has about 200 stock holdings, maintains a fairly modest trading policy. The annual portfolio turnover ratio is 56 percent. The fund is well diversified across industries. Its leading industrial segment is basic industries, which accounts for about 19 percent of assets. Other leading sectors include technology, 10 percent; energy, 9 percent; durables, 8 percent; nondurables (food, tobacco, household products), 8 percent; retail and wholesale, 8 percent; and services, 7 percent. The fund has about $8 billion in assets under management.

PERFORMANCE

The fund has enjoyed solid growth over the past five years. Including dividends and capital gains distributions, the Fidelity Value Fund has provided a total return for the past five years (through early 1998) of 145 percent. A $10,000 investment in 1993 would have grown to $24,500 five years later. Average annual return: 19.6 percent.

CONSISTENCY

The fund has been somewhat inconsistent recently, trailing the Dow Jones Industrial Average in three of the past five years through 1997 (and it was about even with the Dow through the first few months of 1998). Its biggest gain came in 1995, when it jumped 27.1 percent (compared with a 33.5 percent rise in the Dow).

FEES/SERVICES/MANAGEMENT

The fund is a true no-load—no fee to buy and no fee to sell. Its low annual expense ratio of just 0.68 percent (with no 12b-1 fee) compares very favorably with other funds.

The fund offers many of the standard services, such as retirement account availability and automatic checking account deduction. Its minimum initial investment of $2,500 and minimum subsequent investment of $250 are a little high compared with other funds.

Richard Fentin has been with Fidelity since 1979 and has managed the fund since 1996. The Fidelity family of funds includes more than 230 funds.

Top Ten Stock Holdings

1. Rubbermaid
2. Nalco Chemical
3. Dole Food
4. Browning-Ferris
5. AMP

6. R.R. Donnelley
7. Federated Department Stores
8. Wal-Mart
9. United Healthcare
10. Hercules

Asset mix: common stocks—98%; convertible securities: .5%; cash/equivalents—1.5%
Total net assets: $7.91 billion
Dividend yield: 0.70%

Fees

Front-end load	*None*
Redemption fee	*None*
12b-1 fee	*None*
Management fee	0.46%
Other expenses	0.22
Total annual expense	0.68%
Minimum initial investment	$2,500
Minimum subsequent investment	$250

Services

Telephone exchanges	*Yes*
Automatic withdrawal	*Yes*
Automatic checking deduction	*Yes*
Retirement plan/IRA	*Yes*
Instant redemption	*Yes*
Financial statements	*Semiannual*
Income distributions	*Annual*
Capital gains distributions	*Annual*
Portfolio manager: years	2
Number of funds in family	235

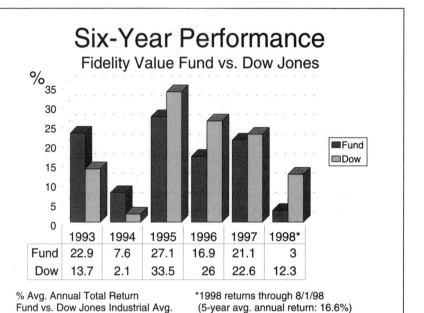

	1993	1994	1995	1996	1997	1998*
Fund	22.9	7.6	27.1	16.9	21.1	3
Dow	13.7	2.1	33.5	26	22.6	12.3

% Avg. Annual Total Return   *1998 returns through 8/1/98
Fund vs. Dow Jones Industrial Avg.   (5-year avg. annual return: 16.6%)

SMALL CAP

Acorn Fund

Acorn Investment Trust
227 West Monroe Street, Suite 3000
Chicago, IL 60606

Fund managers: Ralph Wanger
and Charles P. McQuaid
Fund objective: Small-cap stocks
Web site: www.wanger.com

Toll-free: 800-922-6769
In-state: 312-634-9200
Fax: 312-634-1903

Performance	★ ★
Consistency	★ ★
Fees/Services	★ ★ ★ ★ ★
ACRNX	**9 Points**

For 29 years, Ralph Wanger has kept the Acorn Fund growing like a tall oak. A $10,000 investment in the small-cap stock growth fund when it opened in 1970 would now be worth about $780,000.

The Acorn Fund invests in a diverse cross section of small emerging growth stocks. The fund managers look for attractively priced companies that should benefit from favorable long-term social, economic, or political trends. About 20 percent of the fund's assets are invested in foreign stocks. The fund management takes a long-term approach, buying stocks with the intention of holding them for several years. The fund has a very low portfolio turnover ratio of just 33 percent and stays 90 to 95 percent invested in stocks at almost all times. In all, the fund has more than 250 stock holdings in its portfolio with about 12 percent of its assets in foreign stocks.

Among the Acorn Fund's leading industrial segments are computer-related products and services, 16 percent of assets; health care, 8 percent; financial services, 12 percent; industrial goods and services, 9 percent; energy and minerals, 11 percent; broadcasting and television, 7 percent; and consumer goods and services, 8.5 percent.

PERFORMANCE

The fund has enjoyed solid growth over the last five years. Including dividends and capital gains distributions, the Acorn Fund has provided a total return for the last five years (through mid-1998) of 130 percent. A $10,000 investment in 1993 would have grown to about $23,000 five years later. Average annual return: 18.1 percent.

CONSISTENCY

The fund has been somewhat inconsistent recently, trailing the Dow Jones Industrial Average in three of the last five years through 1997 (but it led the Dow through the first few months of 1998). Its biggest gain came in 1993, when it jumped 32.3 percent (compared with a 13.7 percent rise in the Dow).

FEES/SERVICES/MANAGEMENT

The Acorn Fund is a true no-load—no fee to buy, no fee to sell. The fund's total annual expense ratio of 0.81 percent (with no 12b-1 fee) compares very favorably with other funds.

The fund offers all the standard services, such as retirement account availability, automatic withdrawal, and automatic checking account deduction. Its minimum initial investment of $1,000 and minimum subsequent investment of $100 compare favorably with other funds.

Ralph Wanger, whose comanager is Charles P. McQuaid, has managed the fund since 1970. The Acorn Fund is one of only three funds in the Acorn family of funds.

Top Ten Stock Holdings

1. AES	6. Harley-Davidson
2. Liberty Media	7. International Game Technology
3. Carnival	8. Solectron
4. Lincare Holdings	9. People's Bank Bridgeport
5. Borders	10. HBO

Asset mix: common stocks—91%; cash/equivalents—9%
Total net assets: $3.7 billion
Dividend yield: 0.80%

Fees

Front-end load	*None*
Redemption fee	*None*
12b-1 fee	*None*
Management fee	0.70%
Other expenses	0.11
Total annual expense	0.81%
Minimum initial investment	$1,000
Minimum subsequent investment	$100

Services

Telephone exchanges	*Yes*
Automatic withdrawal	*Yes*
Automatic checking deduction	*Yes*
Retirement plan/IRA	*Yes*
Instant redemption	*Yes*
Financial statements	*Semiannual*
Income distributions	*Semiannual*
Capital gains distributions	*Annual*
Portfolio manager: years	28
Number of funds in family	3

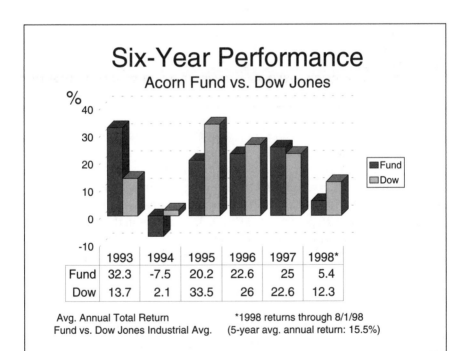

Six-Year Performance
Acorn Fund vs. Dow Jones

	1993	1994	1995	1996	1997	1998*
Fund	32.3	-7.5	20.2	22.6	25	5.4
Dow	13.7	2.1	33.5	26	22.6	12.3

Avg. Annual Total Return
Fund vs. Dow Jones Industrial Avg.

*1998 returns through 8/1/98
(5-year avg. annual return: 15.5%)

SECTOR

83
Fidelity Select Industrial Equipment Portfolio

Fidelity Investments
82 Devonshire Street
Boston, MA 02109

Fund manager: Simon Wolf
Fund objective: Sector
Web site: www.fidelity.com

Toll-free: 800-544-8888
In-state: 801-534-1910
Fax: 617-476-9753

Performance	★ ★ ★ ★
Consistency	★ ★ ★
Fees/Services	★ ★
FSCGX	**9 Points**

The Fidelity Select Industrial Equipment Portfolio has been rolling along recently like a runaway forklift. The fund, which has shunned the glitz and glamour of high-tech stocks in favor of such segments as machine tools, farm machinery, and electrical parts, continues to enjoying outstanding growth. Over the past ten years, the fund has provided an average return of about 16 percent. A $10,000 investment in the fund ten years ago would now be worth about $45,000.

"We are looking for companies whose earnings outlooks are improving dramatically due to changes or catalysts that would allow the firms to accelerate their growth beyond what analysts would expect," says fund manager Simon Wolf. "We are also looking for companies whose current stock valuations versus their growth rates are compelling when compared with the valuations and growth rate of comparable companies."

The fund has about 75 stock holdings in all. Its leading industrial segments include industrial machinery, 24 percent of assets; electrical equipment, 22 percent; aerospace and defense, 10 percent; and computers and office equipment, 6 percent. The fund manager pursues a very aggressive trading policy. The annual portfolio turnover ratio is 261 percent.

PERFORMANCE

The fund has enjoyed outstanding growth over the past five years. Including dividends and capital gains distributions, the Fidelity Select Industrial Equipment Portfolio has provided a total return for the past five years (through early 1998) of 194 percent. A $10,000 investment in 1993 would have grown to about $29,000 five years later. Average annual return: 24.1 percent.

CONSISTENCY

The fund has been fairly consistent, outpacing the Dow Jones Industrial Average in three of the past five years (and again through the first few months of 1998). Its biggest gains came in 1993, when it moved up 43.3 percent.

FEES/SERVICES/MANAGEMENT ★ ★

The fund has a low front-end load of 3 percent and a maximum redemption fee of 0.75 percent if sold out within 29 days. Its annual expense ratio of 1.51 percent (with no 12b-1 fee) is about average among all funds.

The fund offers many of the standard services, such as retirement account availability and automatic checking account deduction. Its minimum initial investment of $2,500 and minimum subsequent investment of $250 are a little high compared with other funds.

Simon Wolf joined Fidelity in 1996 and has managed the fund since 1997. The Fidelity family of funds includes more than 230 funds.

Top Ten Stock Holdings

1. General Electric
2. Pitney-Bowes
3. Xerox
4. Emerson Electric
5. Tyco International
6. Honeywell
7. Chicago Miniature Lamp
8. Illinois Tool Works
9. Chart Industries
10. Ingersoll-Rand

Asset mix: common stocks—90%; cash/equivalents—10%
Total net assets: $47.7 billion
Dividend yield: 0.06%

Fees

Front-end load	3.00%
Redemption fee	0.75
12b-1 fee	*None*
Management fee	0.61
Other expenses	0.90
Total annual expense	1.51%
Minimum initial investment	$2,500
Minimum subsequent investment	$250

Services

Telephone exchanges	*Yes*
Automatic withdrawal	*Yes*
Automatic checking deduction	*Yes*
Retirement plan/IRA	*Yes*
Instant redemption	*Yes*
Financial statements	*Semiannual*
Income distributions	*Semiannual*
Capital gains distributions	*Semiannual*
Portfolio manager: years	1
Number of funds in family	235

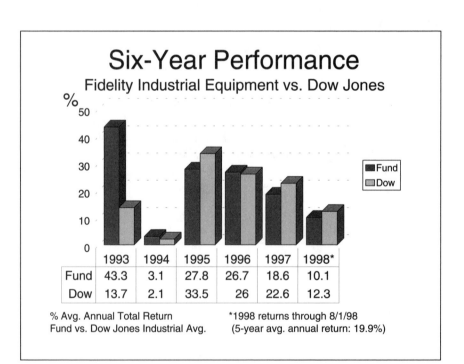

Six-Year Performance
Fidelity Industrial Equipment vs. Dow Jones

	1993	1994	1995	1996	1997	1998*
Fund	43.3	3.1	27.8	26.7	18.6	10.1
Dow	13.7	2.1	33.5	26	22.6	12.3

% Avg. Annual Total Return
Fund vs. Dow Jones Industrial Avg.

*1998 returns through 8/1/98
(5-year avg. annual return: 19.9%)

Fidelity Select
Telecommunications Portfolio

SECTOR

Fidelity Investments
82 Devonshire Street
Boston, MA 02109

Fund manager: Nicholas Thakore
Fund objective: Sector
Web site: www.fidelity.com

Toll-free: 800-544-8888
In-state: 801-534-1910
Fax: 617-476-9753

Performance	★ ★ ★
Consistency	★ ★ ★
Fees/Services	★ ★ ★
FSTCX	**9 Points**

The telecommunications industry has been booming worldwide the past few years, helping boost the Fidelity Select Telecommunications Portfolio to outstanding long-term returns. Over the past ten years, the fund has posted an average annual return of 21 percent. A $10,000 investment in the fund ten years ago would now be worth about $67,000. The fund invests both in service companies such as AT&T and Worldcom and in communications equipment manufacturers such as Tellabs and Motorola.

The telecommunications industry continues to be a volatile but growing sector. "I'll probably continue to pursue my theme of focusing on smaller, developing companies with some kind of competitive advantage that will help them capture market share," says fund manager Nick Thakore.

The leading segment within the Telecommunications Portfolio is the telephone services industry, which accounts for 57 percent of assets. Other leading areas are electronics, 6 percent; electrical equipment, 8 percent; and communications equipment, 8 percent. In all, the fund has about 30 stock holdings, many of which are foreign phone companies. The fund manager maintains a fairly active trading policy, resulting in an annual portfolio turnover ratio of 175 percent.

PERFORMANCE

The fund has enjoyed outstanding growth over the past five years. Including dividends and capital gains distributions, the Fidelity Select Telecommunications Portfolio has provided a total return for the past five years (through early 1998) of 174 percent. A $10,000 investment in 1993 would have grown to about $27,400 five years later. Average annual return: 22.3 percent.

CONSISTENCY

The fund has been fairly consistent, outpacing the Dow Jones Industrial Average in three of the past five years (and again through the first few months of 1998). Its biggest gains came in 1993 and 1995, when it moved up 29.7 percent (both years).

FEES/SERVICES/MANAGEMENT

The fund has a low front-end load of 3 percent and a maximum redemption fee of 0.75 percent if sold out within 29 days. Its annual expense ratio of 1.51 percent (with no 12b-1 fee) is about average among all funds.

The fund offers many of the standard services, such as retirement account availability and automatic checking account deduction. Its minimum initial investment of $2,500 and minimum subsequent investment of $250 are a little high compared with other funds.

Nick Thakore has managed the fund since 1996, but he has been with Fidelity since 1993. The Fidelity family of funds includes more than 230 funds.

Top Ten Stock Holdings

1. MCI Communications
2. WorldCom
3. AT&T
4. LCI International
5. Tel-Save Holdings
6. Alcatel Alsthom CGE
7. Global TeleSystems Group
8. NEXTEL Communications
9. GTE
10. Loral Space & Communications

Asset mix: common stocks—97%; cash/equivalents—3%
Total net assets: $441 billion
Dividend yield: none

Fees

Front-end load	3.00%
Redemption fee	0.75
12b-1 fee	*None*
Management fee	0.60
Other expenses	0.91
Total annual expense	1.51%
Minimum initial investment	$2,500
Minimum subsequent investment	$250

Services

Telephone exchanges	*Yes*
Automatic withdrawal	*Yes*
Automatic checking deduction	*Yes*
Retirement plan/IRA	*Yes*
Instant redemption	*Yes*
Financial statements	*Semiannual*
Income distributions	*Semiannual*
Capital gains distributions	*Semiannual*
Portfolio manager: years	2
Number of funds in family	235

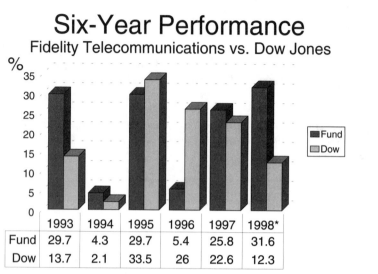

Six-Year Performance
Fidelity Telecommunications vs. Dow Jones

	1993	1994	1995	1996	1997	1998*
Fund	29.7	4.3	29.7	5.4	25.8	31.6
Dow	13.7	2.1	33.5	26	22.6	12.3

% Avg. Annual Total Return   *1998 returns through 8/1/98
Fund vs. Dow Jones Industrial Avg.   (5-year avg. annual return: 20.1%)

LONG TERM

Putnam Investors Fund

Putnam Investments
One Post Office Square
Boston, MA 02109

Fund managers: C. Beth Cotner,
  Richard England, and Manuel Weiss
Fund objective: Long-term growth
Web site: www.putnaminv.com

Toll-free: 800-225-1581
In-state: 617-760-5223
Fax: 617-760-9597

Performance	★ ★ ★
Consistency	★ ★ ★
Fees/Services	★ ★
PINVX	**8 Points**

The Putnam Investors Fund is invested in a broad range of blue chip growth companies, such as General Electric, Microsoft, BankAmerica, Warner-Lambert, and Wal-Mart. Over the past ten years, the fund has posted average annual returns of about 19 percent. A $10,000 investment in the fund ten years ago would now be worth about $56,000.

The fund management team selects its portfolio by examining the general outlook for the economy, the growth prospects for various industries, and the specific prospects for individual companies. They take a fairly active approach in their trading policy. The annual portfolio turnover ratio is 95 percent. The fund stays nearly 100 percent invested in stocks most of the time.

The fund invests in stocks from a diverse range of industries. Leading sectors include consumer cyclicals, 23 percent of assets; financial services, 19 percent; technology, 16 percent; health care, 13 percent; consumer staples, 9 percent; and capital goods, 9 percent.

PERFORMANCE

The fund has enjoyed steady growth over the last five years. Including dividends and capital gains distributions, the Putnam Investors Fund has provided a total return for the last five years (through mid-1998) of 180 percent. A $10,000 investment in 1993 would have grown to about $28,000 five years later. Average annual return: 22.8 percent.

CONSISTENCY

The fund has been fairly consistent recently, outperforming the Dow Jones Industrial Average in three of the last five years through 1997 (and it led the Dow through the first four months of 1998). Its biggest gain came in 1995, when it moved up 37.6 percent (compared with a 33.5 percent rise in the Dow).

FEES/SERVICES/MANAGEMENT

The Putnam Investors Fund has a front-end load of 5.75 percent. Its total annual expense ratio of 1 percent (including a 0.25 percent 12b-1 fee) compares favorably with other funds.

The fund offers all the standard services, such as retirement account availability, automatic withdrawal, and automatic checking account deduction. Its minimum initial investment of $500 and minimum subsequent investment of $50 compare favorably with other funds.

Beth Cotner has been a manager of the fund only since 1995. Richard England and Manuel Weiss joined the management team in 1996. The Putnam family of funds includes 70 funds and allows shareholders to switch from fund to fund by telephone.

Top Ten Stock Holdings

1. General Electric
2. Microsoft
3. Gannett
4. Pfizer
5. Travelers Group
6. CVS
7. BankAmerica
8. American Express
9. Procter & Gamble
10. Warner-Lambert

Asset mix: common stocks—97%; cash/equivalents—3%
Total net assets: $1.9 billion
Dividend yield: 0.28%

Fees

Front-end load	5.75%
Redemption fee	*None*
12b-1 fee	0.25
Management fee	0.56
Other expenses	0.19
Total annual expense	1.00%
Minimum initial investment	$500
Minimum subsequent investment	$50

Services

Telephone exchanges	*Yes*
Automatic withdrawal	*Yes*
Automatic checking deduction	*Yes*
Retirement plan/IRA	*Yes*
Instant redemption	*Yes*
Financial statements	*Semiannual*
Income distributions	*Annual*
Capital gains distributions	*Annual*
Portfolio manager: years	3
Number of funds in family	70

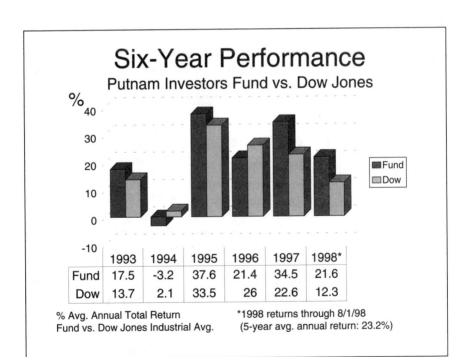

Six-Year Performance
Putnam Investors Fund vs. Dow Jones

	1993	1994	1995	1996	1997	1998*
Fund	17.5	-3.2	37.6	21.4	34.5	21.6
Dow	13.7	2.1	33.5	26	22.6	12.3

% Avg. Annual Total Return
Fund vs. Dow Jones Industrial Avg.

*1998 returns through 8/1/98
(5-year avg. annual return: 23.2%)

86
Alliance Growth Fund

Alliance Funds Group
1345 Avenue of the Americas
New York, NY 10105

LONG TERM

Fund manager: Tyler Smith
Fund objective: Long-term growth
Web site: www.alliancecapital.com

Toll-free: 800-221-5672
In-state: 201-319-4000
Fax: 201-319-4139

Performance	★ ★ ★
Consistency	★ ★
Fees/Services	★ ★ ★
AGRFX	**8 Points**

The Alliance Growth Fund invests in a broad range of stocks, from small emerging growth stocks to major blue chips, such as Merck, Philip Morris, and American Express. The fund is also well diversified across industry groups.

"Our strategy is to look for companies with prospects for above-average earnings growth," explains fund manager Tyler Smith. "In particular, we look for companies where the next few years will be better than the past. That way, investors can potentially benefit from both earnings growth and an expanding price/earnings multiple."

Since 1990, when the fund opened, it has posted an average annual return of 23.5 percent. A $10,000 investment in the fund when it opened in 1990 would have grown to nearly $50,000 by 1998.

The fund has about 100 stock holdings in all. Leading industrial sectors include technology, 29 percent; financial services, 25 percent; consumer noncyclicals, 19 percent; consumer cyclicals, 7 percent; and energy, 6 percent.

Tyler takes a fairly conservative trading approach. The annual turn-over ratio is 48 percent. The fund stays almost 100 percent invested in the stock market most of the time.

PERFORMANCE

The fund has enjoyed excellent growth over the last five years. Including dividends and capital gains distributions, the Alliance Growth Fund has provided a total return for the last five years (through mid-1998) of 175 percent. A $10,000 investment in 1993 would have grown to about $27,500 five years later. Average annual return: 22.3 percent.

CONSISTENCY

The fund has been somewhat inconsistent recently, outperforming the Dow Jones Industrial Average in only two of the last five years through 1997 (and it was just ahead of the Dow through the first few months of 1998). Its biggest gain came in 1995, when it jumped 29.5 percent (compared with a 33.5 percent rise in the Dow).

FEES/SERVICES/MANAGEMENT

The Alliance Growth Fund has a front-end load of 4.25 percent. Its annual expense ratio of 1.26 percent (including a 0.30 percent 12b-1 fee) compares favorably with other funds.

The fund offers all the standard services, such as retirement account availability, automatic withdrawal, and automatic checking account deduction. Its minimum initial investment of $250 and minimum subsequent investment of $50 compare very favorably with other funds.

Tyler Smith has managed the fund since 1990. The Alliance family of funds includes more than 50 funds and allows shareholders to switch from fund to fund by telephone.

Top Ten Stock Holdings

1. Cendant
2. Cisco Systems
3. WorldCom
4. Travelers Group
5. American International Group

6. MBNA
7. Philip Morris
8. American Express
9. Loews
10. Merck

Asset mix: common stocks—95%; outstanding call options—1%; cash/equivalents—4%
Total net assets: $830 million
Dividend yield: none

Fees

Front-end load	4.25%
Redemption fee	*None*
12b-1 fee	0.30
Management fee	0.74
Other expenses	0.22
Total annual expense	1.26%
Minimum initial investment	$250
Minimum subsequent investment	$50

Services

Telephone exchanges	*Yes*
Automatic withdrawal	*Yes*
Automatic checking deduction	*Yes*
Retirement plan/IRA	*Yes*
Instant redemption	*Yes*
Financial statements	*Semiannual*
Income distributions	*Annual*
Capital gains distributions	*Annual*
Portfolio manager: years	8
Number of funds in family	53

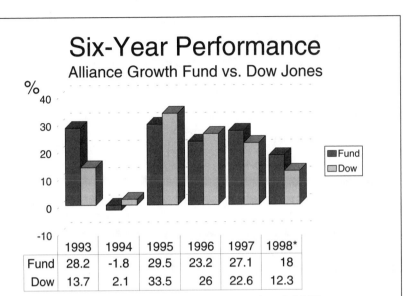

Six-Year Performance
Alliance Growth Fund vs. Dow Jones

	1993	1994	1995	1996	1997	1998*
Fund	28.2	-1.8	29.5	23.2	27.1	18
Dow	13.7	2.1	33.5	26	22.6	12.3

% Avg. Annual Total Return
Fund vs. Dow Jones Industrial Avg.

*1998 returns through 8/1/98
(5-year avg. annual return: 21.1%)

87

Van Kampen American
Capital Emerging Growth Fund

AGGRESSIVE

Van Kampen American Capital Funds
One Parkview Plaza
Oakbrook Terrace, IL 60181

Fund manager: Gary M. Lewis
Fund objective: Aggressive growth
Web site: www.vkac.com

Toll-free: 800-856-3577
In-state: 630-684-6000
Fax: 630-684-6587

Performance	★ ★ ★
Consistency	★ ★
Fees/Services	★ ★ ★
ACEGX	**8 Points**

Founded in 1970, the Van Kampen American Capital Emerging Growth Fund continues to provide strong, steady performance for its shareholders. The fund invests in small and midsize emerging growth stocks, many of which are technology-related.

Over the past ten years, the fund has posted an average annual return of about 20 percent. A $10,000 investment in the fund ten years ago would now be worth about $61,000. Since 1970, a $10,000 investment would have grown to about $800,000.

Fund manager Gary Lewis looks at several factors in selecting stocks: rising earnings estimates, accelerating growth rates in both revenues and per-share earnings, and rising profit margins. "Conversely," says Lewis, "we sell stocks quickly if their earnings estimates or valuations are declining, although we are more patient in holding onto stocks with declining valuations."

Lewis is fairly active in his trading activity, showing a 92 percent annual portfolio turnover ratio. The fund stays almost fully invested in stocks at all times and has more than 200 stock holdings spread across several key industries. Leading sectors include technology, 36 percent of total assets; health care, 10 percent; energy, 9 percent; financial services, 8 percent; consumer distribution, 10 percent; consumer services, 8 percent; and producer manufacturing, 5 percent.

PERFORMANCE

The fund has enjoyed strong growth over the last five years. Including dividends and capital gains distributions, the Van Kampen Emerging Growth Fund has provided a total return for the last five years (through mid-1998) of 163 percent. A $10,000 investment in 1993 would have grown to about $26,000 five years later. Average annual return: 21.3 percent.

CONSISTENCY

The fund has been fairly inconsistent recently, outperforming the Dow Jones Industrial Average in only two of the last five years through 1997 (but it led the Dow through the first few months of 1998). Its biggest gain came in 1995, when it moved up 44.6 percent (compared with a 33.5 percent rise in the Dow).

FEES/SERVICES/MANAGEMENT

The Van Kampen Emerging Growth Fund has a front-end load of 5.75 percent. Its total annual expense ratio of 1.05 percent (including a 0.22 percent 12b-1 fee) compares favorably with other funds.

The fund offers all the standard services, such as retirement account availability, automatic withdrawal, and automatic checking account deduction. Its minimum initial investment of $500 and minimum subsequent investment of $25 compare favorably with other funds.

Gary Lewis has managed the fund since 1989. The Van Kampen family of funds includes 47 funds and allows shareholders to switch from fund to fund by telephone.

Top Ten Stock Holdings

1. Dell Computer	6. BMC Software
2. HBO	7. America Online
3. Compuware	8. Guidant
4. Chancellor Media	9. EMC/Mass
5. PeopleSoft	10. CBT Group

Asset mix: common stocks—94%; cash/equivalents—6%
Total net assets: $2.1 billion
Dividend yield: none

Fees

Front-end load	5.75%
Redemption fee	*None*
12b-1 fee	0.22
Management fee	0.46
Other expenses	0.37
Total annual expense	1.05%
Minimum initial investment	$500
Minimum subsequent investment	$25

Services

Telephone exchanges	*Yes*
Automatic withdrawal	*Yes*
Automatic checking deduction	*Yes*
Retirement plan/IRA	*Yes*
Instant redemption	*Yes*
Financial statements	*Semiannual*
Income distributions	*Annual*
Capital gains distributions	*Annual*
Portfolio manager: years	9
Number of funds in family	47

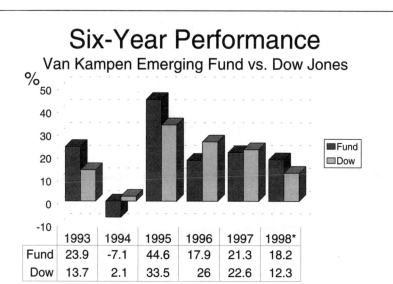

Six-Year Performance
Van Kampen Emerging Fund vs. Dow Jones

	1993	1994	1995	1996	1997	1998*
Fund	23.9	-7.1	44.6	17.9	21.3	18.2
Dow	13.7	2.1	33.5	26	22.6	12.3

% Avg. Annual Total Return
Fund vs. Dow Jones Industrial Avg.

*1998 returns through 8/1/98
(5-year avg. annual return: 20.1%)

88
United New Concepts Fund

SMALL CAP

United Group
6300 Lemar Avenue
P.O. Box 29217
Shawnee Mission, KS 66201-9217

Fund manager: Mark Seferovich
Fund objective: Small-cap stocks
Web site: www.waddell.com

Toll-free: 800-366-5465
In-state: 913-236-2000
Fax: 913-236-1595

Performance	★ ★ ★
Consistency	★ ★
Fees/Services	★ ★ ★
UNECX	**8 Points**

Like a lot of other high-tech, small-stock funds, the United New Concepts Fund has been very volatile recently. Fund manager Mark Seferovich tries to invest in small companies on the verge of big growth. But sometimes the big growth doesn't come. In 1996, for instance, when the Dow Jones Industrial Average was up 26 percent, the fund was up only 4.7 percent. But when the tech sector is strong, this fund thrives.

Founded in 1983, the fund focuses on companies that are relatively new or unseasoned, in the early stages of development, or positioned in new or emerging industries with an opportunity for rapid growth.

Over the past ten years, the fund has posted an average annual return of 17 percent. A $10,000 investment in the fund ten years ago would now be worth about $50,000.

In selecting stocks, Seferovich wants companies with aggressive or creative management, technological or specialized expertise, new or unique products or services, entry into new or emerging industries, and special situations arising out of government priorities and programs. Seferovich takes a fairly conservative buy-and-hold approach and has a modest annual portfolio turnover ratio of just 39 percent.

The fund is heavily weighted in technology stocks. Business services (primarily those that are computer-related, such as Synopsis, America Online, and Parametric Technology) account for 25 percent of assets. Other leading sectors include communications, 9 percent; computer software, 11 percent; health services, 6 percent; and instruments and related products, 5 percent.

PERFORMANCE

The fund has enjoyed strong growth over the last five years. Including dividends and capital gains distributions, the United New Concepts Fund has provided a total return for the last five years (through mid-1998) of 151 percent. A $10,000 investment in 1993 would have grown to about $25,000 five years later. Average annual return: 21 percent.

CONSISTENCY

The fund has been fairly inconsistent recently, outperforming the Dow Jones Industrial Average in only two of the last five years through 1997 (but it led the Dow through the first few months of 1998). Its biggest gain came in 1995, when it moved up 34.1 percent (compared with a 33.5 percent rise in the Dow).

FEES/SERVICES/MANAGEMENT

The United New Concepts Fund has a front-end load of 5.75 percent. Its total annual expense ratio of 1.27 percent (including a 0.18 percent 12b-1 fee) compares favorably with other funds.

The fund offers all the standard services, such as retirement account availability, automatic withdrawal, and automatic checking account deduction. Its minimum initial investment of $500 and minimum subsequent investment of $1 compare favorably with other funds.

Mark Seferovich has managed the fund since 1989. The United Group family of funds includes 17 funds.

Top Ten Stock Holdings

1. America Online
2. Intermedia Communications
3. Steris
4. Parametric Technology
5. Intuit

6. Omnicare
7. INCYTE Pharmaceuticals
8. Stewart Enterprises
9. Harley-Davidson
10. Blyth Industries

Asset mix: common stocks—79%; cash/equivalents—21%
Total net assets: $676 million
Dividend yield: 0.10%

Fees

Front-end load	5.75%
Redemption fee	*None*
12b-1 fee	0.18
Management fee	0.75
Other expenses	0.34
Total annual expense	1.27%
Minimum initial investment	$500
Minimum subsequent investment	$1

Services

Telephone exchanges	*No*
Automatic withdrawal	*Yes*
Automatic checking deduction	*Yes*
Retirement plan/IRA	*Yes*
Instant redemption	*No*
Financial statements	*Semiannual*
Income distributions	*Annual*
Capital gains distributions	*Annual*
Portfolio manager: years	9
Number of funds in family	17

Six-Year Performance
United New Concepts Fund vs. Dow Jones

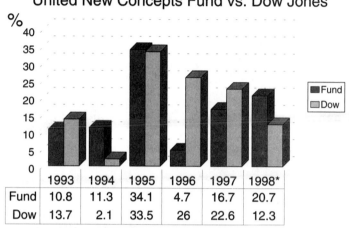

	1993	1994	1995	1996	1997	1998*
Fund	10.8	11.3	34.1	4.7	16.7	20.7
Dow	13.7	2.1	33.5	26	22.6	12.3

% Avg. Annual Total Return   *1998 returns through 8/1/98
Fund vs. Dow Jones Industrial Avg.   (5-year avg. annual return: 18.7%)

89

Alger Growth Portfolio

Alger Funds
30 Montgomery Street
Jersey City, NJ 07302

Fund managers: David Alger,
  Seilai Khoo, and Ronald Tartaro
Fund objective: Long-term growth

Toll-free: 800-992-3863
In-state: 201-547-3600
Fax: 201-434-1459

Performance	★ ★
Consistency	★ ★ ★
Fees/Services	★ ★ ★
AFGPX	**8 Points**

The Alger Growth Portfolio focuses on growing companies with total market capitalizations of $1 billion or more. That emphasis on solid, emerging companies has kept the fund growing consistently for many years.

Over the past ten years, the fund has posted an annual average return of about 20 percent. A $10,000 investment in the fund ten years ago would now be worth about $55,000. The fund managers are fairly aggressive in their trading strategy. The annual portfolio turnover ratio is 128 percent.

The fund stays almost fully invested in stocks most of the time. Although it does invest in some smaller growth stocks, it keeps at least 65 percent of its assets in stocks of companies with over $1 billion in market capitalization.

Alger managers look for stocks of companies that are either still in the developmental stage or are entering a new stage of growth as a result of a change in management or the development of new technology, new products, or broader services.

In all, the fund has about 70 stock holdings. Computers and semiconductor stocks make up 18 percent of total assets. Other leading sectors include communications equipment, 7 percent; financial services, 9 percent; health care–related stocks, 14 percent; and retailing, 6 percent.

PERFORMANCE

The fund has enjoyed strong growth over the last five years. Including dividends and capital gains distributions, the Alger Growth Portfolio has provided a total return for the last five years (through mid-1998) of 157 percent. A $10,000 investment in 1993 would have grown to about $26,000 five years later. Average annual return: 20.8 percent.

CONSISTENCY

The fund has been fairly consistent recently, outperforming the Dow Jones Industrial Average in three of the last five years through 1997 (and it led the Dow through the first few months of 1998). Its biggest gain came in 1995, when it jumped 38.4 percent (compared with a 33.5 percent rise in the Dow).

FEES/SERVICES/MANAGEMENT

Alger Growth Portfolio investors were once limited to "B" shares, which have a maximum redemption fee of 5 percent and a hefty annual expense ratio of 2.08 percent. Alger now offers "A" shares with a 4.75 percent front-end load and a much lower annual expense ratio of 1.30 percent.

The fund offers all the standard services, such as retirement account availability, automatic withdrawal, and automatic checking account deduction. Its minimum initial investment of $500 and minimum subsequent investment of $25 compare very favorably with other funds.

David Alger, who manages the fund along with Seilai Khoo and Ronald Tartaro, has been with the fund since 1986. The Alger family of funds includes six funds and allows shareholders to switch from fund to fund by telephone.

Top Ten Stock Holdings

1. Cendant	6. Sunbeam
2. Tyco International	7. CBS
3. Home Depot	8. AMR
4. Wal-Mart Stores	9. Warner-Lambert
5. Schering-Plough	10. Bank of New York

Asset mix: common stocks—90%; cash/equivalents—10%
Total net assets: $283 million
Dividend yield: none

Fees

Front-end load		4.75%
	("A" shares only)	
Redemption fee (max)		5.00
	("B" shares only)	
	"A" shares	"B" shares
12b-1 fee	*None*	0.75%
Management fee	0.75%	0.75
Other expenses	0.55	0.58
Total annual expense	1.30%	2.08%
Minimum initial investment		$500
Minimum subsequent investment		$25

Services

Telephone exchanges	*Yes*
Automatic withdrawal	*Yes*
Automatic checking deduction	*Yes*
Retirement plan/IRA	*Yes*
Instant redemption	*Yes*
Financial statements	*Semiannual*
Income distributions	*Annual*
Capital gains distributions	*Annual*
Portfolio manager: years	13
Number of funds in family	6

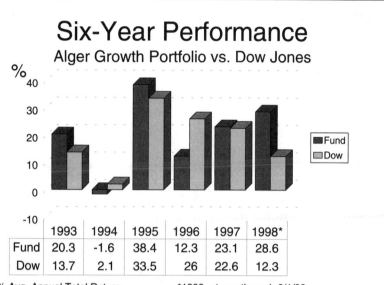

Six-Year Performance
Alger Growth Portfolio vs. Dow Jones

	1993	1994	1995	1996	1997	1998*
Fund	20.3	-1.6	38.4	12.3	23.1	28.6
Dow	13.7	2.1	33.5	26	22.6	12.3

% Avg. Annual Total Return
Fund vs. Dow Jones Industrial Avg.

*1998 returns through 8/1/98
(5-year avg. annual return: 22.7%)

90

Putnam Voyager Fund

AGGRESSIVE

Putnam Investments
One Post Office Square
Boston, MA 02109

Fund managers: Roland Gillis,
   Charles Swanberg, and Robert Beck
Fund objective: Aggressive growth
Web site: www.putnaminv.com

Toll-free: 800-225-1581
In-state: 617-760-5223
Fax: 617-760-9597

Performance	★ ★
Consistency	★ ★ ★
Fees/Services	★ ★ ★
PVOYX	**8 Points**

The Putnam Voyager Fund has grown very big by betting small. With more than $18 billion in assets under management, the fund continues to thrive by investing in a wide universe of small and midsize stocks. Over the past ten years, the fund has posted an average annual return of about 20 percent. A $10,000 investment in the fund ten years ago would now be worth about $60,000.

Although the fund does have a few well-known blue chips, such as Warner-Lambert, Exxon, and American Express, most of its holdings are lesser-known companies on the rise. As the fund's assets have grown, so has its portfolio. It now has about 300 stock holdings across a wide range of industries. Leading sectors include retailing, 10 percent; medical-related companies, 13 percent; computer-related businesses, 19 percent; business services, 5 percent; and banks and financial services, 13 percent.

The fund stays almost 100 percent invested in stocks under normal circumstances. The fund managers take a fairly modest trading approach. The annual portfolio turnover ratio is 60 percent.

PERFORMANCE

The fund has enjoyed solid growth over the last five years. Including dividends and capital gains distributions, the Putnam Voyager Fund has provided a total return for the last five years (through mid-1998) of 155 percent. A $10,000 investment in 1993 would have grown to about $25,000 five years later. Average annual return: 20.6 percent.

CONSISTENCY

The fund has been fairly consistent recently, outperforming the Dow Jones Industrial Average in three of the last five years through 1997 (and it led the Dow through the first few months of 1998). Its biggest gain came in 1995, when it moved up 40.2 percent (compared with a 33.5 percent rise in the Dow).

FEES/SERVICES/MANAGEMENT

The Voyager Fund has a front-end load of 5.75 percent. Its total annual expense ratio of 1.02 percent (including a 0.25 percent 12b-1 fee) compares favorably with other funds.

The fund offers all the standard services, such as retirement account availability, automatic withdrawal, and automatic checking account deduction. Its minimum initial investment of $500 and minimum subsequent investment of $50 compare very favorably with other funds.

Roland Gillis, Charles Swanberg, and Robert Beck have managed the fund since 1995. The Putnam family of funds includes 70 funds and allows shareholders to switch from fund to fund by telephone.

Top Ten Stock Holdings

1. Computer Associates	6. American Express
2. Cendant	7. FHLMC
3. Costco	8. Telecom-TCI Ventures
4. CBS	9. Fannie Mae
5. Tele-Comm TCI Group	10. Compuware

Asset mix: common stocks—99%; cash/equivalents—1%
Total net assets: $13.8 billion
Dividend yield: none

Fees

Front-end load	5.75%
Redemption fee	*None*
12b-1 fee	0.25
Management fee	0.49
Other expenses	0.28
Total annual expense	1.02%
Minimum initial investment	$500
Minimum subsequent investment	$50

Services

Telephone exchanges	*Yes*
Automatic withdrawal	*Yes*
Automatic checking deduction	*Yes*
Retirement plan/IRA	*Yes*
Instant redemption	*Yes*
Financial statements	*Semiannual*
Income distributions	*Annual*
Capital gains distributions	*Annual*
Portfolio manager: years	4
Number of funds in family	70

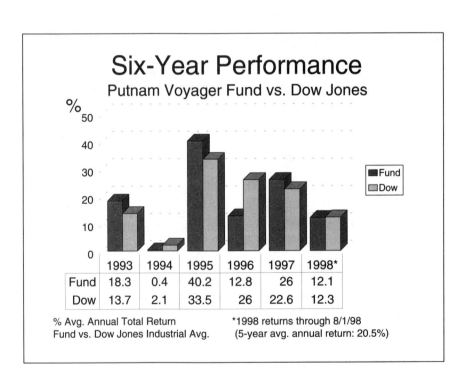

Six-Year Performance
Putnam Voyager Fund vs. Dow Jones

	1993	1994	1995	1996	1997	1998*
Fund	18.3	0.4	40.2	12.8	26	12.1
Dow	13.7	2.1	33.5	26	22.6	12.3

% Avg. Annual Total Return
Fund vs. Dow Jones Industrial Avg.

*1998 returns through 8/1/98
(5-year avg. annual return: 20.5%)

LONG TERM

91
MainStay Capital Appreciation Fund

MainStay Funds
260 Cherry Hill Road
Parsippany, NJ 07054

Fund managers: Bob Centrella, Edmon Spelman, Rudolph Carryl, and Eileen Cook
Fund objective: Long-term growth
Web site: www.mainstayfunds.com

Toll-free: 800-522-4202
In-state: 201-331-2000
Fax: 973-316-4793

Performance	★ ★
Consistency	★ ★ ★
Fees/Services	★ ★ ★
MCSAX	**8 Points**

Fast-growing small to midsize stocks are the mainstay of the MainStay Capital Appreciation Fund. Its management team focuses on companies with "positive growth characteristics, strong management, new products and other innovations with potential to fuel rapid and sustained earnings growth."

The fund, which opened in 1986, has enjoyed excellent returns the past decade, with an average annual return of about 19 percent. A $10,000 investment in the fund ten years ago would now be worth about $56,000.

The managers take a very conservative buy-and-hold approach. The annual portfolio turnover ratio is just 16 percent. The fund, which has about 50 stock holdings, is heavily weighted in technology-related issues. Its leading industrial sectors include computers, software and related technology, 17 percent of assets; drugs, 8 percent; health care, 5 percent; medical equipment, 6 percent; retailing, 12 percent; and financial services, 15 percent.

PERFORMANCE

The fund has enjoyed solid growth over the last five years. Including dividends and capital gains distributions, the MainStay Capital Appreciation Fund has provided a total return for the last five years (through mid-1998) of 154 percent. A $10,000 investment in 1993 would have grown to about $25,000 five years later. Average annual return: 20.5 percent.

CONSISTENCY

The fund has been fairly consistent recently, outperforming the Dow Jones Industrial Average in three of the last five years through 1997 (and it led the Dow through the first few months of 1998). Its biggest gain came in 1995, when it moved up 35.1 percent (compared with a 33.5 percent rise in the Dow).

FEES/SERVICES/MANAGEMENT

The fund has a front-end load of 5.50 percent. Its total annual expense ratio of 1.09 percent (including a 0.25 percent 12b-1 fee) compares favorably with other funds.

The fund offers all the standard services, such as retirement account availability, automatic withdrawal, and automatic checking account deduction. Its minimum initial investment of $500 and minimum subsequent investment of $50 compare favorably with other funds.

A management team (currently consisting of Bob Centrella, Edmon Spelman, Rudolph Carryl, and Eileen Cook) has managed the fund since 1990. The MainStay family of funds includes 15 funds and allows shareholders to switch from fund to fund by telephone.

Top Ten Stock Holdings

1. Cendant
2. Tyco International
3. Computer Associates
4. SunAmerica
5. Eli Lilly
6. Travelers Group
7. Schering-Plough
8. Medtronic
9. Safeway
10. MGIC Investment

Asset mix: common stocks—93%; cash/equivalents—7%
Total net assets: $1.9 billion
Dividend yield: none

Fees

Front-end load	5.5%
Redemption fee	*None*
12b-1 fee	0.25
Management fee	0.58
Other expenses	0.26
Total annual expense	1.09%
Minimum initial investment	$500
Minimum subsequent investment	$50

Services

Telephone exchanges	*Yes*
Automatic withdrawal	*Yes*
Automatic checking deduction	*Yes*
Retirement plan/IRA	*Yes*
Instant redemption	*Yes*
Financial statements	*Semiannual*
Income distributions	*Quarterly*
Capital gains distributions	*Annual*
Portfolio manager: years	8
Number of funds in family	15

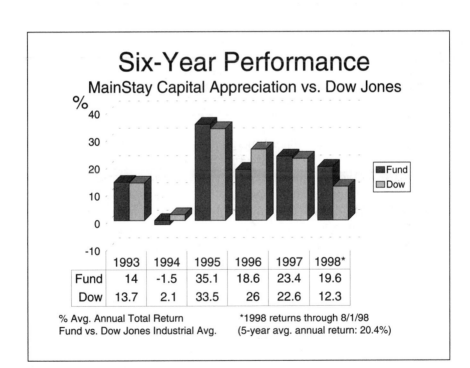

Six-Year Performance
MainStay Capital Appreciation vs. Dow Jones

	1993	1994	1995	1996	1997	1998*
Fund	14	-1.5	35.1	18.6	23.4	19.6
Dow	13.7	2.1	33.5	26	22.6	12.3

% Avg. Annual Total Return
Fund vs. Dow Jones Industrial Avg.

*1998 returns through 8/1/98
(5-year avg. annual return: 20.4%)

92
Principal Mid Cap Fund

Principal Mutual Funds
Princor Financial Services Corp.
P.O. Box 10423
Des Moines, IA 50306

SMALL CAP

Fund manager: Michael R. Hamilton
Fund objective: Small-cap stocks

Toll-free: 800-247-4123
In-state: 515-246-7503
Fax: 515-248-0112

Performance	★ ★
Consistency	★ ★ ★
Fees/Services	★ ★ ★
PEMGX	**8 Points**

Formerly known as the Princor Emerging Growth Fund, the Principal Mid Cap Fund focuses on young, fast-growing companies from a wide range of industries. Over the past ten years, the fund has posted an average annual return of about 18 percent. A $10,000 investment in the fund ten years ago would now be worth about $54,000.

Started in 1987, the fund tends to stay 80 to 95 percent invested in stocks under normal circumstances. Fund manager Mike Hamilton maintains a very conservative buy-and-hold approach and so the annual portfolio turnover ratio is just 10 percent.

The fund's stated investment policy is to "invest for any period of time, in any industry, and in any kind of growth-oriented company." Hamilton particularly likes companies that "focus on controlling costs while at the same time improving their productivity."

The fund has about 100 stock holdings in all, covering about 50 different industries. Leading sectors include banks and trusts, 13 percent of assets; data processing, 9 percent; computer and office equipment, 6 percent; drugs and health care, 6 percent; and electronic components, 6 percent.

PERFORMANCE

The fund has enjoyed solid growth over the last five years. Including dividends and capital gains distributions, the Principal Mid Cap Fund has provided a total return for the last five years (through mid-1998) of 150 percent. A $10,000 investment in 1993 would have grown to about $25,000 five years later. Average annual return: 20.1 percent.

CONSISTENCY

The fund has been fairly consistent recently, outperforming the Dow Jones Industrial Average in three of the last five years through 1997 (and it led the Dow through the first few months of 1998). Its biggest gain came in 1995, when it moved up 34.2 percent (compared with a 33.5 percent rise in the Dow).

FEES/SERVICES/MANAGEMENT

The Mid Cap Fund has a front-end load of 4.75 percent. Its total annual expense ratio of 1.26 percent (including a 0.25 percent 12b-1 fee) compares favorably with other funds.

The fund offers all the standard services, such as retirement account availability, automatic withdrawal, and automatic checking account deduction. Its minimum initial investment of $1,000 and minimum subsequent investment of $100 compare favorably with other funds.

Michael Hamilton has managed the fund since 1987. The Principal family of funds includes 18 funds and allows shareholders to switch from fund to fund by telephone.

Top Ten Stock Holdings

1. EVI
2. EMC
3. Mercantile Bancorp
4. Diamond Offshore Drilling
5. Cadence Design Systems
6. Apogee Enterprises
7. Solectron
8. Synopsys
9. North Fork Bancorp
10. Associated Banc-Corp

Asset mix: common stocks—91%; convertible issues—2%; cash/equivalents—7%
Total net assets: $351 million
Dividend yield: 0.10%

Fees

Front-end load	4.75%
Redemption fee	*None*
12b-1 fee	0.25
Management fee	0.59
Other expenses	0.42
Total annual expense	1.26%
Minimum initial investment	$1,000
Minimum subsequent investment	$100

Services

Telephone exchanges	*Yes*
Automatic withdrawal	*Yes*
Automatic checking deduction	*Yes*
Retirement plan/IRA	*Yes*
Instant redemption	*Yes*
Financial statements	*Semiannual*
Income distributions	*Annual*
Capital gains distributions	*Annual*
Portfolio manager: years	11
Number of funds in family	18

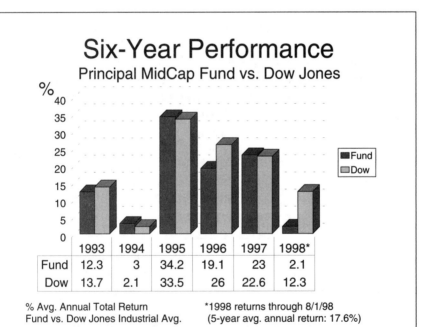

Six-Year Performance
Principal MidCap Fund vs. Dow Jones

	1993	1994	1995	1996	1997	1998*
Fund	12.3	3	34.2	19.1	23	2.1
Dow	13.7	2.1	33.5	26	22.6	12.3

% Avg. Annual Total Return
Fund vs. Dow Jones Industrial Avg.

*1998 returns through 8/1/98
(5-year avg. annual return: 17.6%)

LONG TERM

93

Oppenheimer Quest Opportunity Value Fund

Oppenheimer Funds
10200 East Girard-Suite A
Denver, CO 80231-5516

Fund manager: Richard Glasebrook II
Fund objective: Long-term growth
Web site: www.oppenheimerfunds.com

Toll-free: 800-525-7048
In-state: 212-323-0200
Fax: 212-645-0765

Performance	★ ★
Consistency	★ ★ ★
Fees/Services	★ ★ ★
QVOPX	**8 Points**

Richard Glasebrook II, the fund manager of the Oppenheimer Quest Opportunity Value Fund, has a different view of value than most investment managers. Standard procedure on Wall Street is to evaluate a stock's value based primarily on earnings and sales growth, but Glasebrook peers a bit deeper into the balance sheet to study the company's cash flow and return on capital. He prefers companies that have a high return on invested capital and a strong enough grip on their market niche to sustain that same level of return well into the future.

The fund invests primarily in well-established blue chip companies from a broad range of industries, such as Dow Chemical, McDonald's, Nike, and Boeing. The fund has about 40 stock holdings in all. The leading industrial sectors include chemicals, 10 percent of assets; consumer cyclicals, 12 percent; financial services, 28 percent; industrial, 8 percent; and technology, 18 percent.

Glassbrook takes a conservative trading approach and has an annual portfolio turnover ratio of 30 percent. The fund generally stays invested primarily in stocks, although it often has as much as 20 percent of assets in short-term corporate notes and government bonds.

PERFORMANCE

The fund has enjoyed solid growth over the last five years. Including dividends and capital gains distributions, the Quest Opportunity Value Fund has provided a total return for the last five years (through mid-1998) of 150 percent. A $10,000 investment in 1993 would have grown to about $25,000 five years later. Average annual return: 20.1 percent.

CONSISTENCY

The fund has been fairly consistent recently, outperforming the Dow Jones Industrial Average in two of the last five years through 1997, and it was within a few percentage points of the Dow the other three years. Its biggest gain came in 1995, when it moved up 42 percent (compared with a 33.5 percent rise in the Dow).

FEES/SERVICES/MANAGEMENT

The fund has a front-end load of 5.75 percent. Its total annual expense ratio of 1.54 percent (including a 0.50 percent 12b-1 fee) is in line with other funds.

The fund offers all the standard services, such as retirement account availability, automatic withdrawal, and automatic checking account deduction. Its minimum initial investment of $1,000 and minimum subsequent investment of $25 is in line with other funds.

Richard Glasebrook II has managed the fund since 1991. The Oppenheimer family of funds includes 50 funds and allows shareholders to switch from fund to fund by telephone.

Top Ten Stock Holdings

1. Citicorp	6. Boeing
2. duPont (EI) de Nemours	7. Caterpillar
3. McDonald's	8. ACE
4. FHLMC	9. BankBoston
5. Time Warner	10. Diageo

Asset mix: common stocks—81%; government securities—5%; cash/equivalents—14%
Total net assets: $2.0 billion
Dividend yield: 0.43%

Fees

Front-end load	5.75%
Redemption fee	*None*
12b-1 fee	0.50
Management fee	0.87
Other expenses	0.17
Total annual expense	1.54%
Minimum initial investment	$1,000
Minimum subsequent investment	$25

Services

Telephone exchanges	*Yes*
Automatic withdrawal	*Yes*
Automatic checking deduction	*Yes*
Retirement plan/IRA	*Yes*
Instant redemption	*Yes*
Financial statements	*Semiannual*
Income distributions	*Annual*
Capital gains distributions	*Annual*
Portfolio manager: years	7
Number of funds in family	50

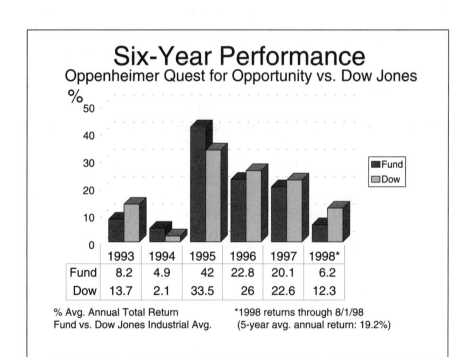

Six-Year Performance
Oppenheimer Quest for Opportunity vs. Dow Jones

	1993	1994	1995	1996	1997	1998*
Fund	8.2	4.9	42	22.8	20.1	6.2
Dow	13.7	2.1	33.5	26	22.6	12.3

% Avg. Annual Total Return
Fund vs. Dow Jones Industrial Avg.

*1998 returns through 8/1/98
(5-year avg. annual return: 19.2%)

94

Piper Emerging Growth Fund

Piper Funds
Piper Jaffray Tower
222 South 9th Street
Minneapolis, MN 55402-3804

SMALL CAP

Fund manager: Sandra K. Shrewsbury
Fund objective: Small-cap stocks
Web site: www.piperjaffray.com

Toll-free: 800-866-7778
In-state: 612-342-1100
Fax: 612-342-5745

Performance	★ ★
Consistency	★ ★ ★
Fees/Services	★ ★ ★
PJEGX	**8 Points**

The Piper Emerging Growth Fund loves that "home cookin'." The fund invests at least 65 percent of its assets in small and midsize companies based in the northern and northwestern states where Piper Jaffray has offices.

Over the past five years, the fund has posted an average annual return of about 19 percent. Fund manager Sandra Shrewsbury focuses on companies that have annual revenues between $10 million and $1 billion, and market capitalization between $250 million and $4 billion. The fund may also invest in some larger companies whose rates of earnings growth are expected to accelerate because of such special factors as new management, new products, changes in consumer demand, or changes in economic circumstances.

Opened in 1990, the fund has about 70 stock holdings in all. The fund manager takes a fairly conservative trading approach. The annual portfolio turnover ratio is 51 percent.

The fund is well diversified across a wide range of industry groups. Leading sectors include financial services, 16 percent of total assets; technology, 19 percent; health care, 13 percent; consumer services, 9 percent; energy, 8 percent; capital goods and services, 8 percent; retailing, 6 percent; and commercial services, 6 percent.

PERFORMANCE

The fund has enjoyed solid growth over the last five years. Including dividends and capital gains distributions, the Piper Emerging Growth Fund has provided a total return for the last five years (through mid-1998) of 140 percent. A $10,000 investment in 1993 would have grown to about $23,000 five years later. Average annual return: 19 percent.

CONSISTENCY

The fund has been fairly consistent recently, outperforming the Dow Jones Industrial Average in three of the last five years through 1997 (and it led the Dow through the first few months of 1998). Its biggest gain came in 1995, when it moved up 39.4 percent (compared with a 33.5 percent rise in the Dow).

FEES/SERVICES/MANAGEMENT

The Piper Emerging Growth Fund has a front-end load of 4 percent. Its total annual expense ratio of 1.23 percent (includes a 0.34 percent 12b-1 fee) compares favorably with other funds.

The fund offers all the standard services, such as retirement account availability, automatic withdrawal, and automatic checking account deduction. Its minimum initial investment of $250 and minimum subsequent investment of $1 compare very favorably with other funds.

Sandra Shrewsbury has managed the fund since 1990. The Piper family of funds includes 11 funds and allows shareholders to switch from fund to fund by telephone.

Top Ten Stock Holdings

1. Elan
2. Stewart Enterprises
3. Danaher
4. EMC/Mass
5. Clear Channel Communications
6. Stage Stores
7. TCF Financial
8. FINOVA Group
9. Sola International
10. Chancellor Media

Asset mix: common stocks—97%; cash/equivalents—3%
Total net assets: $262 million
Dividend yield: none

Fees

Front-end load	4.00%
Redemption fee	*None*
12b-1 fee	0.34
Management fee	0.69
Other expenses	0.20
Total annual expense	1.23%
Minimum initial investment	$250
Minimum subsequent investment	$1

Services

Telephone exchanges	*Yes*
Automatic withdrawal	*Yes*
Automatic checking deduction	*Yes*
Retirement plan/IRA	*Yes*
Instant redemption	*Yes*
Financial statements	*Semiannual*
Income distributions	*Annual*
Capital gains distributions	*Annual*
Portfolio manager: years	8
Number of funds in family	11

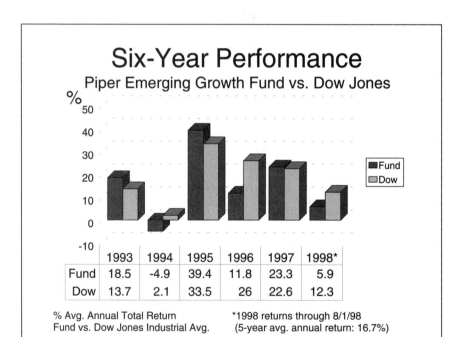

Six-Year Performance
Piper Emerging Growth Fund vs. Dow Jones

	1993	1994	1995	1996	1997	1998*
Fund	18.5	-4.9	39.4	11.8	23.3	5.9
Dow	13.7	2.1	33.5	26	22.6	12.3

% Avg. Annual Total Return
Fund vs. Dow Jones Industrial Avg.

*1998 returns through 8/1/98
(5-year avg. annual return: 16.7%)

LONG TERM

95
Putnam Vista Fund

Putnam Investments
One Post Office Square
Boston, MA 02109

Fund managers: Carol McMullen,
  Anthony Santosus, and David Santos
Fund objective: Long-term growth
Web site: www.putnaminv.com

Toll-free: 800-225-1581
In-state: 617-760-5223
Fax: 617-760-9597

Performance	★ ★
Consistency	★ ★ ★
Fees/Services	★ ★ ★
PVISX	**8 Points**

The Putnam Vista Fund invests in a broad "vista" of stocks, including small-cap, midcap, and large-cap growth stocks from a wide range of industry groups. Typically, its stock holdings range in size from $300 million to $5 billion in market capitalization.

Over the past ten years, the fund has posted an average annual return of about 18 percent. A $10,000 investment in the fund ten years ago would now be worth about $43,000.

The fund managers consider several factors in selecting stocks, such as a company's financial strength, competitive position, and projected future earnings. The fund has about 100 stock holdings in all, including such familiar names as Harley-Davidson, Sherwin-Williams, and Honeywell. For the most part, however, the fund invests in lesser-known emerging growth stocks, such as Apollo Group, Paychex, and Parametric Technology.

The fund stays almost fully invested in stocks at all times. The fund managers take a fairly active trading approach. The annual portfolio turnover ratio is 83 percent.

The fund invests in a wide range of industries. Leading sectors include medical-related companies, 16 percent of assets; retailing, 9 percent; computer-related business, 14 percent; banks and thrifts, 7 percent; and financial services and insurance, 8 percent.

PERFORMANCE

The fund has enjoyed solid growth over the last five years. Including dividends and capital gains distributions, the Putnam Vista Fund has provided a total return for the last five years (through mid-1998) of 147 percent. A $10,000 investment in 1993 would have grown to about $25,000 five years later. Average annual return: 18.1 percent.

CONSISTENCY

The fund has been fairly consistent recently, outperforming the Dow Jones Industrial Average in three of the last five years through 1997 (and about even with the Dow through the first few months of 1998). Its biggest gain came in 1995, when it moved up 39.4 percent (compared with a 33.5 percent rise in the Dow).

FEES/SERVICES/MANAGEMENT

The Vista Fund has a front-end load of 5.75. Its total annual expense ratio of 1.04 percent (including a 0.25 percent 12b-1 fee) compares favorably with other funds.

The fund offers all the standard services, such as retirement account availability, automatic withdrawal, and automatic checking account deduction. Its minimum initial investment of $500 and minimum subsequent investment of $50 compare very favorably with other funds.

Carol McMullen, Anthony Santosus, and David Santos have managed the fund since 1991. The Putnam family of funds includes 70 funds and allows shareholders to switch from fund to fund by telephone.

Top Ten Stock Holdings

1. Costco Companies
2. TJX Companies
3. Teleport Communications Group
4. Omnicom Group
5. Clear Channel Communications

6. Coca-Cola
7. America Online
8. Pier 1 Imports
9. Northern Trust
10. Rite Aid

Asset mix: common stocks—97%; cash/equivalents—3%
Total net assets: $3.2 billion
Dividend yield: none

Fees

Front-end load	5.75%
Redemption fee	*None*
12b-1 fee	0.25
Management fee	0.51
Other expenses	0.28
Total annual expense	1.04%
Minimum initial investment	$500
Minimum subsequent investment	$50

Services

Telephone exchanges	*Yes*
Automatic withdrawal	*Yes*
Automatic checking deduction	*Yes*
Retirement plan/IRA	*Yes*
Instant redemption	*Yes*
Financial statements	*Semiannual*
Income distributions	*Annual*
Capital gains distributions	*Annual*
Portfolio manager: years	4
Number of funds in family	70

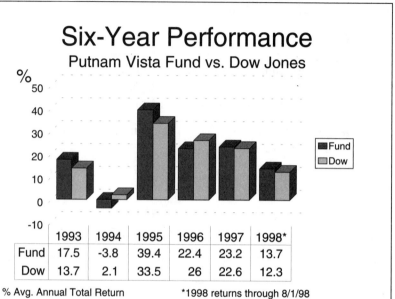

Six-Year Performance
Putnam Vista Fund vs. Dow Jones

	1993	1994	1995	1996	1997	1998*
Fund	17.5	-3.8	39.4	22.4	23.2	13.7
Dow	13.7	2.1	33.5	26	22.6	12.3

% Avg. Annual Total Return   *1998 returns through 8/1/98
Fund vs. Dow Jones Industrial Avg.   (5-year avg. annual return: 20.2%)

SMALL CAP

96

Morgan Stanley Dean Witter Developing Growth Securities Fund

Dean Witter Funds
Two World Trade Center
New York, NY 10048

Fund manager: Jayne Stevlingson
Fund objective: Small-cap stocks
Web site: www.deanwitter.com/intercapital

Toll-free: 800-869-3863
In-state: 212-392-2550
Fax: 212-392-7204

Performance	★ ★
Consistency	★ ★
Fees/Services	★ ★ ★
DGRBX	**7 Points**

Small stocks with big potential—that's the focus of the Morgan Stanley Dean Witter Developing Growth Securities Fund. The fund concentrates on stocks of companies with annual sales in the range of $50 million to $500 million, although it also holds some larger stocks.

In selecting stocks for the portfolio, fund manager Jayne Stevlingson looks for companies with certain key traits: a commitment to quality in their product or service; a competitive edge in their respective markets; hands-on managers who own a large stake in the company; the ability to maintain pricing and business flexibility; the ability to respond quickly to market shifts; and above-average price appreciation potential.

Over the past ten years, the fund has posted an average annual return of about 16 percent. A $10,000 investment in the fund ten years ago would now be worth about $42,000.

Stevlingson is aggressive in her trading policies, so the annual portfolio turnover ratio is 154 percent. In all, the fund has about 250 stock holdings and stays almost fully invested in stocks most of the time.

The fund is well diversified across several growing industrial sectors. The leading sectors include computer software and services, 7 percent;

medical-related companies, 10 percent; telecommunications, 6 percent; oil and gas, 8 percent; and semiconductors, 8 percent.

PERFORMANCE

The fund has enjoyed strong growth over the last five years. Including dividends and capital gains distributions, the Developing Growth Securities Trust has provided a total return for the last five years (through mid-1998) of 155 percent. A $10,000 investment in 1993 would have grown to about $26,000 five years later. Average annual return: 20.7 percent.

CONSISTENCY

The fund has been somewhat inconsistent recently, trailing the Dow Jones Industrial Average in three of the last five years through 1997 (but it led the Dow slightly through the first few months of 1998). Its biggest gain came in 1995, when it jumped 47.7 percent (compared with a 33.5 percent rise in the Dow).

FEES/SERVICES/MANAGEMENT

The fund is available in "A" shares that carry a 5.25 percent front-end load or in "B" shares that have a 5 percent redemption fee that declines gradually to zero if the fund is held for more than six years. Class "A" shares have a very low annual expense ratio of 0.93 percent, while "B" shares carry a much higher 1.68 percent annual expense ratio.

The fund offers all the standard services, such as retirement account availability, automatic withdrawal, and automatic checking account deduction. Its minimum initial investment of $1,000 and minimum subsequent investment of $100 compare favorably with other funds.

Jayne Stevlingson has managed the fund since 1994. The Dean Witter family of funds includes more than 60 funds and allows shareholders to switch from fund to fund by telephone.

Top Ten Stock Holdings

1. Steris
2. Outdoor Systems
3. Mail Well
4. Saville Systems
5. Lason

6. Iron Mountain
7. Jacor Communications
8. Mitzler Group
9. The Bisys Group
10. Safeguard Scientifics

Asset mix: common stocks—90%; cash/equivalents—10%
Total net assets: $810 million
Dividend yield: none

Fees

		"A"	"B"
Front-end load	5.25% *("A" shares only)*		
Redemption fee	5.00 *("B" shares only)*		
12b-1 fee		0.25%	1.00%
Management fee		0.49	0.49
Other expenses		0.19	0.19
Total annual expense		0.93%	1.68%
Minimum initial investment	$1,000		
Minimum subsequent investment	$100		

Services

Telephone exchanges	*Yes*
Automatic withdrawal	*Yes*
Automatic checking deduction	*Yes*
Retirement plan/IRA	*Yes*
Instant redemption	*Yes*
Financial statements	*Semiannual*
Income distributions	*Annual*
Capital gains distributions	*Annual*
Portfolio manager: years	4
Number of funds in family	62

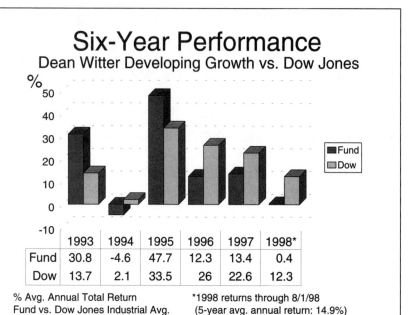

Six-Year Performance
Dean Witter Developing Growth vs. Dow Jones

	1993	1994	1995	1996	1997	1998*
Fund	30.8	-4.6	47.7	12.3	13.4	0.4
Dow	13.7	2.1	33.5	26	22.6	12.3

% Avg. Annual Total Return   *1998 returns through 8/1/98
Fund vs. Dow Jones Industrial Avg.   (5-year avg. annual return: 14.9%)

97
Mentor Growth Fund

Mentor Funds
901 East Byrd Street
Richmond, VA 23219

Fund managers: Ted Price,
  Linda Ziglar, and Jeff Drummond
Fund objective: Long-term growth

Toll-free: 800-382-0016
In-state: 804-782-3754
Fax: 804-782-6604

Performance	★ ★
Consistency	★ ★
Fees/Services	★ ★ ★
MGAAX	**7 Points**

The Mentor Growth Fund focuses on small and midsize stocks with strong growth momentum and the potential for continued earnings growth. The management team, led by Ted Price, who has been with the fund since its inception in 1985, looks at several criteria in selecting stocks. It wants companies with emerging leadership in rapidly growing industries, strong market share, proprietary products and services, and product leadership in niche markets. Most of the stocks in the Mentor Growth portfolio have market capitalizations of under $500 million.

Over the past ten years, the fund has posted an average annual return of about 17 percent. A $10,000 investment in the fund ten years ago would now be worth about $46,000.

The fund managers take a fairly active trading approach. The annual portfolio turnover ratio is 77 percent. They are quick to unload stocks at the first sign of trouble, selling when quarterly earnings come in below expectations, when companies have unfavorable changes, and when the price drops dramatically relative to the market. They also sell when a stock grows so quickly that it reaches an overweighted position in the portfolio.

In all, the fund has about 120 stock holdings, heavily weighted in health and technology stocks. Leading sectors include technology, 23 percent of assets; health care, 21 percent; consumer cyclicals, 15 percent; energy, 9 percent; financial services, 5 percent; and transportation, 5 percent.

PERFORMANCE

The fund has enjoyed solid growth over the last five years. Including dividends and capital gains distributions, the Mentor Growth Fund has provided a total return for the last five years (through mid-1998) of 150 percent. A $10,000 investment in 1993 would have grown to about $25,000 five years later. Average annual return: 20.1 percent.

CONSISTENCY

The fund has been somewhat inconsistent recently, trailing the Dow Jones Industrial Average in three of the last five years through 1997 (but it led the Dow through the first few months of 1998). Its biggest gain came in 1995, when it moved up 39.4 percent (compared with a 33.5 percent rise in the Dow).

FEES/SERVICES/MANAGEMENT

The Mentor Growth Fund has a front-end load of 5.75 percent. Its total annual expense ratio of 1.28 percent (with no 12b-1 fee) compares favorably with other funds.

The fund offers all the standard services, such as retirement account availability, automatic withdrawal, and automatic checking account deduction. Its minimum initial investment of $1,000 and minimum subsequent investment of $100 compare favorably with other funds.

Ted Price has managed the fund since 1985. Also serving on the management team are Linda Ziglar and Jeff Drummond. The Mentor family of funds includes ten funds and allows shareholders to switch from fund to fund by telephone.

Top Ten Stock Holdings

1. Outdoor Systems
2. National Commerce Bancorp
3. Markel
4. Core Laboratories
5. Fairfield Communities
6. Dollar General
7. Chancellor Media
8. Richfood Holdings
9. AHL Services
10. Concord EFS

Asset mix: common stocks—92%; cash/equivalents—8%
Total net assets: $123 million
Dividend yield: none

Fees

Front-end load	5.75%
Redemption fee	*None*
12b-1 fee	*None*
Management fee	0.70
Other expenses	0.58
Total annual expense	1.28%
Minimum initial investment	$1,000
Minimum subsequent investment	$100

Services

Telephone exchanges	*Yes*
Automatic withdrawal	*Yes*
Automatic checking deduction	*Yes*
Retirement plan/IRA	*Yes*
Instant redemption	*Yes*
Financial statements	*Semiannual*
Income distributions	*Annual*
Capital gains distributions	*Annual*
Portfolio manager: years	13
Number of funds in family	10

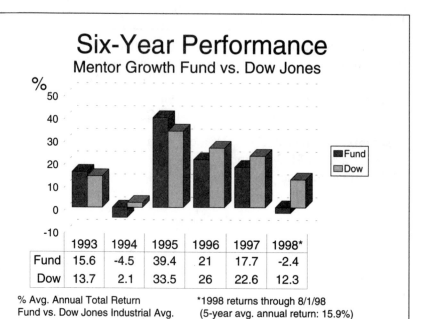

Six-Year Performance
Mentor Growth Fund vs. Dow Jones

	1993	1994	1995	1996	1997	1998*
Fund	15.6	-4.5	39.4	21	17.7	-2.4
Dow	13.7	2.1	33.5	26	22.6	12.3

% Avg. Annual Total Return   *1998 returns through 8/1/98
Fund vs. Dow Jones Industrial Avg.   (5-year avg. annual return: 15.9%)

AGGRESSIVE

American Century–Twentieth Century Giftrust

American Century Investments
P.O. Box 419200
Kansas City, MO 64179-9965

Fund managers: Glenn Fogle
and John Seitzer
Fund objective: Aggressive growth
Web site: www.americancentury.com

Toll-free: 800-345-2021
In-state: 816-531-5575
Fax: 816-340-4753

Performance	★ ★
Consistency	★ ★
Fees/Services	★ ★ ★
TWGTX	**7 Points**

The American Century–Twentieth Century Giftrust is an aggressive growth fund that has produced outstanding returns for long-term investors. But short-term investors need not apply.

The Giftrust Fund is designed as a trust to be used to set aside money for children or foundations. The fund has a minimum ten-year holding period intended to encourage a long-term growth philosophy. Because of its ten-year requirement, it may not be appropriate as a college savings vehicle for children who will be attending college in less than ten years. The Giftrust fund is irrevocable.

The fund, which was opened in 1983, is very aggressive and fairly volatile, but its long-term performance has been exceptional. Over the past ten years, it has posted an average annual return of nearly 21 percent. A $10,000 investment in the fund ten years ago would now be worth about $65,000.

The fund invests primarily in small to midsize companies on a fast growth track and, generally speaking, stays fully invested in stocks. It maintains a fairly aggressive trading policy. The annual portfolio turnover ratio is 121 percent.

In all, the fund has about 70 stock holdings, heavily weighted in the high-tech area. Leading sectors include computer software and services, 11 percent of total assets; energy services, 14 percent; medical-related companies, 8 percent; biotechnology, 9 percent; communications equipment, 9 percent; and electrical and electronic components, 14 percent.

PERFORMANCE

The fund has enjoyed solid growth over the last five years. Including dividends and capital gains distributions, the Giftrust fund has provided a total return for the last five years (through mid-1998) of 140 percent. A $10,000 investment in 1993 would have grown to about $24,000 five years later. Average annual return: 19 percent.

CONSISTENCY

The fund has dropped off considerably the past three years after posting exceptional returns for many years prior to 1996. But the fund trailed the market in 1996, and it actually showed a loss in 1997 when the Dow Jones Industrial Average was up 22.6 percent. It also trailed the Dow through the first few months of 1998.

FEES/SERVICES/MANAGEMENT

Like all American Century funds, the Giftrust fund is a true no-load fund—no fee to buy, no fee to sell. And it has a very low total annual expense ratio of 1 percent (with no 12b-1 fee).

Because of its unusual nature, the fund offers very few of the standard services most other funds offer. As mentioned above, you can't invest in the fund in your own name. It is to be used strictly as a trust for others. The fund's $500 minimum initial investment and $50 minimum contribution for existing accounts compare very favorably with other funds.

Glen Fogle has been manager of the fund since 1990, and John Seitzer was recently added to the management team. The American Century family of funds includes more than 20 funds.

Top Ten Stock Holdings

1. Trico Marine Services
2. CBT Group
3. Jabil Circuit
4. P-COM
5. Applied Graphics Technologies

6. Vitesse Semiconductor
7. Family Dollar Stores
8. Agouron Pharmaceuticals
9. Tekelec
10. Clear Channel Communications

Asset mix: common stocks—97%; cash/equivalents—3%
Total net assets: $986 million
Dividend yield: none

Fees

Front-end load	*None*
Redemption fee	*None*
12b-1 fee	*None*
Management fee	1.00%
Other expenses	0.00
Total annual expense	1.00%
Minimum initial investment	$500
Minimum subsequent investment	$50

Services

Telephone exchanges	*Yes*
Automatic withdrawal	*No*
Automatic checking deduction	*Yes*
Retirement plan/IRA	*No*
Instant redemption	*No*
Financial statements	*Semiannual*
Income distributions	*Annual*
Capital gains distributions	*Annual*
Portfolio manager: years	8
Number of funds in family	22

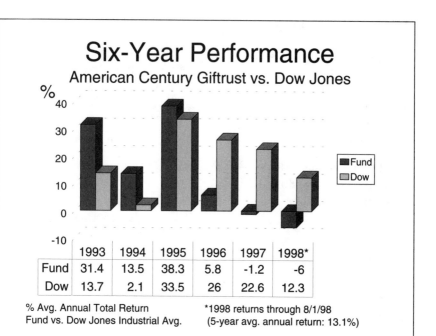

Six-Year Performance
American Century Giftrust vs. Dow Jones

	1993	1994	1995	1996	1997	1998*
Fund	31.4	13.5	38.3	5.8	-1.2	-6
Dow	13.7	2.1	33.5	26	22.6	12.3

% Avg. Annual Total Return   *1998 returns through 8/1/98
Fund vs. Dow Jones Industrial Avg.   (5-year avg. annual return: 13.1%)

AGGRESSIVE

99

AIM Constellation Fund

AIM Funds Group
11 Greenway Plaza, Suite 100
Houston, TX 77046-1173

Fund managers: Robert Kippes, Ken Zschappel, Charles Scavone, and Dave Barnard
Fund objective: Aggressive growth

Toll-free: 800-347-4246
In-state: 713-626-1919
Fax: 713-993-9890
Web site: www.aimfunds.com

Performance	★ ★
Consistency	★ ★
Fees/Services	★ ★ ★
CSTGX	**7 Points**

After years of outstanding growth, the AIM Constellation Fund hit a couple of years of subpar growth as many of the nation's high-tech stocks went through a sobering market correction. But long term, this has been one of the nation's top-performing funds. Opened in 1976, the fund has provided an average annual return over the past ten years of about 20 percent. A $10,000 investment in the fund ten years ago would now be worth about $64,000.

The fund managers try to load the fund with the fastest-growing stocks available. Earnings momentum is the primary criterion they consider in selecting stocks. The fund management takes a bottom-up (based on a company-by-company evaluation) rather than a top-down approach (which puts the emphasis on the economy and the big picture).

One key to the fund's success is the strict sell discipline of the fund managers. They emphasize the sell side, quickly unloading stocks that have lost momentum. The fund managers are more concerned with present earnings than future earnings projections. Nor do they try to project sales of a new product. Rather, they wait and see how it does and make future projections based on its initial market results.

The AIM funds were started by Harry Hutzler in 1976. Hutzler, who retired in 1993, began the Value Line Investment Survey in the 1950s and 1960s. He started the very successful Weingarten Fund in 1969 and then added the AIM Constellation Fund seven years later.

The fund maintains a portfolio of about 300 stocks selected from thousands of small-cap, midcap, and large-cap stocks that fund managers evaluate on an ongoing basis. The portfolio consists of about 40 percent emerging growth stocks, 40 percent medium-size firms, and 20 percent large-capitalization companies.

The AIM Constellation Fund is heavily weighted with high tech–related stocks. Leading sectors include computer-related products and services, 15 percent of total assets; electronics, 6 percent; health care and medical, 11 percent; oil and gas, 8 percent; retailing, 13 percent; and communications equipment, 3 percent. The fund stays almost fully invested in stocks at all times and has a modest annual portfolio turnover ratio of about 67 percent.

PERFORMANCE

The fund has enjoyed solid growth over the last five years. Including dividends and capital gains distributions, the AIM Constellation Fund has provided a total return for the last five years (through mid-1998) of 135 percent. A $10,000 investment in 1993 would have grown to about $23,500 five years later. Average annual return: 18.7 percent.

CONSISTENCY

The fund has been rather inconsistent recently, trailing the Dow Jones Industrial Average in three of the last five years through 1997 (but it led the Dow through the first few months of 1998). Its biggest gain came in 1995, when it moved up 35.5 percent (compared with a 33.5 percent rise in the Dow).

FEES/SERVICES/MANAGEMENT

The fund has a front-end load of 5.50 percent. Its total annual expense ratio of 1.11 percent (with a 0.30 percent 12b-1 fee) compares favorably with other funds.

The fund offers all the standard services, such as retirement account availability, automatic withdrawal, and automatic checking account deduction. Its minimum initial investment of $500 and minimum subsequent investment of $50 compare favorably with other funds.

The fund is managed by a four-person team led by Robert Kippes, who has been there since 1993. The AIM family of funds includes 30 funds and allows shareholders to switch from fund to fund by telephone.

Top Ten Stock Holdings

1. HEALTHSOUTH
2. MGIC Investment
3. Health Management Associates
4. Tenet Healthcare
5. Service International
6. Compuware
7. Household International
8. Safeway
9. ADC Telecommunications
10. Maxim Integrated Products

Asset mix: common stocks—93%; cash/equivalents—7%
Total net assets: $14 billion
Dividend yield: none

Fees

Front-end load	5.50%
Redemption fee	*None*
12b-1 fee	0.30
Management fee	0.61
Other expenses	0.20
Total annual expense	1.11%
Minimum initial investment	$500
Minimum subsequent investment	$50

Services

Telephone exchanges	*Yes*
Automatic withdrawal	*Yes*
Automatic checking deduction	*Yes*
Retirement plan/IRA	*Yes*
Instant redemption	*Yes*
Financial statements	*Semiannual*
Income distributions	*Annual*
Capital gains distributions	*Annual*
Portfolio manager: years	12
Number of funds in family	30

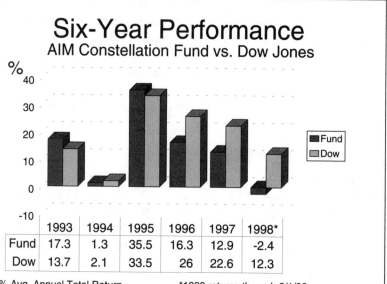

Six-Year Performance
AIM Constellation Fund vs. Dow Jones

	1993	1994	1995	1996	1997	1998*
Fund	17.3	1.3	35.5	16.3	12.9	-2.4
Dow	13.7	2.1	33.5	26	22.6	12.3

% Avg. Annual Total Return   *1998 returns through 8/1/98
Fund vs. Dow Jones Industrial Avg.   (5-year avg. annual return: 16.9%)

AGGRESSIVE

Fidelity Emerging Growth Fund

Fidelity Investments
82 Devonshire Street
Boston, MA 02109

Fund manager: Erin Sullivan
Fund objective: Aggressive growth
Web site: www.fidelity.com

Toll-free: 800-544-6666
In-state: 801-534-1910
Fax: 617-476-9743

Performance	★ ★
Consistency	★ ★
Fees/Services	★ ★
FDEGX	**6 Points**

The Fidelity Emerging Growth Fund has the flexibility to diversify across a broad range of industrial sectors. But, like many of the best funds of the 1990s, this fund's portfolio is loaded with high-tech stocks. Fund manager Erin Sullivan has invested nearly 50 percent of the fund's assets in technology and health-related stocks. (Retail and wholesale stocks account for about 19 percent and services make up 9 percent.)

The objective of the fund is to invest at least 65 percent of its assets in small, emerging stocks that "are in the developing stage of their life cycle and offer the potential for accelerated growth." The fund may also invest in larger companies such as Microsoft and Oracle that continue to have strong growth prospects. It also has some foreign stock holdings.

"I always look for companies that have the potential for strong earnings growth," says Sullivan. "They also must have effective management teams that can capitalize on opportunities for new business in the marketplace."

The fund, which opened in 1990, has experienced outstanding performance the past five years with an average annual return of about 20.5 percent. The fund has well over 200 stock holdings in its portfolio. Sullivan pursues a fairly active trading strategy and has a 212 percent annual portfolio turnover ratio.

PERFORMANCE

The fund has enjoyed outstanding growth over the past five years. Including dividends and capital gains distributions, the Fidelity Emerging Growth Fund has provided a total return for the past five years (through early 1998) of 154 percent. A $10,000 investment in 1993 would have grown to $25,400 five years later. Average annual return: 20.5 percent.

CONSISTENCY

The fund has been somewhat inconsistent recently, trailing the Dow Jones Industrial Average in three of the last five years through 1997 (but it led the Dow through the first few months of 1998). Its biggest gain came in 1995, when it jumped 35.9 percent (compared with a 33.5 percent rise in the Dow).

FEES/SERVICES/MANAGEMENT

The fund has a low front-end load of 3 percent and a maximum redemption fee of 0.75 percent if sold out within 29 days. Its low annual expense ratio of 1.09 percent (with no 12b-1 fee) compares favorably with other funds.

The fund offers many of the standard services, such as retirement account availability and automatic checking account deduction, but it does not offer an automatic withdrawal plan. Its minimum initial investment of $2,500 and minimum subsequent investment of $250 are a little high compared with other funds.

Erin Sullivan has managed the fund only since 1997. The Fidelity family of funds includes more than 230 funds.

Top Ten Stock Holdings

1. McKesson
2. Guidant
3. BMC Software
4. CVS
5. Tyco International

6. HEALTHSOUTH
7. Microsoft
8. Medtronic
9. Consolidated Stores
10. Proffitt's

Asset mix: common stocks—97%; cash/equivalents—3%
Total net assets: $1.98 billion
Dividend yield: none

Fees

Front-end load	3.00%
Redemption fee	0.75
12b-1 fee	*None*
Management fee	0.77
Other expenses	0.32
Total annual expense	1.09%
Minimum initial investment	$2,500
Minimum subsequent investment	$250

Services

Telephone exchanges	*Yes*
Automatic withdrawal	*No*
Automatic checking deduction	*Yes*
Retirement plan/IRA	*Yes*
Instant redemption	*Yes*
Financial statements	*Semiannual*
Income distributions	*Annual*
Capital gains distributions	*Annual*
Portfolio manager: years	1
Number of funds in family	235

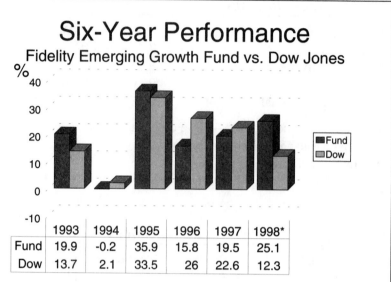

Six-Year Performance
Fidelity Emerging Growth Fund vs. Dow Jones

	1993	1994	1995	1996	1997	1998*
Fund	19.9	-0.2	35.9	15.8	19.5	25.1
Dow	13.7	2.1	33.5	26	22.6	12.3

% Avg. Annual Total Return   *1998 returns through 8/1/98
Fund vs. Dow Jones Industrial Avg.   (5-year avg. annual return: 20.5%)

Honorable Mentions

Corporate Bond Funds

Fund	Load (%)	Average Annual Return (%) 3-yr.	5-yr.	Minimum Investment	Telephone
Strong Corporate Bond	None	10.67	10.59	$2,500	800-368-1030
Alliance Bond Fund Corporate Bond Portfolio	4.25	12.52	10.13	250	800-227-4618
Managers Bond Fund	None	10.01	9.41	2,000	800-835-3879
Invesco Select Income Fund	None	9.55	8.66	1,000	800-525-8085
Westcore Long-Term Bond Fund	None	9.68	8.52	1,000	800-392-2673
IDS Bond Fund A	5.00	9.13	8.49	2,000	800-328-8300
Ivy Bond Fund A	4.75	9.87	8.37	1,000	800-456-5111
New England Bond Income Fund A	4.50	9.19	8.06	2,500	800-225-7670
Principal Bond Fund A	4.75	8.19	7.90	1,000	800-451-5447

High-Yield Bond Funds

Fund	Load (%)	Average Annual Return (%) 3-yr.	5-yr.	Minimum Investment	Telephone
Northeast Investors	None	15.18	14.21	$ 1,000	800-225-6704
Fidelity Spartan High Income	None	15.46	14.18	10,000	800-544-8888
Value Line Aggressive Income	None	16.90	12.55	1,000	800-223-0818
Seligman High-Yield Bond Fund A	4.75	14.53	12.98	1,000	800-221-2783
MainStay High-Yield Corporate Bond B	5.00	13.78	12.79	500	800-624-6782
Eaton Vance Income of Boston	4.75	14.00	11.70	1,000	800-225-6265
State Street Research High-Income Fund A	4.50	13.90	11.55	2,500	800-882-0052
Pilgrim America High-Yield Fund A	4.75	14.40	11.49	1,000	800-334-3444
Fidelity Capital and Income Fund	None	13.43	11.38	2,500	800-544-8888
Colonial High-Yield Securities Fund A	4.75	12.91	11.35	1,000	800-426-3750

International Funds

Fund	Load (%)	Average Annual Return (%)		Minimum Investment	Telephone
		3-yr.	5-yr.		
IDEX Global Fund A	5.50	29.46	22.93	$ 500	888-223-4339
United International Growth Fund A	5.75	23.88	20.52	500	800-366-5465
Oppenheimer Global Growth and Income Fund A	5.75	23.66	18.95	1,000	800-525-7048
Phoenix Worldwide Opportunity Fund A	4.75	21.90	18.64	500	800-243-4361
Oppenheimer Global Fund A	5.75	20.52	18.61	1,000	800-525-7048
Capital World Growth and Income Fund	5.75	21.26	18.59	1,000	800-421-4120
Seligman Henderson Global Small Companies A	4.75	19.16	18.39	1,000	800-221-2450
Putnam International Growth Fund	5.75	22.15	18.26	500	800-225-1581
American Century-Twentieth Century International Growth Fund	None	23.48	17.58	2,500	800-345-2021

Tax-Exempt Bond Funds

Fund	Load (%)	Average Annual Return (%)		Minimum Investment	Telephone
		3-yr.	5-yr.		
United Municipal High-Income Fund A	4.25	9.39	8.27	$ 500	800-366-5465
Smith Barney Managed Municipals Fund A	4.00	7.86	7.91	1,000	800-451-2010
Excelsior Long-Term Tax-Exempt Fund	None	7.96	7.87	500	800-446-1012
Delaware National High-Yield Municipal Bond Fund	3.75	8.42	7.38	1,000	800-523-4640
Eaton Vance National Municipals Fund B	5.00	8.59	7.23	1,000	800-225-6265
Prudential Municipal Bond Fund (High-Yield)	3.00	7.90	7.15	1,000	800-225-1852
STI Classic Investment Grade Tax-Exempt Bond Fund	3.75	6.71	7.08	2,000	800-428-6970
Sit Tax-Free Income Fund	None	7.81	7.08	2,000	800-332-5580
T. Rowe Price Tax-Free High-Yield Fund	None	7.99	7.08	2,500	800-638-5660

Glossary

American Depository Receipt (ADR) A foreign stock sponsored by a U.S. bank and re-issued on a U.S. stock exchange. Although ADRs do not trade at the same price in the United States as they do at home (because the sponsoring bank issues them at a different price), their prices move exactly in concert with the price movements of the original stock.

annual expense ratio Yearly mutual fund fee assessed to cover the fund's expenses, including management fees, transaction fees, and marketing expenses. Annual expense ratios usually vary from 0.60 percent to about 3 percent of the fund's net asset value. The expense ratio is deducted directly from each shareholder's holdings.

assets The amount of money invested in a mutual fund by shareholders. The largest mutual fund is Fidelity Magellan, which boasts about $72 billion in total assets. Most funds have assets of $25 million to $3 billion.

back-end load A fee charged investors by some mutual funds when the investors sell their shares in the fund. The fees, which range from about 1 to 6 percent, typically diminish about 1 percent each year the investor holds the fund. For instance, a fund with a maximum 5 percent back-end load will charge the full 5 percent the first year. But the fee normally drops to 4 percent the second year, 3 percent the third, 2 percent the fourth, 1 percent the fifth, and zero after the fifth year. The two types of back-end loads are *deferred sales charges* and *redemption fees;* deferred sales charges are definitely preferred. Funds with deferred sales fees base charges on the net asset value of the shares when you bought them, whereas redemption fees are based on the price of your shares at the time you sell. Thus, if your fund has a strong gain, you'll pay much more in redemption fees than you would in deferred sales charges. (See also *load, no-load, front-end load, redemption fee,* and *deferred sales charge.*)

bottom up Investment method in which an investor selects stocks based on the merits of each individual stock without regard to the overall economy. This is the opposite of a top-down approach in which an investor looks at broad economic patterns to determine which investment sectors would make the most timely investments. Most stock mutual fund managers use a *bottom-up* approach, although some use a blend of both. (See also *top down.*)

cash equivalent An investment that has a monetary value equal to a specified sum.

cash equivalent investments Interest-bearing securities of high liquidity and safety—such as commercial paper, certificates of deposit, and Treasury bills—that are considered virtually as good as cash. Money market funds invest almost exclusively in cash equivalents. When stock mutual fund managers sense a looming downturn in the market, they often lighten their stock portfolios and move more assets to cash equivalents for safety and a little income in the short term while they await a turnaround in the market.

classes of mutual fund shares Mutual fund companies often issue fund shares of several classifications. The shares, which normally are referred to as "A" class, "B" class, "C" class, "D" class, and so on, usually have the same asset mix but different investor requirements. For instance, "A" shares may have a front-end sales load and a low annual expense ratio, whereas "B" shares may have a back-end load and a slightly higher annual expense ratio, "C" shares may have no sales load but a very high annual expense ratio and "D" shares may be geared to institutional and affluent investors and may require a minimum investment of $100,000 or more.

deferred sales charge A sales fee or back-end load charged shareholders by some mutual funds when the shareholders sell their fund shares. (See *back-end load*.)

dividend A portion of a company's earnings that is paid to its shareholders. Funds holding dividend-paying stocks pass those dividends onto shareholders in lump-sum payments either quarterly, semiannually, or annually, depending on the fund. Investors in most funds may have dividends automatically reinvested in additional shares.

dividend yield The annual dividend payment divided by its market price per share. If a stock is trading at $100 a share and it pays a $10 dividend, the dividend yield is 10 percent.

equity investment A security (usually common stock or preferred stock) that represents a share of ownership in a business entity (usually a corporation).

front-end load The sales fee a mutual fund charges investors to buy shares of the fund. The fee (usually in the range of 3 to 8.5 percent) is deducted directly from the investor's contribution. For instance, a $1,000 investment in a fund with a 5 percent front-end load would result in $50 in load fees and $950 in actual fund shares. (See also *load, no-load, back-end load*.)

load A sales fee charged to mutual fund investors. Loads normally vary from about 3 percent to 8.5 percent of the total purchase amount. (See *no-load, front-end load, back-end load*, and *redemption fee*.)

money market fund A mutual fund that invests in high-quality, short-term debt instruments such as Treasury bills or certificates of deposit. Money market fund investors earn a steady stream of interest income that varies with short-term interest rates and generally may cash out at any time.

Morgan Stanley Capital Investment and Europe, Australasia, Far East index (MSCI/ EAFE) An index that gauges the performance of the foreign stock market.

net asset value (NAV) The total worth of all the investments of a mutual fund. The NAV changes daily to reflect fluctuations in the price of a fund's stock and bond holdings.

no-load fund A mutual fund that charges no sales fee to buy and no sales fee to sell. (Also see *load, front-end load*, and *back-end load*.)

open-end mutual fund A mutual fund that allows investors to buy shares directly from the mutual fund company and stands ready to redeem shares whenever shareholders are ready to sell. Open-end funds may issue new shares any time there is a demand for more shares from investors. Shareholders buy and sell shares at the fund's net asset value (plus sales fees), in contrast to a closed-end mutual fund, which trades like stock on a stock exchange. Rather than selling at net asset value, closed-end fund shares trade at whatever price the market is willing to pay.

price-earnings ratio (PE) A company's stock price divided by its earnings per share over the past 12 months. It is Wall Street's most commonly used ratio to determine a stock's value to investors. PEs are a lot like golf scores: the lower the better. For instance, a company with a stock price of $20 and earnings-per-share of $1 has a 20 PE ($20 divided by $1), while a company with a stock price of $10 and the same $1 in earnings-per-share has a 10 PE. The higher a stock's PE, the more expensive the stock is relative to its earnings.

redemption fee Sales fee or back-end load charged by some mutual funds to shareholders when they sell their shares. (See *back-end load*.)

top down An investment strategy in which the investor looks at broad economic trends to decide which types of investments appear to be best positioned for growth, and then selects individual investments based on that economic assessment. It is the opposite of a bottom-up strategy, in which an investor assesses an individual investment strictly on its own merits irrespective of the overall economy. (Also see *bottom up*.)

12b-1 fee A small fee assessed annually by some mutual funds to cover advertising and marketing expenses. The fee is deducted directly from each shareholder's holdings and usually represents less than 1 percent of net asset value.

Index